Time and the Macroeconomic Analysis of Income

Time and the Macroeconomic Analysis of Income

Alvaro Cencini

Foreword by
Meghnad Desai

St. Martin's Press, New York

 For information, write:
St. Martin's Press, Inc., 175 Fifth Avenue, New York, NY 10010
Printed in Great Britain
First published in the United States of America in 1984

Library of Congress Cataloging in Publication Data

Cencini, Alvaro,
Time and the macroeconomic analysis of income.

Includes index.
1. Income. 2. Multiplier (Economics) 3. Time and economic reactions. 4. Macroeconomics. I. Title.
HB522.C42 1984 339.4'1 83-40201
ISBN 0-312-80502-0

To my parents

Contents

Foreword

by Meghnad Desai

This book will undoubtedly puzzle, stimulate, infuriate, or annoy many readers. Alvaro Cencini challenges so many of the commonly held notions which are perpetuated in elementary textbooks and taken for granted in learned journals that a first reaction is bound to be that the author must be naïve or ignorant. I would, however, advise readers to persist, as I did myself when Alvaro Cencini came to LSE as a research student. After close and long arguments, he convinced me that the questions he raises about the logical foundations of macroeconomic theory are original. I am still not wholeheartedly convinced of his answers. I wish, therefore, in this brief foreword to examine the questions he raises and attempt to provide an alternative answer.

Even at the price of doing this work some injustice, it is best to summarise at the outset what it is about. The book argues that the treatment of time in economics—reflected in controversies over such matters as stocks versus flows, continuous versus discrete analysis—is logically faulty. In particular the notion that flows such as income are functions of time does not bear careful examination. In particular, the early Lerner–Hansen–Samuelson exposition of the income–expenditure theory is untenable as a *causal* mechanism. The circular flow of income is not a causal scheme whereby expenditures *generate* income.

The drastic implication of this objection is that the conventional story of the multiplier mechanism does not hold. The problem is that if we take Savings equals Investment as an identity (as Keynes did in the *General Theory*), then corresponding to any initial injection I_0 there should correspond an exactly equal amount of saving. The multiplier story relies on the idea that in the first round a fraction cI_0 (c being the marginal propensity to consume) is consumed and $(1-c)I_0$ is saved. So for $0 < c < 1$ the Savings–Investment identity is violated. If the identity is to be preserved then the only value of the multiplier which is sensible is unity!

This is clearly an astounding result and if valid it is very depressing for anyone advocating 'Keynesian' policies for employment generation. Cencini is not at all dismayed by this and proceeds to argue for a 'quantum time' approach to economics. As he well knows, I am not prepared to go along with him down this path. I do, however, wish to counter his critique constructively and retain the public-policy usefulness of the *General Theory* analysis, without in any way evading the objections. This is what I shall do briefly below.

The key, I believe, is already present in this book. As many others who have sought to rehabilitate Keynes (Paul Davidson, for example) have said, there is a need to marry the analysis of the *Treatise on Money* with that of the *General Theory*. In the *Treatise*, Keynes's definition of income excludes profits, which are treated as a disequilibrium element. In analogy with Wicksell's conditions, Keynes takes zero macroeconomic profits as an equilibrium condition where prices are stable.

Now, while the *Treatise* includes this dynamic disequilibrium condition and the associated 'fundamental equations', the analysis in the *Treatise* is static. The *General Theory*, on the other hand, has a static framework, especially in Keynes's insistence on the Savings–Investment identity, but much of the analysis is a mixture of equilibrium comparative statics and disequilibrium dynamics. The paradox is that while in the *General Theory* Keynes works out the theory of the level of aggregate output, he is concerned with the ways in which output (or employment) can be changed. In the *Treatise*, the focus is on the changing price level but the Wicksell problem of conditions for a stable price level dominate the analysis. Indeed, despite all the recent writings on fixed-price 'Keynesian' models, Keynes says more about changes in the aggregate price level in Chapters 19–21 of the *General Theory* than he does in the *Treatise*.

The implications of all this are quite simple. The multiplier process is a disequilibrium dynamic one whereby output changes from one level to another. The converging geometric series merely sets a definite limit to the resultant increase in output between the two equilibrium situations but of course the multiplier as a number being a long-run value is only a potential not an actual. Thus it is of relevance for policy purposes to know that the multiplier of a certain tax change is higher than that of another but the actual income change from one year to the next will not fully reflect the multiplier. This is why econometric model builders have always distinguished between impact multipliers and dynamic multipliers.

Cencini insists absolutely that the $S \equiv I$ identity must hold at all times. I disagree. I believe it holds if you could artifically observe the economy in a state of rest as in the analogous condition of an unchanging price level. In an actual economy where banks actively give loans and advances to finance investment expenditure to which no 'real' savings correspond, the Savings–Investment equality is not the relevant one. As long as banks balance their books and do not go bankrupt, the actual source of finance for an investment programme is not of issue. This is because we are in a monetary economy and financial solvency is the only binding constraint on banks and other financial intermediaries.

Thus while the multiplier process is working itself out, we adopt the *Treatise* definitions but, unlike in the *Treatise*, the consequence of an injection into aggregate demand is that both the price level and the output level change. As events progress the share of output change and price change consequent upon an injection will vary. This can easily be seen if we realise that what we should be modelling is not the consumption–income relationship but the consumers' expenditure–income relationship. Consumption can only be measured ex-post and for reasons Keynes made eloquently clear in Chapter 4 of the *General Theory*, in a monetary economy what interests us for ex-ante decision making are quantities which are easily measurable and aggregatable. Real output, real capital and consumption do not fall into this category. If we now model the nominal consumers' expenditure and nominal income as a dynamic disequilibrium relation then the short-run (total, not partial) response of consumers' expenditure to income will be a variable not a constant. This varying partial response will be a consequence of the changing output and changing price response during the multiplier process. Being a variable coefficient, we cannot immediately translate that into a converging geometric series $1 + c + c^2$, etc. That formula is an idealisation, which holds only if either there are no price changes and the output change is constant, as in the textbook consumption function, or if the sum of price and output changes is constant for the entire process. These are textbook conditions unlikely to be met in real life.

Thus the multiplier has to be seen as a dynamic process and the equation defining its value as an idealisation but nothing more. When theorising about a monetary economy, we must be careful always to specify our relations in nominal terms and not fall into the bad old habits of thinking in the dichotomous real/monetary ways of neoclassical economics. 'Real' changes are then approximated by differences between aggregate nominal quantities and aggregate price level changes.

The task of constructing a theory of a monetary economy is however still unfinished. A few economists are working away at this. Alvaro Cencini comes from the French–Swiss School of Bernard Schmitt who has been uncompromising in his determination to build a theory for a monetary economy. We do not as yet have such a theory, nor can one hope that it will come from an individual's effort alone, Keynes's own example notwithstanding. I welcome this book as a contribution to the collective social effort that must be undertaken if we are to construct such an alternative theory.

Acknowledgements

I am particularly grateful to Bernard Schmitt of the Universities of Dijon (France) and Fribourg (Switzerland) who has constantly followed and encouraged this research, which is based on the theory he has been developing since 1953, and to Meghnad Desai, the supervisor of my Ph.D. dissertation at the London School of Economics, whose support and critical contribution have played an important role in the progress of this work.

Mauro Baranzini of The Queen's College, Oxford, invited me to his seminar on macroeconomics where I participated in many stimulating discussions, and he encouraged this research by publishing in his readings *Advances in Economic Theory* two articles relating to the new quantum approach to macroeconomics, introduced here mainly in Chapters 3 and 4. My thanks go also to Jerry Coackley of the Open University, who read the first draft of this work and gave me useful criticisms and suggestions. I would like to thank Christine Webb of London University for her invaluable help in improving the style of the English manuscript. Finally, I would like to record that the Fonds National Suisse de la Recherche Scientifique financed a major part of this research.

Introduction

Economic theories are becoming ever more complex. This phenomenon can be explained by the increasing intricacy of our economic apparatus, which deals with an increasing number of variables and complicated situations. Inflation, crisis and international payments are the main causes of disturbances in the system, and their effect is evident in many attempts at theoretical understanding.

The existence of a correlation between the intricacy of the economic world and the complexity of actual theories is surely obvious. Yet, a theory should lead us to a better understanding of the real world; it should go beyond appearances and tell us how to read reality. Unfortunately this does not seem to be the case with most economic theories. A 'descriptive picture' is, in fact, the most appropriate definition of many theories whose aim is to explain the past and present, and to forecast the future. As long as we simply try to describe observable facts, any insight into their logical interrelation will be unattainable.

The definition and measurement of national income cannot merely be derived from observation and abstraction from the real process of production. This process can simply try to describe the physical characteristics of the product, but it cannot express its economic and social value. This information results from an inductive analysis which necessarily goes beyond purely factual observation.

We shall therefore try to develop our analysis along logical lines capable of penetrating the 'defensive belt' of appearances to get to the 'hard core' of economics. Our main purpose is to throw some light on the relation between time and economics, with particular reference to the problem of income determination.

We certainly do not need to remind the reader of the importance of time in economics. As Marshall pointed out, the 'element of Time is the centre of the chief difficulty of almost every economic problem'.[1] This difficulty has been currently identified with the necessity of integrating time into a given set of equations. Accordingly, economic variables have been expressed as continuous or discontinuous functions of time.

One of the first attempts to integrate time was the use of the distinction between flow and stock variables introduced by Fisher. Thereafter, conditions of equilibrium for the whole system were elaborated in terms of flow and stock.[2] Now, these conditions do not explain the passage from one situation to another. In the general equilibrium models, time is in some respect put aside, since a state of equilibrium is a timeless concept.[3]

Therefore, new attempts were made to take time fully into account. Analysis of capital is undoubtedly one of the most serious examples of such an attempt. Unfortunately, neither Hicks's study of the 'traverse' nor Bliss's work on intertemporal and temporary equilibrium systems represents a definitive answer to this difficult question.[4] The working of a dynamic system has still to be fully understood and in this respect it could prove worthwhile to re-examine critically some of the widely accepted axioms of our science in their relation to time.

Income is one of the variables which are supposed to be a function of time. Now, the question should be asked whether it is right or not to analyse income as a continuous or discontinuous function of time. If we define time as a one-way stream whose main characteristic is irreversibility and whose main consequence is the distinction between past and future,[5] the flow description of income seems applicable. Yet, the ensuing 'earning through spending' theory of income remains a vicious circle, and, moreover, this circularity is unavoidable as long as income is considered a function of time.

The logical weakness of the 'earning through spending' theory of income lies in its incapacity to establish any relation between income and production. The result is an explanation of economics which does not account for the existence of a net product.

A further undermining of the traditional definition of income as a flow of expenditures results from Keynes's identity between total supply and total demand. Now, this identity finds its logical consequence in his analysis of the *instantaneous* multiplier, which proves once and for all that the value of the multiplier is necessarily always one.

Despite Keynes's effort, traditional theorists have not

abandoned the concept of income as a function of time. This functional relation is, however, neither a necessary nor a sufficient condition for the determination of income. The traditional theory of production, which results from an unfortunate analogy between physical mechanics and economics, is logically inconsistent with the economic definition of expenditure. In particular, the equivalence of expenditure and its instantaneous result points to a new analysis of production and to a new approach with respect to time. The instantaneousness of the expenditure defining national income is, in fact, related to a positive and indivisible period of time: a *quantum of time.*

The importance of the quantum-theory approach to economics becomes evident once it is proved that Keynes's identities are logically related to quantum time. By means of this analysis it can thus be eventually established that production is a process of creation, and not merely a process of physical transformation. Accordingly, the expenditure defining the creation of income is an *emission*, i.e. an instantaneous event which quantises time. The final expenditure of income is then also an emission (of the same amount and of the same time dimension as its corresponding production, but of opposite sign), so that the identity of total demand and total supply is definitively established by quantum analysis.

The theory of emissions, first developed by Bernard Schmitt, introduces a new approach to macroeconomics. Traditional general equilibrium analysis can then be rejected and substituted by a theory where the dichotomy between the real and monetary world is finally overcome. The definition of the product in terms of wage units means, in fact, that the commodities are instantaneously determined as a monetary entity and not as the physical counterpart of wages. The integration between money and product is thus one of the main results of quantum analysis. Some other important results are the formal proof that there is only one factor of production, and that, although necessarily equal in quantum time, saving and investment adjust to one another in continuous time.

This last result, which is based on the distinction between quantum time and continuous time, allows the equalisation of S and I *within a given income*, i.e. within the identity of total demand and total supply. This adjustment explains the variation of the rate of interest and is only one example of the analysis yielded by the new quantum theory. Many others can be obtained if we follow Keynes's suggestion and try to develop a macroeconomic approach to economics.

> The classical theorists resemble Euclidean geometers in a non-Euclidean world who, discovering that in experience straight lines apparently parallel often meet, rebuke the lines for not keeping straight—as the only remedy for the unfortunate collisions which are occurring. Yet, in truth, there is no remedy except to throw over the axiom of parallels and to work out a non-Euclidean geometry. Something similar is required to-day in economics.[6]

Accordingly, our study will be concerned with a critical appraisal of the functional determination of income, as well as with the introduction of some elements supporting the new theory. The categories of stock and flow, and the concepts of period and continuous analysis, identity and equilibrium, static and dynamic, provide the context of our four chapters.

In the first we analyse Keynes's fundamental identities, $Y \equiv C + I$ and $I \equiv S$, with respect to time and equilibrium. The second chapter deals with a critical appraisal of income determination through multiplier analysis and leads us to a new, timeless definition of a finite period of time (Chapter 3). The quantum theory of income is the subject of this chapter. Finally, in the fourth chapter, we underline a fundamental role played by the distinction between continuous and quantum time.

NOTES

1. A. Marshall, *Principles of Economics*, London, Macmillan, 1950, p. vii.
2. J. R. Hicks, *Capital and Growth*, London, Oxford University Press, 1965.
3. J. R. Hicks, 'Some questions of time in economics', in *Evolution, Welfare and Time in Economics*, ed. A. M. Tang, Lexington, Mass., Lexington Books, 1976.
4. J. R. Hicks, *Capital and Time*, London, Oxford University Press, 1973, and C. J. Bliss, *Capital Theory and the Distribution of Income*, Amsterdam, North-Holland/American Elsevier, 1975.
5. J. Robinson, *Collected Economic Papers*, Vol. IV, Oxford, Blackwell, 1973, and Hicks, 'Some questions of time', op. cit.
6. J. M. Keynes, *The General Theory of Employment, Interest and Money*, London, Macmillan, 1973, p. 16.

1 The Definition of National Income

PART I: INCOME AS A FLOW OF EXPENDITURES

1. Stocks and flows

Time, 'the great independent variable of human experience', has been introduced into economic analysis by way of a distinction between aggregates which are timeless concepts and aggregates which have a positive time dimension. Stocks and flows are the terms which, most conveniently, describe these concepts. 'When we speak of a certain quantity of wealth we may refer either to a quantity existing at a particular instant of time, or to a quantity produced, consumed, exchanged or transported during a period of time. The first quantity is a '*stock* (or *fund*) of wealth; the second quantity is a *flow* (or *stream*) of wealth.'[1] A good picture of this distinction is given by Lerner.

The relationship between the stock and the flow is illustrated in Figure 1.1. The *stock* of water in the tank at any point of time is measured on the scale that tells by the height of the water how many cubic feet are in the tank. The *flow* of water out of the tank is measured by means of the meter which tells you how many cubic feet have passed through the meter in the

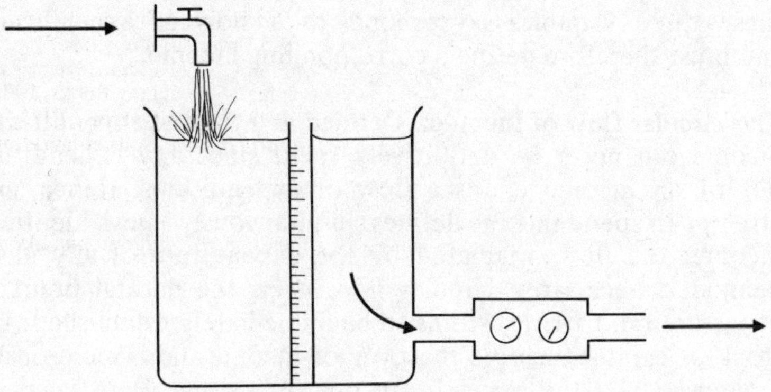

Fig. 1.1.

period that has elapsed since the last time the meter was read. The stock refers to a *point* in time and is measured simply as so many cubic feet. The flow refers to a *period* and is measured not as so many cubic feet, but as so many cubic feet *per hour* or *per month* or other period.[2]

This analysis, until now never rejected by any economist, establishes the functional relation between time and a certain number of economic variables. Thereafter, every economic concept has been classified according to whether it can be expressed as a function of time or not.

The traditional definition of income. Definitions of income and capital are the clearest example of the implications inherent in this approach.

The distinction between a fund and a flow has many applications in economic science. The most important application is to differentiate between capital and income. Capital is a fund and income a flow. This difference between capital and income is, however, not the only one. There is another important difference, namely, the capital is *wealth* and income is the *service* of wealth. We have therefore the following definitions: A *stock of wealth* existing at an *instant* of time is called *capital*. A *flow of services* through a *period* of time is called income.[3]

The definition of income as a *flow of expenditures* is a very broad one and tends toward a generalisation capable of explaining the relationship between such apparently different concepts as consumption, saving and investment. In fact, it is said, all these three variables correspond to a flow of expenditures and must therefore define a corresponding income.

The circular flow of income. Defined as a flow of expenditures, income can never be definitively spent since any expenditure out of an income elicits a flow of expenditures. Hence, any attempt to spend income defines simultaneously a new, identical, income: the flow originated by the expenditure of any given income is necessarily circular. Moreover, the natural point of departure (and arrival) seems to be immediately established: the stock of capital finances the flow of income and is reciprocally replenished by the expenditure out of income. Here again we can refer to Lerner's illustration of the circuit.

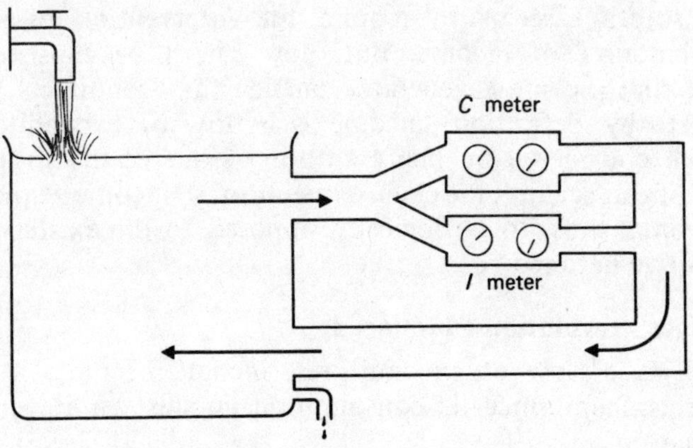

Fig. 1.2.

> [Figure 1.2] illustrates the division of the flow of spending into consumption and investment. The large flow above represents consumption and the small flow below represents investment, each of these flows being measured by its own meter. The two flows together add up to the total of spending.[4]

In this representation the stream of income does not affect capital, whose magnitude remains constant through time.

Net income. This last description is therefore incomplete since it does not take into account the increase in capital due to the net income produced by the banking system. 'As we widen our assumptions to bring them nearer reality, the more tenuous does a definition by "constant income stream" become.'[5] In fact, the theory should not only explain how the stock of capital is maintained by the flow of income, but also how it can be increased once the system produces a positive net income.

Unfortunately, the 'earning through spending' theory of income is of no help here, since it does not account for the existence of a net income. Being a flow of expenditures, income cannot increase since expenditures cannot be greater than the income which feeds them. Thus, if capital is supposed to be the only source of income, the theory must conclude that the flow of income will always maintain the stock of capital. In fact, how could capital increase, given that its expenditure necessarily gives birth to an equivalent income whose expenditure is its own definition?

The solution seems to require the intervention of some external source of income. But, how can it be consistently claimed that income is generated outside the economic system and that, by definition, income is a flow of expenditures? Although considered by many authors as one of the strongest axioms of our science, the chain expenditures→income→expenditures seems, thus, to be logically opposed to the existence of any positive net income.

2. Keynes's revolution announced

Defined as a flow of expenditures, income becomes a very peculiar concept since its consumption implies simultaneously its formation.

> The *income* earned in any period of time is always *exactly equal* to the *spending* in that period of time. Income must be exactly equal to spending simply because the two words refer to the same thing looked at from different points of view. Every receipt of a dollar of income is also the outlay of a dollar of spending.[6]

Coming from one of the most faithful followers of Keynes, this statement deserves to be examined closely. At first sight it seems to reproduce conscientiously Keynes's analysis. In fact, the Keynesian identity between Y and $C + I$ could easily be interpreted as a relation establishing the equivalence of income earning and income spending: the flow of income, Y, is exactly equal to the flow of expenditures on consumption and investment goods. Now, if we accept the definition of income as a flow of expenditures, $Y \equiv C + I$ would appear to be a simple formalisation which does not improve our understanding of the problem. If we did not care about words we should say that Keynes's contribution is reduced here to a mere truism.

Yet, this misinterpretation of Keynes's fundamental identity unfortunately goes far beyond the platitude of a truism: the identity of Y and $C + I$ is used to prove the existence of a logically uninterrupted chain of incomes.

> The sum of the incomes of all the individuals in the economy, Y, is equal to the sum of the expenditures of all kinds by the individuals of the economy, since these expenditures *are* nothing but the payments, the receipt of which constitutes all the incomes. The sum of all the payments must be equal to the sum of all receipts in the same period, since these are the same thing, only looked at from different angles.[7]

The subsequent statement that 'only spending on currently produced goods and services creates income'[8] does not substantially modify the result. Even when limited to the spending on currently produced goods and services, the principle is accepted that *income spending does not destroy but creates new income.*

Attempting to consolidate the validity of $Y \equiv C + I$, Lerner thinks he has a proof in the statement that income created is necessarily spent because income spending is a creation of income.

> The total income of society (Y) is made up of the income earned in making consumption goods (C) and the income earned in making investment goods (I). $Y = C + I$.
>
> Now C, which stands for income earned in making consumption goods, must also stand for the amount spent on buying consumption goods, since these two are in fact the same thing. (Similarly I stands also for the amount of money spent on investment goods.)[9]

In reality it can be shown, and that will be one of the main tasks of our work, that Keynes's identity does not rely upon such a circular definition. In particular, we shall prove that the two terms of $Y \equiv C + I$ are not tautologically identical and do not imply any functional link between succeeding incomes. A veritable revolution in economic thinking, Keynes's analysis introduces a new concept of income which can no longer be considered a flow of expenditures. More precisely, we shall see that Keynes's theory reconciles two apparently opposing requirements.

1. Income is necessarily equal to final expenditures on consumption and investment.
2. No income is created by C and I.

Before pursuing our analysis, let us briefly point out an inconsistency present in Lerner's theory of income determination. Having claimed that income earning is equal to income spending for the economy as a whole, Lerner gives us the following example.

> To simplify our example to the extreme, let us suppose that no investment takes place at all so that we can for the time being leave it out

of the picture. Income is then created only by the spending on consumption goods and is equal to consumption. This gives us our first equation, $Y = C$, where Y stands for income and C stands for consumption.

The second equation is provided by the *propensity to consume*, which is the way in which consumers adjust their consumption to their income. Let us suppose that $C = 40 + 2/3\ (Y - 40)$. This means that the propensity to consume is such that the people in the country will consume 40 billion dollars a year plus two-thirds of any excess of their income over 40 billion dollars.

We have two equations:

$$Y = C, \tag{1}$$

$$C = 40 + 2/3\ (Y - 40). \tag{2}$$

The first equation enables us to substitute Y for C in (2), obtaining an equation with a single unknown:

$$Y = 40 + 2/3\ (Y - 40).$$

Solving this by easy steps we have

$$Y = 40 + 2/3(Y) - 2/3(40),$$

$$Y - 2/3(Y) = 40 - 2/3(40)$$

$$\frac{Y}{3} = \frac{40}{3},$$

$$Y = 40.$$

Or, without algebra, we can see without much difficulty that it is impossible for any income other than 40 billion dollars to satisfy both the equality of income to consumption and the propensity to consume which is supposed to rule.[10]

Now, if 'income is created only by the spending on consumption goods' the propensity to consume can have no influence at all on the determination of income, which is always equal to C. Whatever the consumption, Y will perfectly adjust to it so that there will never be a difference between the two. Therefore, the only compatible value of the propensity to consume is 1. Obviously enough, if C is necessarily always equal to $Y (Y \equiv C)$, and c is the propensity to consume, in the relation $C = cY$, c can only be equal to 1.

This result is not surprising, since identity $Y = C$ states that all income is necessarily consumed. It then follows that Lerner's second equation is completely useless for the determination of income. This can also be easily verified mathematically: whatever propensity to consume is chosen, Y will always be equal to the constant term of the consumption equation. If, for example, the propensity to consume is 1/2 instead of 2/3, we have $C = 40 + 1/2\ (Y - 40)$ whence, given $Y = C$, it follows that

$$Y = 40 + 1/2\ (Y - 40) = 1/2\ Y - 20 = 40.$$

Analogously, for a propensity to consume of 2/5, we have

$$Y = 40 + 2/5\ (Y - 40) = 2/5\ Y - 24 = 40,$$

and so on for any conceivable value of the propensity to consume. Generally, from

$$Y = C \text{ and}$$

$$C = a + c(Y - a),$$

it necessarily follows that

$$Y = a + cY - ac,$$

$$Y(1 - c) = a(1 - c),$$

$$Y = a.$$

Now, it could be said that this result is based on a particular numerical example and cannot be applied to the more general case where the consumption function is expressed by

$$C = a + bY. \tag{1.1}$$

In fact, it can be shown that even in this case income is always equal to the constant term of the consumption function, a. Equation (1.1), given that

$$Y = C,$$

can also be written as follows:

$$Y = a + bY.$$

Thus:

$$Y(1-b) = a,$$

$$Y = \frac{a}{1-b}.$$

But the expression

$$\frac{1}{1-b}$$

is nothing other than the algebraical expression of the multiplier k. Now, anticipating the result of Chapter 2, we can write

$$\frac{1}{1-b} = k = 1.$$

From which it follows that

$$Y = a.$$

Let us start again with the definition of income as a stream of expenditures. We already know that acceptance of this hypothesis implies a chain of causalities whose result can at most account for the maintenance of capital and the constancy of income. The logical impossibility of explaining any increase in income and capital seems therefore unavoidable. Yet, many authors believe that the increase of income can be easily explained, their reason being the interaction of saving and investment.

3. The controversy on saving and investment

Provided it is agreed that income is equal to the value of current output, that current investment is equal to the value of that part of current output which is not consumed, and that saving is equal to the excess of income over consumption—all of which conform both to common sense and to traditional usage by the great majority of economists—the equality of saving and investment necessarily follows. In short

income = value of output = consumption + investment;
saving = income − consumption;
therefore saving = investment.

Thus any set of definitions which satisfy the above conditions leads to the same conclusion. It is only by denying the validity of one or other of them that the conclusion can be avoided.[11]

This and other passages of *The General Theory* have been the cause of one of the most exciting controversies among economists.

On one side there were, and still are, those who believe that the identity is a simple matter of definition, whereas on the other side we find those who interpret the identity as a condition of equilibrium. Though very different in their conclusions, both of these schools accept as their starting point Keynes's fundamental identity between income, Y, and final expenditures on consumption and investment goods, $C + I$. 'By definition, *national income* (at market prices), Y, can initially be set equal to the sum of consumption expenditure, C, and *net investment*, I: $Y = C + I$.'[12]

Even if Keynes never affirms the existence of a causal relation between income spending, $C + I$, and income earning, Y, we shall momentarily admit this hypothetical circularity to suit our analysis to the generally accepted interpretation of Keynes's identity.[13]

Now, given these premises, our two schools of thought have first to face a simple and logical test. Each of the two hypotheses:

$$S \text{ and } I \text{ are always equal by definition,} \tag{1.2}$$
$$S = I \text{ is a condition of equilibrium,} \tag{1.3}$$

must be confronted with the accepted axiom of the identity between Y and $C + I$. Bearing in mind that *we are dealing only with actual or realised quantities*, so that Hansen's distinction between actual and desired as well as Klein's distinction between desired and virtual quantities do not apply here,[14] we can easily verify that one of the two hypotheses is inconsistent with $Y \equiv C + I$.

$Y \equiv C + I$ and the equilibrium of S and I. For the sake of clarity let us suppose that $C = 0$. $Y \equiv C + I$ is therefore reduced to the simpler form of $Y \equiv I$. Thus, I is the measure of Y, which means that Y can only be known through final spending on investment goods. Consider now $S = I$ as a condition of equilibrium. The adjustability between S and I implies their possible quantitative difference: $S \gtrless I$ at any point outside equilibrium. Yet, saving is unanimously defined as 'that part of the income of the period which has not passed into consumption.'[15] Given $C = 0$ it immediately follows that S represents all the income of the period, $Y = S$, and therefore that I and S are necessarily equal.

Not surprisingly, this result holds even if we do not put C equal to zero. The main reason is that C and I are the *total* measure of Y, so that $S \gtrless I$ could only be possible if there were an income which did not correspond to $C + I$. Once we accept that saving is the excess of income over consumption, the definition of income imposes the necessary equality of S and I.

Equilibrium of S and I has also been analysed in terms of flows. According to a widely accepted definition, income, saving and investment are flow variables. Income is a stream of expenditures and so are saving and investment. Now, the equilibrium hypothesis considers S and I as two opposed forces trying to neutralise each other, leaving income at a constant level. In terms of flows, this proposition sounds extremely odd. How could it be possible, in fact, for one flow to neutralise another and thus maintain the main flow (Y)?

> The rate of change of income depends upon the difference between savings and investment such that income rises when investment exceeds savings, and income falls when savings exceed investment. In equilibrium, income has a zero rate of change; it is neither rising nor falling. Equilibrium, in this sense, implies that there is no difference between savings and investment. Thus the Keynesian savings–investment equation can be looked upon as the equilibrium solution of a dynamical system.[16]

Let us try to represent such a dynamic process. The first step is the refusal of any diagram of the kind shown in Figure 1.3,

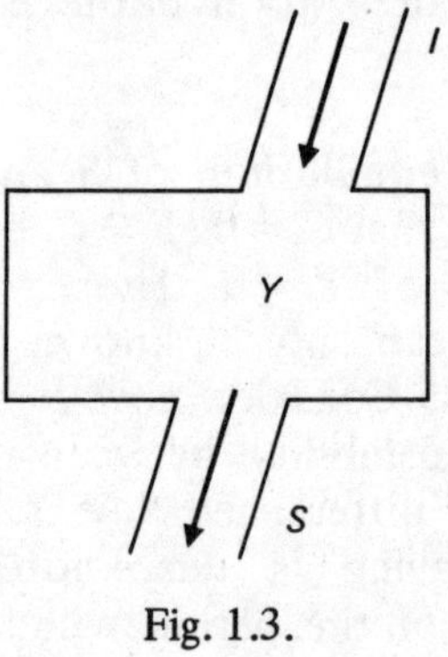

Fig. 1.3.

where income is transformed into a stock. The representation in Figure 1.4, although it respects the flow component of our three variables, does not take into account that I is a part of Y. We have, therefore, the representation of income shown in Figure 1.5. In this case, what does the equilibrium of S and I

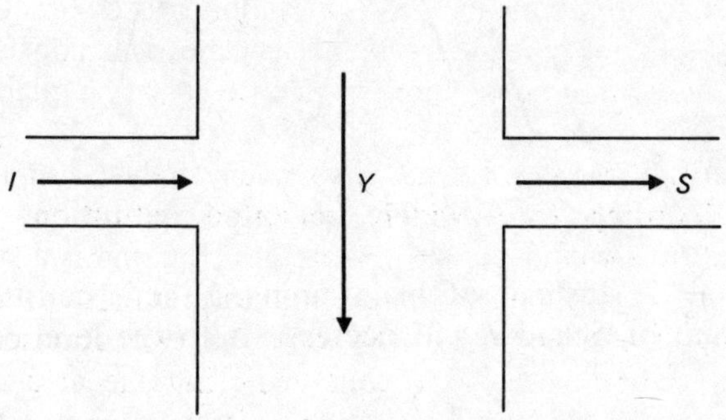

Fig. 1.4.

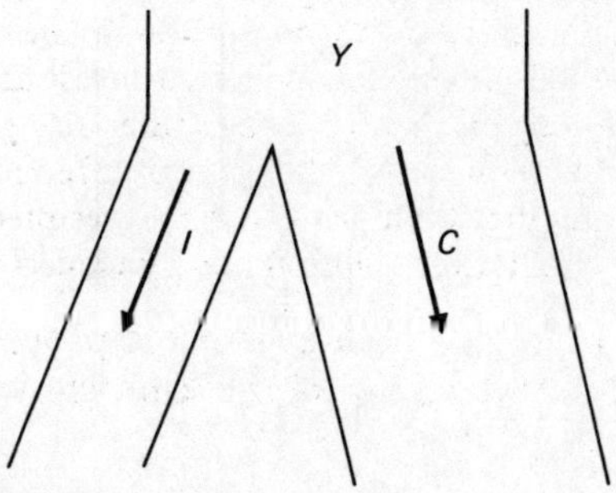

Fig. 1.5.

mean? If we consider equilibrium as a state in which opposite forces, applied to the same object, neutralise each other and leave the object at rest, how can we represent S in our diagram? Perhaps like a flow of the same strength as I but flowing in the opposite direction? (See Figure 1.6.) Whether or not we were able to represent it in a diagram, the result of the equilibrium between S and I would be unacceptable in any case, since Y would be reduced to C, so contradicting our starting point:

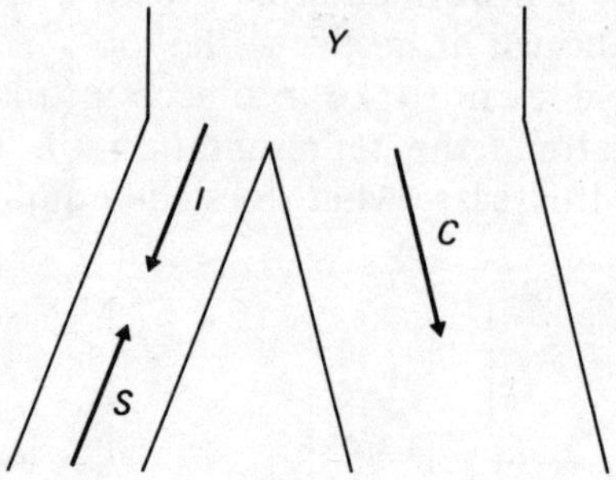

Fig. 1.6.

$Y \equiv C + I$. Instead of maintaining Y at a constant level, equilibrium of S and I will decrease it to the level of C. (See Figure 1.7.)

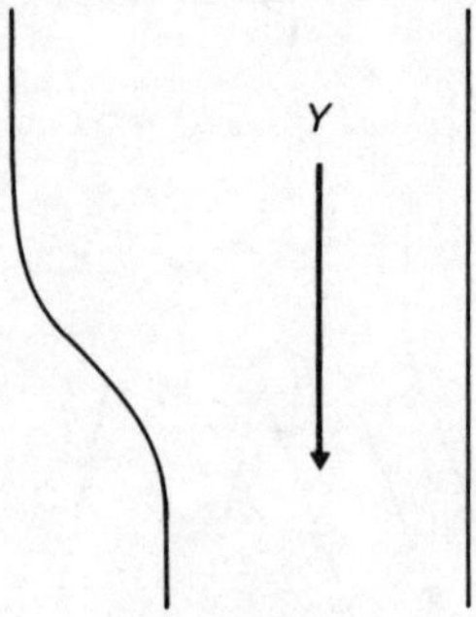

Fig. 1.7.

An alternative analysis of the flow of income is offered by Lipsey, who states that saving and investment can be represented respectively as a leakage from and an injection into the circuit of income (see Figure 1.8). If saving and investment are the only withdrawal and the only injection into the circular flow of income and if, moreover, 'any internal lag-generated fluctuation is removed', then the system is in equilibrium when saving equals investment. According to Lipsey, this situation is very rarely, if ever, realised: saving and investment are usually different, and even when they are equal their equality is not sufficient to ensure the equilibrium of the flow of income.

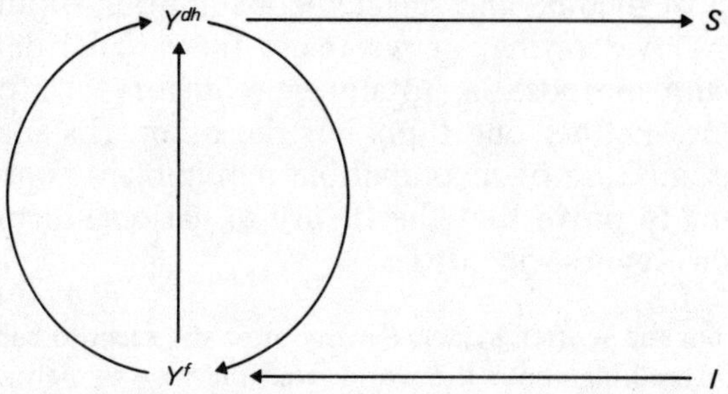

Fig. 1.8.

Leaving aside the problem of lags, and assuming that there are no injections other than investment and no withdrawals other than saving,[17] let us prove that Lipsey's analysis is inconsistent with the definition of income as a flow of expenditures. Firstly, let us note that saving and investment are also considered as flows of expenditures. In particular, saving is defined as that part of income which is spent by households to buy bonds, and 'investment is defined as expenditure on capital goods and inventories'.[18]

Now, according to the 'earning through spending' theory of income, saving and investment are expenditures that can only originate from a pre-existent income. This is evident as far as saving is concerned, since the purchase of bonds is financed by the income earned by households. The case of investment is apparently equally simple. In fact, expenditure on capital goods and inventories could be financed by saving, thus respecting the circular flow of income. The difficulty arises, however, when it is said that saving and investment can be different. How can investment be greater than saving, if saving is the only income which can be spent for the purchase of investment goods? Unless we accept the metaphysical idea of 'spontaneous creation and destruction of goods and money',[19] no positive difference between investment and saving can be accounted for within an 'earning through spending' theory of income. Where could an excess of investment come from, given that investment is an expenditure and that every expenditure comes out of an income? The only possible answer within the circular flow of income is saving, which means that either we accept this definition of income and reject the assumption of an excess of investment over saving, or we reject the circular definition of income and propose a totally new theory. Unfortunately, Lipsey does neither one thing nor the other. His analysis is an erroneous mixture of incompatible requirements introduced in an attempt to prove that the theory of national income cannot be built on Keynes's identities.

> Judging from the written evidence many of us still seem to believe that we can learn something about the world from the way we define our terms, and that there are key and important definitions (identities) which somehow exist in the world waiting to be discovered by a genius such as Keynes.[20]

Given the importance of the argument developed by Lipsey, we shall analyse it later in some detail. For the time being, let us stick to the problem of the definition of income as a flow of expenditures.

Hoarding and equilibrium. A solution allowing an equilibrium analysis of S and I seems nevertheless to be possible once we introduce the concept of hoarding.

> A more common-sense objection to the proposition that saving and investment must always and inevitably be equal to each other is to be found in the query whether the identity of these two cannot be upset by *hoarding.* In the case of any individual it is clear that there is no need for his saving to be equal to his investment. When an individual saves more than he invests he is said to *hoard* the difference. Why cannot society do the same? And if society hoards (or dishoards) will that not make saving greater (or less) than investment?[21]

Hoarding is, by definition, that part of income which is not spent to purchase either consumption or investment goods. Saving is, also by definition, the excess of income over consumption. It seems therefore reasonable to say that hoarding is a part of saving.[22] Thereafter any increase in income can be devoted to three different usages: it can be consumed, invested or hoarded. Moreover it would always be true that

$$\text{saving} = \text{investment} + \text{hoarding},$$

so that income can be represented by $Y = C + S$ or, equivalently, by $Y = C + I + H$. It then follows that S and I are equal only when $H = 0$: identity of S and I has become a condition of equilibrium.

Now, despite its powerful simplicity, this solution is mistaken because it is widely inconsistent with the accepted definition of income. Let us suppose that hoarding is positive. Income, which is measured by $C + S$, is then greater than $C + I$, since $S = I + H$ where $H > 0$. But how can the income produced be greater than the income spent when final spending *is the measure* of income earning? How can we have $Y > C + I$ when, by definition, $Y \equiv C + I$? Obviously, the inequality is inconsistent with the identity and, since an identity can never be dismissed, the initial hypothesis of positive hoarding must be rejected: macroeconomic hoarding is necessarily nil.

This astonishing result is also confirmed by another short analysis. Unlike income, consumption and investment, hoarding is not a flow.

> Sometimes 'hoarding' means a reduction in the velocity of circulation, the irrelevance of which has been shown. Sometimes it means simply holding stocks of money. Sometimes it means increasing one's stock of money. And most frequently it mysteriously means all three of these simultaneously, as well as a lengthening of the period an individual holds particular coins or notes. The concept of *stock* inherent in all of these usages renders irrelevant any validity that the particular meaning of 'hoarding' may retain.[23]

As it is a stock, hoarding cannot be included in the measure of income which represents a *flow* of expenditures on C and I. Positive hoarding will decrease the flow of income and will therefore be excluded from its measure. Symbolically, income cannot be represented by $C + I + H$ since 'anybody is hoarding who does something "calculated", as the police would say, to cause a hitch up in the flow of money income'.[24]

Lerner is therefore perfectly right in pointing out that positive (negative) hoardings are inconsistent with a circular definition of income. Since income is formed through spending, hoarding is never a part of it because hoarding represents an income which is not spent and, therefore, an income which does not exist.[25] I and C are positive incomes since expenditures on C and I maintain income at its previous level; hoarding, on the contrary, is an income which negates itself. 'The *income* earned in any period of time is always *exactly* equal to the *spending* in that period of time. Income must be exactly equal to spending simply because the two words refer to the same thing looked at from different points of view'.[26]

4. $I = S$: a tautology?

According to the circular definition of income, hoarding is necessarily always nil and investment necessarily always equal to saving.

The income of the whole society is earned by the members of the society in producing either consumption goods or other kinds of goods. We call these other goods investment goods. This gives us our first equation. The total income of society (Y) is made up of the income earned in making consumption goods (C) and the income earned in making investment goods (I). $Y = C + I$.

Now C, which stands for income earned in making consumption goods, must also stand for the amount spent on buying consumption goods, since these two are in fact the same thing. (Similarly I stands also for the amount of money spent on investment goods.) The aggregate amount of saving in any period (S) is defined as the excess of aggregate income in the period over the expenditure on consumption goods. This, the almost universal definition of saving, gives us our second equation $S = Y - C$ (definition).

From these two equations it follows that saving must always be equal to investment. $S = I$.[27]

Again, according to the circular definition of income, saving and investment are equal precisely because their definition is one and the same. This argument is not surprising, since Keynes himself calls both saving and investment the 'excess of income over consumption' and concludes that '*saving* and *investment* have been so defined that they are necessarily equal in amount, being, for the community as a whole, merely different aspects of the same thing'.[28]

As a matter of fact, $S \equiv I$ seems to be already implied in $Y \equiv C + I$.

Total spending and therefore total income consist of consumption plus investment. This is seen when we look at income to see how it is created. If we look at what is done with the income, we see that a part of it is consumed. The remainder is what we call 'saving'. Income is then also equal to consumption plus saving. Consumption plus investment is thus equal to consumption plus saving, both being equal to the same thing—income—and so equal to each other. It follows that the investment that takes place in any period is always equal to the saving that takes place in the same period.[29]

The starting point is always the same: income is created by spending. Since expenditures are only related to C and I, it follows that $Y \equiv C + I$. Now this same income can be looked at from a different point of view. Instead of analysing its formation we can consider its utilisation, and immediately we find that it can be either consumed or saved. But consumption and saving are the utilisation of an income which is created by its own expenditure. Therefore, if we refer to the income of a given period its utilisation is nothing but its conservation through spending, which implies the necessary equality of S and I.

Formed by $C + I$, income can be consumed or saved, yet in both cases it is necessarily spent, since a non-spent income is a contradiction in terms. This means that saving must be invested, since investment alone is that part of income which is spent but not consumed. The necessary equality of S and I is then fully implied in the definition of income as a causal chain of earning through spending. This is because expenditures on C and I are simultaneously the creation of income and its utilisation.

> All incomes are derived either from producing consumption goods or from producing investment goods. And all income either is spent on consumption goods or is saved. The income derived from producing consumption goods is equal to what is spent on them. Therefore what is saved is equal to the income derived from producing investment goods. In short, the rate of saving is equal to the rate of investment.[30]

The central point here is the identity of the two equations

$$Y \equiv C + I, \text{ defining the formation of income, and} \quad (1.4)$$

$$Y \equiv C + S, \text{ defining its utilisation.} \quad (1.5)$$

If we consider (1.4) and (1.5) as relating to the same object, identity $I \equiv S$ follows immediately or, according to Robertson, tautologically. 'Evidently, if we define our terms suitably this statement is true, because it is what is called a tautology.'[31]

As we already know, $H = 0$ is also a result of the identity between (1.4) and (1.5). In fact, from the statement

$$\text{income creation} = \text{income utilisation,}$$

and since income is created through spending, it follows that income utilisation = income spending.

Since it is that part of income which is not spent, hoarding is consequently excluded from (1.5), which implies that H is necessarily always nil.

Consider the income of a period chosen arbitrarily, say p_x. According to the 'creating through spending' theory of income, Y of p_x is formed by the expenditure of an equivalent preceding income which is therefore '*conserved*' through spending. Income of p_x comes from consumption and investment of p_{x-1}, which in turn comes from C and I of p_{x-2}, and so on. Y of p_x is also spent for the purchase of consumption and investment goods, which means that it is also conserved through its spending. Thus the analysis seems to result very naturally in an uninterrupted succession of incomes through time.

Before exploring this point let us take a last critical glance at the identity of I and S.

Returning to the possible disequilibrium of *I* and *S*. As was first pointed out by M. Curtis in her brilliant article 'Is money saving equal to investment?',[32] equations (1.4) and (1.5) do not refer to the same aspect of income. Equation (1.4) is concerned with income formation, equation (1.5) with income disposal. They define two different processes referring to the same object, and must logically be kept separate. It is obviously true that $C + I$ and $C + S$ give us the same numerical value of Y, nevertheless $S \equiv I$ cannot be deduced from this simple arithmetical relation. The reason is that I refers to the spending of a preceding income, whereas S is related to the income resulting from this spending. I is the part of Yp_{x-1} which is spent for the purchase of investment goods, while S is the part of Yp_x which is not spent in buying consumption goods. By imposing the necessary equality of I and S we would therefore impose a constancy upon the amount of investment, which does not seem to be implied in (1.4) and (1.5).

In fact income Yp_x, created by the spending of Yp_{x-1}, could be partially hoarded, the only effect of this decision being a reduction in the flow of income: Yp_{x+1} will be smaller than Yp_x. But what about the objection that hoarding is a non-existent income? Here again the answer is very clear. Even if it is true that an income which is not spent is an income which does not reproduce itself, this does not at all imply its non-existence.

If this analysis is correct it follows that the value of hoarding ($\gtrless 0$) modifies income formation which can thereafter be greater or smaller than income utilisation or equal to it. Suppose that income created in p_x is equal to 100 and that hoarding takes the following successive values: +10 in p_x; 0 in p_{x+1}, −10 in p_{x+2}. Then, income earned in p_x is less than income spent in the same period, since only 90 units are spent on C and I. In p_{x+1} income formation and income spending are equal, whereas in p_{x+2} income spent is greater than income formed, the difference being caused by a dishoarding of 10. Yet these results, which imply a possible inequality of I and S, do not respect the numerical identity of $C + I$ and $C + S$. Each of these expressions refers to the same income, which is indifferently measured by the total spending that creates it, $C + I$, or by its final use, $C + S$. This equality could be said to be respected in the first two periods of our example. In fact, there is no reason why the positive hoarding of p_x could not be accounted for in $C + S$. In this case, income earned in p_x, $C + I = 100$, would be equal to the use made of it, $C + S$, where $S = I' + H = I$. Although not spent, hoarding is considered a disposable income, so that its inclusion in $C + S$ is fully justified. In our second period, p_{x+1}, the equality is immediately respected, since hoarding is zero; but what about p_{x+2}?

In this third period income utilisation is increased by the amount of dishoarding and this introduces an irreducible gap between $C + S$ and $C + I$. Since it is still available for disposal, the income previously hoarded can be spent at any moment, but when it is, the new expenditures, $C + S$, are increased. This, however, leaves unaltered $C + I$, the income created before the spending of $C + S$. Clearly inconsistent with the definitional identity of $C + I$ and $C + S$, this analysis corroborates our previous result: the rejection of hoarding as a possible factor of inequality between saving and investment. Does this vindicate the analysis supporting the identity of I and S within an 'earning by spending' theory of income?

5. The 'vicious' circle

Robertson is right in pointing out the vicious circularity implied in a theory which explains income through its own expenditure. 'But it is clear that this disconcerting result only follows if we insist on identifying the income received in any small slice of time with the income whose expenditure (*plus* or *minus* certain other items) generates the income received in this small slice of time.'[33] How can it be said that income can be created only by its own spending? How can society spend an income which does not exist before its expenditure? In other words, spending cannot be the cause of income formation, since income is the necessary source of spending.

Like Descartes, who was desperately trying to break his famous 'Cartesian circle' in an attempt to prove the existence of God, we would struggle in vain against the inconsistency represented by the causal chain of incomes. Nevertheless suppose, absurdly, that income earning and income spending can be confused. As a result we would have a constant income stream, which logically would last for ever. Finally, in this hypothesis, income is never created nor spent: it is 'preserved' through time. If Y were used to purchase C and I it would be inconsistent to infer that Y has been spent, since the same income would be simultaneously earned by society. Analogously, no positive income could ever be formed, since income earning would always correspond, instantaneously and for the same subject, to an income spending of exactly the same amount. Thus income conservation is what earning through spending is all about.

Consequently, neither income spending nor income earning are theoretically explained. The question of the source of income remains unanswered. Referring earning to spending and spending to earning *ad infinitum* is no solution: which comes first, earning or spending, the chicken or the egg? Being an infinite series of sequences, the income chain is incapable of solving this problem and must therefore be rejected.

Does this imply the analytical rejection of $S \equiv I$? Since the identity of saving and investment seems to rely upon zero hoarding, and since zero hoarding is a consequence of income conservation, the answer is apparently positive. Once we reject the restrictive hypothesis of earning through spending there seems to be no reason for hoarding to be constantly zero, and once hoarding is varying freely identity of S and I becomes a condition of equilibrium.

The idea of regarding any observed value of national income as the equilibrium value corresponding to an equation between savings and investment, in the schedule sense, is somewhat artificial. A more realistic view is that the observed levels of national income are observed as the result of a continuous dynamical process . . . In this model, savings depend upon the level of income; investment depends upon the level of income; the rate of change of income depends upon the difference between savings and investment such that income rises when investment exceeds savings, and income falls when savings exceed investment. In equilibrium, income has a zero rate of change; it is neither rising nor falling. The equilibrium, in this sense, implies that there is no difference between savings and investment. Thus the Keynesian savings–investment equation can be looked upon as the equilibrium solution of a dynamical system.[34]

Klein's analysis is very clear: S and I are regarded as two separate forces whose interaction determines the equilibrium level of income. Whether or not it is the result of a continuous dynamic adjustment, the equality of S and I is conditional and not necessarily true as, for example, in Lerner's analysis.

After being thrown out of the window, equilibrium analysis seems to come back triumphantly through the front door! But what about Keynes's identity, $Y \equiv C + I$? Is there any inconsistency between accepting the identity of Y and $C + I$ and considering $I = S$ a condition of equilibrium? Should we share, after all, Samuelson's authoritative advice?

Moreover, there is reason to believe that Keynes' thinking remained fuzzy on one important analytical matter throughout all his days: the relationship between 'identity' and functional (or equilibrium-schedule) equality; between 'virtual' and observable movements; between causality and concomitance; between tautology and hypothesis.[35]

6. Identity $I \equiv S$ and the rejection of the 'vicious' circle

Before starting a critical analysis of Keynes's identities, it would be useful to examine the conditional interpretation of $S = I$ once again. In particular, we would like to point out that, although they refuse the identity of saving and investment, the paladins of an equilibrium analysis do not fundamentally reject the 'earning through spending' theory of income.

Let us take R. G. Allen as an example. In his *Macro-Economic Theory* he analyses the 'circular flow of income' as follows.

We must be clear at the outset on the relation between demand Z and income Y on the one hand and output Q on the other. The relation can be viewed as a conceptual one, the circular flow of income in the economy;

or it can be put in the framework of the aggregates of national income accounting.

The circular flow of income is illustrated in [Figure 1.9] in purely schematic terms. It does not matter where we start but we must follow the direction of the flow of income.[36]

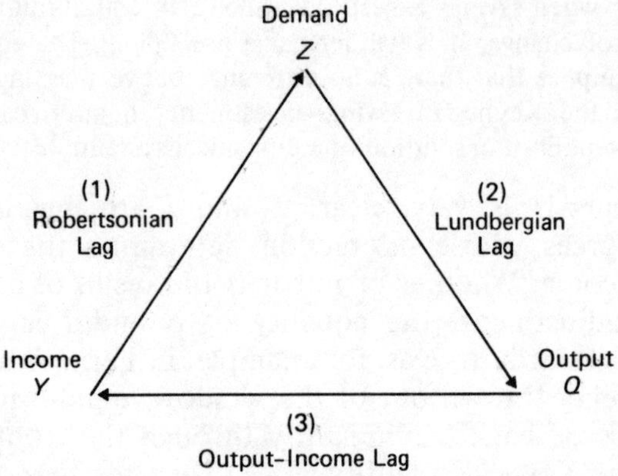

Fig. 1.9.

The circularity is explicit: wherever we start we shall come back to the same point, since income moves in a circular flow. This hypothesis becomes even more evident once we are told that output Q and income Y are in fact the same object.

The third lag is not of the same importance as the other two, and in the models we treat in the present text, we always assume that there is no lag between output and income.

Taking a zero lag of the third type, we can write output Q and income Y interchangeably. When we concentrate attention on the production aspects of the economy, e.g. in writing a production function, then we may use Q for output. But in general it is enough to write Y for income and output alike.

Effectively, then, there are two distinct aggregates, demand Z and income (output) Y.[37]

Now, if demand Z and income Y are the only two distinct concepts and if, moreover, income is moving in a circular flow it necessarily follows that income is conserved through its own demand (expenditure). This result is stressed by Allen himself when he represents the flow of national income.

The circular-flow scheme of [Figure 1.9] can be translated into national income terms. We show the translation in the form of [Figure 1.10]. Apart from lags, the aggregate of incomes is the national income Y; the aggregate demand is the sum of all purchases of goods and services or the national expenditure Z; and the aggregate of output is the production of all goods and services or the national product Q. The three aggregates, by definition, are equal in any given period.[38]

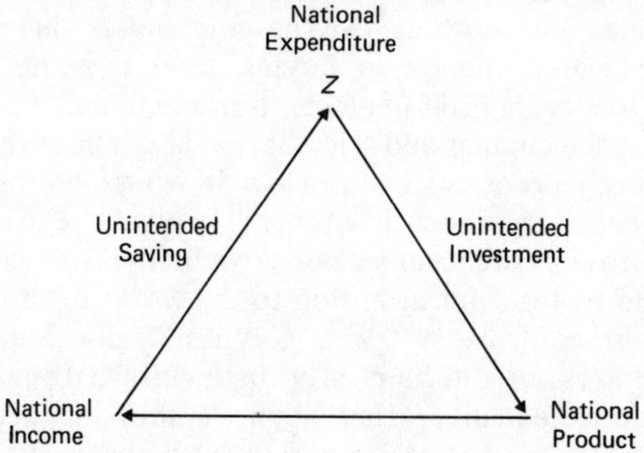

Fig. 1.10.

National income and national expenditure are equal 'in any given period' and circularly related: income is conserved through time. Given that

> All macro-models, whether of equilibrium or disequilibrium dynamics, are based on the flow conditions assumed for the product market. The conditions express the circular flow of income and allow for lags between income and demand and between demand and output.[39]

are we not kept, hopelessly, in a trap? In fact, as has been extensively argued, the 'earning by spending' theory of income is definitely inconsistent with any equilibrium analysis of S and I. Thus any attempt at refuting $S \equiv I$ by maintaining the hypothesis of a circular flow of income is necessarily contradictory. Identity of saving and investment is a logical consequence of the circular theory of income; acceptance of the latter necessarily implies acceptance of the former. There is no way out of the pitfall unless we give up the circularity.

A last remark: though the 'earning by spending' concept of income does necessarily imply the identity of saving and investment, the causality does not work the other way round; $S \equiv I$ does not imply an uninterrupted chain of expenditures. In other words, it is a logical possibility for S to be necessarily equal to I within a theoretical framework substantially distinct from the one based upon the concept of an autogeneous income. Lerner's attempt to prove that $I \equiv S$ relies upon a circular hypothesis. 'The earning of income is thus identical with the selling of services or of goods incorporating such services. But nothing can be sold unless there is somebody who spends money in buying what is being sold. The earning of income is itself dependent on spending.'[40]

Rejecting the circular and 'vicious' explanation of income, we reject Lerner's proof of $S \equiv I$. Now it would be mistaken to infer the necessary inconsistency of S 'always equal to I': a failure to prove existence does not prove non-existence.

It is time to turn our attention to the works of the man who started this controversy. Was Keynes really confused, as Samuelson says, or did he clearly distinguish between identity and functional equality? Has Keynes's thinking been understood correctly or has it been frequently betrayed, as Hicks seems to admit when he says:

> The 'Keynesian revolution' went off at half-cock; so the line, which I believe to be a vital line, was smudged over. The equilibrists, therefore, did not know that they were beaten; or rather (for I am not claiming that they had been altogether beaten) they did not know that they had been challenged. They thought that what Keynes had said could be absorbed into their equilibrium systems; all that was needed was that the scope of their equilibrium systems should be extended. As we know, there has been a lot of extension, a vast amount of extension; what I am saying is that it has never quite got to the point.[41]

PART II: THE KEYNESIAN DEFINITION OF NATIONAL INCOME

1. The 'Treatise on Money'

Income. We propose to mean identically the same thing by the three expressions: (1) *the community's money income*: (2) *the earnings of the factors of production*; and (3) *the cost of production*; and we reserve the term *profits* for the difference between the cost of production of the current output and its actual sale proceeds, so that profits are not part of the community's income as thus defined.[42]

So in his great book of 1930, described by Schumpeter as 'a splendid achievement', Keynes does not include profits in his definition of national income. This exclusion will play a determinant role in the relation between saving and investment and will represent the main cause of a great dispute conducted by Keynes, Robertson and Hayek immediately after the *Treatise* was published. Before looking at this dispute let us underline some aspects of Keynes's income analysis.

First let us consider the importance of money. Keynes's decision to analyse concepts like income, profit, saving and investment in a book dedicated to the study of money is more than symptomatic. Production is not considered as the possible interaction of two distinct objects, real and money product, corresponding to a dichotomic appraisal of the economic world. This kind of approach, so widely accepted among economists, before as well as after the *Treatise*, is implicitly rejected by Keynes, who analyses production in purely monetary terms. Yet it would be wrong to deduce that he avoids the dichotomy by rejecting one of its terms. In fact, both aspects of production are taken into account but one is subsumed under the other: the monetary value of production is the *form* of the real product. There are not two different objects, but one and the same object whose social measure is unique and given in terms of money. As a consequence, Keynes includes only monetary expenditures in his definition of income.

> More particularly we include in income:
>
> (*a*) Salaries and wages paid to employees, including any payments made to unemployed or partially employed or pensioned employees—these being in the long run a charge on industry just as much as other outgoings to remunerate the factors of production.
> (*b*) The normal remuneration of entrepreneurs.
> (*c*) Interest on capital (including interest from foreign investments).
> (*d*) Regular monopoly gains, rents and the like.[43]

A second point which can be raised here is the absolute independence of income from any subjective evaluation. Direct and indirect salaries and wages, including the normal remuneration of entrepreneurs, interest on capital, rents and monopoly gains are all money expenditures which do not depend on any kind of individual evaluation of national product. Whatever individual preferences or utilities are, income is defined by an objective amount of money representing the total money cost of production. The second aspect of Keynes's analysis, like the first, is distinctive of a fundamentally new way of looking at economics. Thus two of the main concepts characterising neo-classical thought are put aside by Keynes in his attempt at 'getting rid of the ideas which I used to have and of finding my way to those which I now have'.[44]

Let us go back to Chapter 9 of the *Treatise* and in particular to Keynes's definition of saving and investment.

> *Savings.* We shall mean by savings the sum of the differences between the money incomes of individuals and their money expenditure on current consumption . . .
>
> *Investment.* We shall mean by the rate of investment the net increment during a period of time of the capital of the community (as defined in the next section of this chapter); and by the value of investment, not the increment of value of the total capital, but the value of the increment of capital during any period. We shall find, therefore, that the value of current investment, as thus defined, will be equal to the aggregate of savings and profits, as thus defined.[45]

Thus profits, which have been excluded from the definition of national income, are not a part of saving but, as an increment of the existing capital, they do represent a part of investment. Profits, saving and investment can therefore be represented by the following relation, $Q = I - S$. 'Total profits on output as a whole are equal to the difference between the *value* of new investment and savings, being negative when savings exceed the value of new investment.'[46]

If we call Y the total money income, I' the cost of production of new investment and C' the cost of production of consumption goods we have: $Y = C' + I'$. Now, whereas this expression gives us the cost of production aspect of income, $Q = I - S$ is concerned with income spending. How are these two aspects of income interrelated? Since income can either be measured by its final expenditure or by its cost of production, and since profits are not part of it, the solution is immediately given by $Y = C' + I' = C + S$.

Given the previous definitions, equality of saving and investment is a matter of equilibrium. Profits, Q, are determinant; equilibrium between I and S is realised only when $Q = 0$.

We have seen in the previous chapter that, since the profits (Q) are the difference between the value of current output and E, its cost of production, we have

$$Q = I - S,$$

so that entrepreneurs make a profit or a loss according as the money value of current investment exceeds or falls short of current savings.

Thus we have profits = value of output − cost of production = value of investment − savings; profits being the balancing figure not only between cost of production and value of output, but also between savings and the value of net investment, both in terms of money . . .[47] In equilibrium, therefore, both the value and the cost of current investment must be equal to the amount of current savings, and profits must be zero.[48]

2. From 'The General Theory' to the 'Treatise'

Did Keynes exclude profits from his definition of national income to allow I and S to be numerically different or did he find $S \neq I$ only as a consequence of his considering profits to be the main cause of monetary disequilibrium? This question is fundamental to an understanding of Keynes's contribution in the *Treatise* and his subsequent modified version in *The General Theory*. Unfortunately, no easy answer can be found since Keynes himself seems to support both interpretations. Thus, in his reply to Hayek, Keynes says

> Has he, moreover, apprehended the significance of my equation $S + Q = I$, namely that savings *plus* profits are always exactly equal to the value of new investment? It follows from this that, if we define *income* to include profits, and savings as being the excess of income thus defined over expenditure on consumption, then savings and the value of investment are identically the same thing.[49]

And he is even more explicit in his preface to the German and Japanese editions of the *Treatise*.

> My definition of *income* is thought paradoxical because I exclude from it (as explained below) windfall profits and losses, and my definition of *saving*, being the excess of income thus defined over expenditure on consumption, corresponds to my definition of *income*. But those who object to these definitions have not, I think, followed out to the end the consequences of rejecting them. For if windfall profits and losses are included in income, i.e. if income is defined as being not E but $E + Q$ . . . and saving as the excess of income thus defined over expenditure on consumption, it follows that saving is in all cases exactly equal to the value of current investment.[50]

This seems to support the idea that Keynes's particular definition of income follows from his opposition to the identity of S and I. Yet, reading *The General Theory* we get just the opposite impression. 'For the system as a whole the amount of income which is saved, in the sense that it is not spent on current consumption, is and must necessarily be exactly equal to the amount of net new investment.'[51]

If we take into account only Keynes's two main books the dilemma cannot be solved, since the *Treatise* introduces a definition of income apparently inconsistent with the one proposed by *The General Theory*. At this point, all seems lost. Yet a solution is perhaps not impossible. Its condition, at least, is very simple: each definition of income must refer to a different object or to a different aspect of the same object. But how can this be possible, given that both are concerned with the definition of national income? In other words, how can we reconcile the following propositions?

(I) Profits are not a part of national income.
(II) Profits are included in the measure of national income.

From the *Treatise* to *The General Theory*, Keynes moves from one definition to the other under the pressure exercised upon him by two great economists of his time: F. A. Hayek and D. H. Robertson. After a long and sharp controversy Keynes decides to modify his first definition by introducing profits into national income.

> Let E be the amount of earnings or cost of current net output, i.e. the sum of fixed and variable costs and of entrepreneurs' inducement.
>
> Q the net profit of entrepreneurs, i.e. the amount of their actual net receipts in excess of entrepreneurs' inducement. So that $E + Q = E'$, which is total income in Hawtrey's, Hayek's and D.H.R.'s sense, and in the sense to which I have now bowed the knee.[52]

In reality Keynes did not definitively give up the definition of the *Treatise*. His acceptance of Robertson's definition seems rather tactical than substantial. Aware of the difficulties his theory represents for the reader, Keynes steps back in order to be better understood, but does not consider his previous analysis to be mistaken. In *The General Theory*, having redefined income he affirms that

> The above definitions of income and of net income are intended to conform as closely as possible to common usage. It is necessary, therefore, that I should at once remind the reader that in my *Treatise on Money* I defined income in a special sense . . . I am afraid that this use of terms has caused considerable confusion, especially in the case of the correlative use of saving . . . For this reason, and also because I no longer require my former terms to express my ideas accurately, I have decided to discard them—with much regret for the confusion which they have caused.[53]

This seems to corroborate our thesis that Keynes in *The General Theory* was mainly trying to formulate the analytical basis necessary for an understanding of the *Treatise*: this means that the chronological order of publication of these works does not correspond to their logical succession. In other words, chronology notwithstanding, *The General Theory* helps to understand the *Treatise*. If this is correct, we have to start from $Y \equiv C + I$ and the necessary equality of S and I in order to understand $I \neq S$ and $Q = I - S$. Obviously this new approach to Keynes's thought has to be supported by a proof of the consistency between propositions (I) and (II). Though a formal proof is necessary, it will represent the final result of our analysis more than its premiss. Nevertheless, even at this stage it is possible to give some elements of it.

Let us start again with the *Treatise* and try to identify its proper object. That money is this object is beyond doubt, but we need to get closer to our subject. We are finally led to a concept of great importance: the purchasing power of money. In fact, an attentive reader of the *Treatise* will certainly notice that windfall profits play a fundamental role in the stability of purchasing power.

> It is important for the reader to appreciate that the definition of *profits* given above, and the division of the total value of the product between what we call *income* or *earnings* and what we call *profits*, are not arbitrary. The essential characteristic of the entity which we call *profits* is that its having a zero value is the usual condition in the actual economic world of today for the equilibrium of the purchasing power of money. It is the introduction of this *fact* from the real world which gives significance to the particular fundamental equations which we have selected and saves them from the character of being mere identities.[54]

Thus we are taught that the stability of purchasing power depends on the nullity of windfall profits. This point becomes even more evident once we consider that profits as defined in the *Treatise* correspond to inflationary expenditures. 'We may have a rise or fall of Q, the total profits above or below zero, due to an inequality between saving and the value of investment. We shall call this *profit inflation* (or *deflation*).'[55]

This inflationary character of profits was already present in Keynes's definition of national income. By excluding profits from the money cost of production Keynes is explicitly considering them as non-income. It is because they are not part of income that positive or negative profits are a cause of monetary disequilibrium. They represent an amount of money with no correspondence to any produced income, so that their very existence has a necessary consequence for the purchasing power of money, whose equilibrium is assured by a perfect correspondence between money and income. Moreover, expenditure of this false income instead of destroying it assures its maintenance: every time a profit is spent, a profit of the same amount is created. This continues indefinitely, in an uninterrupted chain which Keynes calls a 'widow's cruse'.

> There is one peculiarity of profits (or losses) which we may note in passing, because it is one of the reasons why it is necessary to segregate them from income proper, as a category apart. If entrepreneurs choose to spend a portion of their profits on consumption (and there is, of course, nothing to prevent them from doing this), the effect is to *increase* the profit on the sale of liquid consumption goods by an amount exactly equal to the amount of profits which have been thus expended. This follows from our definitions, because such expenditure constitutes a diminution of saving, and therefore an increase in the difference between I' and S. Thus, however much of their profits entrepreneurs spend on consumption, the increment of wealth belonging to entrepreneurs remains the same as before. Thus profits, as a source of capital increment for entrepreneurs, are a widow's cruse which remains undepleted however much of them may be devoted to riotous living.[56]

The circularity of profit spending is a logical consequence of Keynes's definitions. In fact, from $Q = I - S$ and $Y = C' + I' = C + S$ we have $Q = I - (C' + I') + C = C + I - (C' + I')$. For any positive profit, $C + I$, the sum of final expenditures on consumption and investment goods, is greater than $C' + I'$, the total cost of production. Now, when a profit, Q, is spent it increases $C + I$ with respect to $C' + I'$, thus eliciting a new profit equal to the previous one. The fact that profits are replenished as soon as they are spent means that profits are formed by their own expenditure. No net expenditure of profit is logically possible: once it has been created, a windfall profit lasts forever, the widow can never fill the cruse with her tears.

It should be clear by now that Keynes in his *Treatise* was concerned with a particular kind of profit whose existence is symptomatic of a monetary disequilibrium or, in medical terms, of a pathological state of the system. Inflation and deflation are diseases whose cause is recognised to be the existence of such profits or losses. Let us call these profits *external.*[57]

Having described and defined external profits, Keynes was confronted with strong opposition, which he attributed to a lack of explanation of his theoretical framework. In an attempt to overcome this situation he went back to work and developed his analysis of income along new lines, considering in particular a kind of profit he did not investigate in the *Treatise*: *internal* profits. What we call, conventionally, internal profits are such categories of income as rents, dividends and monopoly gains which do not correspond to a direct cost of production. Unlike external profits, internal profits are part of income and their existence does not characterise a pathological state of the economy. This is the kind of profit in which Keynes is interested in *The General Theory*.

Thus Keynes goes back to some of the implicit concepts of the *Treatise* aware of the fact that he has to set down very clearly the laws upon which his theory is based. Just as the understanding of a disease requires previous knowledge of the healthy state of the body, so an economic disequilibrium can be defined only in relation to the laws corresponding to a 'healthy' state of the economy.

In the light of what has been said, *The General Theory* appears as the first analytical step towards a deeper understanding of the *Treatise*. It also emerges that these two main works, with their apparently different definitions of income, do not refer to the same object, and are therefore perfectly consistent with one another. Effectively, the *Treatise* analyses a system characterised by pathological disequilibria, such as inflation and deflation, and is consequently concerned with external profits which are, quite consistently, excluded from the definition of income. On the other hand, *The General Theory* studies a situation in which no disequilibrium can logically take place and which is described by a definition of income incorporating the value of internal profits.

We can now see that, despite appearances to the contrary, the two definitions of income are not contradictory. While $Y \equiv C + I$ measures income in the absence of any inflationary or deflationary gap, $Y \equiv C + S \equiv C + I - Q$ represents the value of income when a disequilibrium, $Q = I - S$, affects the purchasing power of money. Though different in their symbolical expressions, both measures give the same numerical results, which is not surprising since what Keynes is looking for is a measure of income independent of any amount of nominal money: only money costs of production are a valid measure of income.

> Accordingly, whilst the amount of the entrepreneurs' normal remuneration must be reckoned, whether their actual remuneration exceeds it or falls short, as belonging to the income of the individuals who perform entrepreneurial functions, the profits must be regarded not as part of the earning of the community (any more than an increment in the value of existing capital is part of current income), but as increasing (or, if negative, as diminishing) the value of the accumulated wealth of the entrepreneurs.[58]

Finally, both identities, $Y \equiv C + I - Q$ and $Y \equiv C + I$, refer to national income net of any double accounting or of any nominal money.

It is time to turn our attention to Keynes's analysis of the 'healthy' state of the economy in order to understand its fundamental laws and their implications.

3. 'The General Theory'

> We have defined income as equal to the sum of investment and of consumption; and we have defined saving as equal to the excess of income over consumption. It follows that, for the community as a whole, investment and saving are necessarily, and by definition, equal. There can be no escape from this conclusion—which, after all, is in full harmony with common sense and the common usage of the world—unless we so define income that is not equal to the sum of investment and of consumption, or so define saving that it is not equal to the excess of incomes over consumption.[59]

In *The General Theory* inflationary or deflationary profits are no longer taken into account. It is true that Keynes accepts the inclusion of profits in his definition of national income, yet his capitulation is only apparent: profits included in national income are what we have called internal profits, that is, indirect incomes like rents, dividends and interests, and not the external ones. According to this interpretation Keynes never failed to resist his critics who wanted him to change radically his definitions. In resisting Hayek and Robertson's sharp attack, Keynes was pointing out the logical impossibility of explaining any monetary disequilibrium once we include external profits in national income.

The last paragraph of his [Robertson's §8] of which I can make nothing, makes me think that he does not quite see the difficulty. For if, as he suggests, we are to define 'income' to mean 'earnings *plus* profits' ($E + Q$ in my notation) and 'saving' to mean the difference between income thus defined and expenditure on consumption ($S = E + Q - PR$), then it would follow that savings and the value of new investment would always be exactly equal (for $Q = PR + I - E$, so that $S = I$).[60]

The necessary equality of S and I which follows from $Y \equiv C + I$ (where $Q \in Y$) does not allow any disequilibrium and is therefore unable to explain exogenous variations of purchasing power. Keynes's bowing the knee must be understood within this framework. His acceptance of the definition of income as 'the amount of earnings or cost of current net output, i.e. the sum of fixed and variable costs and of entrepreneurs' inducement'[61] could be interpreted as a turnaround if Q corresponds to external profits. What we are maintaining, on the contrary, is that Keynes did not betray his first analysis when accepting $Y \equiv C + I$ as the definition of national income, since he was not including external profits in his definition of Y. In other words, Keynes agreed to investigate a new object rather than change the definition of the previous one. Having clarified this point, let us consider $Y \equiv C + I$ more closely. According to this identity, income is measured in such a way that no distinction can ever be found between I and S once we define saving as the excess of income over consumption. In the absence of any monetary disequilibrium I and S are always necessarily equal, as is consistently maintained by Keynes.

The prevalence of the idea that saving and investment, taken in their straightforward sense, can differ from one another, is to be explained,

I think, by an optical illusion due to regarding an individual depositor's relation to his bank being a one-sided transaction, instead of seeing it as the two-sided transaction which it actually is. It is supposed that a depositor and his bank can somehow contrive between them to perform an operation by which savings can disappear into the banking system so that they are lost to investment, or, contrariwise, that the banking system can make it possible for investment to occur, to which no saving corresponds. But no one can save without acquiring an asset, whether it be cash or a debt or capital-goods; and no one can acquire an asset which he did not previously possess, unless *either* an asset of equal value is newly produced *or* someone else parts with an asset of that value which he previously had. In the first alternative there is a corresponding new investment; in the second alternative someone else must be dis-saving an equal sum.[62]

The central point of Keynes's argument is that saving is not an unspent income: consumption and saving are two different ways of spending a given income. Thus, each act of saving is a purchase of an asset, either capital or a financial good. In the first case, saving and investment are the same thing while in the second, investment is the necessary consequence of saving; in both cases $I \equiv S$. Another way of obtaining this result is by proving that macroeconomic hoarding is necessarily nil. Y is always necessarily equal to $C + I$ and not to $C + I + H$, so that from $S \equiv Y - C$ it immediately follows $S \equiv I$.

Let us mean by current *income* the value of current output, which, I understand is what Mr. Robertson means by it. If we define savings as the excess of income during a period over expenditure on consumption during that period, it follows that savings are exactly equal to the value of output added to accumulated wealth, i.e. to investment.[63]

When he defines income as the sum of expenditures on consumption and investment Keynes is implicitly assuming $H = 0$. Thus, being a part of income, savings are also an expenditure. Now, both saving and investment are income expenditures and both are the complementary part of consumption into Y: S and I are always necessarily equal.

But what if only consumption goods are produced and if the income holders decide to save part of their income? Is such a saving different from investment? The answer appears to be positive; yet we should not forget that any act of saving is simultaneously a purchase of a financial asset. Thus, in the case at issue, income saved is indirectly spent, through the financial market, for the purchase of consumption goods. Now, since we define saving as that part of income which is not spent in purchasing consumption goods, we come to the conclusion that no saving can logically be determined when only consumption goods are produced.

> Thus the old-fashioned view that saving always involves investment, though incomplete and misleading, is formally sounder than the newfangled view that there can be saving without investment or investment without 'genuine' saving. The error lies in proceeding to the plausible inference that, when an individual saves, he will increase aggregate investment by an equal amount. It is true, that, when an individual saves he increases his own wealth. But the conclusion that he also increases aggregate wealth fails to allow for the possibility that an act of individual saving may react on someone else's savings and hence on someone else's wealth.[64]

What Keynes is very clearly sustaining here is that individual or microeconomic saving should not be confused with macroeconomic saving: what is valid for an individual is not automatically valid for the community as a whole. In particular, if an individual is saving part of his income this does not necessarily imply positive saving by the whole of society. In our previous example, income saved by income holders is spent by sellers of financial assets for the purchase of consumption goods still available so that, macroeconomically, no positive saving can be observed. According to Keynes's analysis, saving can only be positive when total income expenditure is greater than total expenditure on consumption, when there is an 'excess of income over consumption'. Then, as long as we keep to Keynes's macroeconomic definitions, no difference can be found between saving and investment. 'There can, however, be no escape from the conclusion that saving and net investment are, necessarily and by definition, equal.'[65]

Further on Keynes gives a different proof of $S \equiv I$.

> The reconciliation of the identity between saving and investment with the apparent 'free-will' of the individual to save what he chooses irrespective of what he or others may be investing, essentially depends on saving being, like spending, a two-sided affair. For although the amount of his own saving is unlikely to have any significant influence on his own income, the reactions of the amount of his consumption on the incomes of others

makes it impossible for all individuals simultaneously to save any given sums.[66]

Suppose that we want to increase our saving. In order to do so we decrease our consumption:

$$S = Y - C.$$

Now income, which is measured by $C + I$, will also decrease by the same amount:

$$Y = C + I.$$

Finally saving will remain at its previous level, since both income and consumption are simultaneously and equally decreasing:

$$S = Y - C.$$

Hence Keynes's conclusion: 'Every such attempt to save more by reducing consumption will so affect incomes that the attempt necessarily defeats itself.'[67]

Whilst asserting the necessary equality of S and I, Keynes seems to suggest that this result is a logical consequence of an 'earning through spending' conception of income. Suppose, in fact, that income is formed through its expenditure. In this case any variation in spending would instantaneously represent an identical variation in income, and $I = S$ would then be observed for any level of consumption. When spending on C decreases, Y decreases and S remains stable and equal to I. Now our claim is that Keynes's rejection of $S \neq I$ holds even if the hypothesis of the circular generation of income by income expenditures is forfeited. Though his example is not very clear on this subject, the following analysis should allow a better understanding of what we could call, paraphrasing K. Popper, 'the hard core' of Keynes's revolution.

4. Keynes and the 'flow of income'

I propose, therefore, to break away from the traditional method of setting out from the total quantity of money irrespective of the purpose on which it is employed, and to start instead—for reasons which will become clear as we proceed—with the flow of the community's earnings or money income, and with its twofold division (1) into the parts which have been *earned* by the production of consumption goods and of investment goods respectively, and (2) into the parts which are *expended* on consumption goods and on savings respectively.[68]

Keynes's twofold division of income is essential. Clearly understood, it means that income can equally be measured by the costs of production of the final expenditures on consumption and investment. Although the two measures are numerically equal, they are related to two different processes. Let us analyse them separately.

Income creation. Income creation is concerned with production; in fact it is its main result. By producing consumption and investment goods the factors of production create an income corresponding to their costs or earnings. 'We propose to mean identically the same thing by the three expressions: (1) *the community's money income;* (2) *the earnings of the factors of production*; and (3) *the cost of production*.'[69] Thus income is measured by $C' + I'$, where C' and I' represent the money cost of production for consumption and investment goods respectively:

$$Y \equiv C' + I'.$$

As can be easily seen, this identity tells us nothing about any conceivable relation between saving and investment for the very simple reason that saving and investment are categories related to income spending and not to income earning. Looking at the payment of the factors of production tells us how much income has been created, but it does not give us any information about the way it will be spent.

Income utilisation. In this case income is seen from the point of view of its expenditure. Any given income can be spent for the purchase of consumption, C, or investment goods, I, so that $Y \equiv C + I$ represents an alternative way of measuring income. Now Keynes proves,[70] introducing the financial market, that $C + I$ is always equal to $C + S$. Therefore identity of I and S establishes that, for the community as a whole, any income saved is necessarily spent for the purchase of investment goods.

Identity of income creation and income utilisation: $C' + I' \equiv C + I$. From $Y \equiv C' + I'$, $Y \equiv C + I$ and $S = I$ we immediately deduce the necessary equality of $C' + I'$ and $C + I$: income spent for the final purchase of consumption and investment goods is always equal to income earned by the factors of production. This identity, then, implies that production of consumption and investment goods creates the income necessary and sufficient for their final purchases:

$$C' + I' \equiv C + I.$$

'Income = value of output = consumption + investment'[71] where value of output is equal to 'the earnings of the factors of production', $C' + I'$. Thus, $C' + I'$ and $C + I$, are two faces of the same object. Like the example of a convex surface in which convexity and concavity are bound to go together, being two aspects of one and the same thing, creation and final expenditure are the two identical aspects of income. Neither $C' + I'$, nor $C + I$ can exist without one another. Being one and the same thing, there can be no relation of causality between $C' + I'$ and $C + I$, or vice versa. First used by Spinoza in his *Ethics* to prove the 'parallelism' of body and mind (Part III, Proposition 2), this kind of analysis is applied here in another domain. Identity of $C' + I'$ and $C + I$ implies that income earning and income spending are determined simultaneously. The chain of causality characterising so many pre- and post-Keynesian theories appears, then, to be widely inconsistent with Keynes's own analysis. Every time that an income is created by a given production we know instantaneously what the final purchase, direct and indirect, of this same production will be. This perfect correspondence between what is created and what is spent is autonomously established for every production. Thus, the income spent on the final purchase of a given set of goods is the income earned by producing these same goods.

Earning and spending of Y are identical, in the same way that the two faces of a coin are inseparable. Logically, the two faces of a coin are not two distinct objects which, despite their physical differences, are practically inseparable. If we call these two faces A and B, the coin is, by definition, the perfect unity of A and B. In other words, the coin cannot exist except through the unity of its two faces. Moreover, A cannot exist without B nor B without A. The existence of only one face is a contradiction *in adjecto*, since the face of a coin exists only if the coin exists, and a coin cannot exist without its two faces. Finally, the identity of A and B results directly from the identity of the coin with itself. Analogously, as the coin is defined by its two faces, so income is defined by the identity of its creation and its final expenditure, and, exactly as every coin is independent of any other coin, successive incomes are not causally related.

Identity of saving and investment tells us that the totality of income, Y, is necessarily spent, directly and through the financial market, for the purchase of consumption and investment goods. Now, does $C' + I' \equiv C + I$ give us any additional information about this relation? In fact, it does. From the statement that income created by producing consumption and investment goods, $C' + I'$, is spent for the purchase of these same goods, $C + I$, and from $I \equiv S$, it follows $C' \equiv C$ and $I' \equiv I \equiv S$: consumption goods and investment goods are purchased by the income corresponding to their respective cost of production. This last result is not surprising since, if $C' + I'$, represents the income necessary and sufficient to purchase C and I and if, conversely, $C + I$ represents the total income created, the income necessary and sufficient to purchase C can only be C' and, similarly, to purchase I it is necessary and sufficient to spend an income equal to I'.

Suppose, for instance, that only consumption goods are produced. In this case, income is measured either by C', the cost of producing consumption goods, or by C the final expenditure to purchase them: $Y \equiv C' \equiv C$. Similarly, if only investment goods are produced we have $Y \equiv I' \equiv I \equiv S$. Keynes's identity can therefore be restated as follows: every production creates the income necessary and sufficient for its own purchase. Finally, identity of income earning and income spending is verified for every act of production.

5. Identities versus conditions of equilibrium

Although unanimously accepted as definitions, Keynes's equations are frequently considered the result of an adjustment between separate forces. According to this conditional analysis of income, saving and investment or total supply and total demand are kept in equality by a continuous process of adjustment. S and I adjust instantaneously through a variation, also instantaneous, of income, so that $S = I$ is a condition of equilibrium constantly fulfilled, but not an identity.

This hypothesis of instantaneous adjustment is often attributed to Keynes himself. In fact, in Chapter 14 of *The General Theory* he says:

The traditional analysis has been aware that saving depends on income but it has overlooked the fact that income depends on investment, in such fashion that, when investment changes, income must necessarily change in just that degree which is necessary to make the change in saving equal to the change in investment.[72]

L. R. Klein does not hesitate and considers 'this latter statement referred to a process of adjustment which achieves an equilibrium'.[73] Thus, income is changing every time that a difference appears between saving and investment, and it is changing instantaneously in order to maintain the equality of S and I. 'Thus the Keynesian savings–investment equation can be looked upon as the equilibrium solution of a dynamical system. In exactly the same way, the usual supply–demand equation can also be looked upon as the equilibrium solution of a dynamical system.'[74] Accordingly, total supply, Y, and total demand, $C + I$, are continuously adjusted, transforming $Y \equiv C + I \, (S \equiv D)$ into a condition of equilibrium.

Now, apart from the analytical difficulties already set forth in Part I of this chapter, another short critique can be raised here. In order to reconcile the condition of equilibrium aspect of S and I (Y and $C + I$) with their necessary equality, the conditional relation between S and I (Y and $C + I$) is supposed to be continuously verified at any instant in real time. That is the meaning of the instantaneous adjustment of S and I (Y and $C + I$). It seems possible, therefore, to consider $S = I$ as an equivalence defining the equilibrium level of income, in the same way as $Y = C + I$ defines income. Actually, this inference is mistaken, since the very idea of instantaneous adjustment is self-contradictory. Adjustment takes time—a finite, though sometimes very short, period of time—and not a mere instant which is timeless. So, if we are to consider a finite period of adjustment between demand and supply, $Y = C + I$ can no longer be thought of as the definition of national income, since a definition implies a relation of equivalence, i.e. a relation which is verified at any point in time. Finally we are confronted with a logical alternative. Either we consider $Y = C + I$ (and $S = I$) a condition of equilibrium, in which case income has still to be defined or, with Keynes, we regard $Y = C + I$ (and $S = I$) as an identity defining national income, in which case no adjustment can ever take place between total supply and total demand.

Consistent with our previous analysis and relying on Keynes, we think it peremptory to reject the first term of this alternative. As definitions of national income, $Y = C + I$, and $Y = C' + I'$, (and $S = I$) are irreducible identities.

> There can, however, be no escape from the conclusion that saving and net investment are, necessarily and by definition, equal—which, after all, is in full harmony with common sense and the common usage of the world—unless (as in my *Treatise on Money*) we so define income that it is not equal to the sum of net investment and consumption, or (like Mr Robertson) so define saving that it is not equal to the excess of income over consumption.[75]

An identity is the strongest relation we can think of, a relation which can never be dismissed or transformed into a mere condition of equilibrium. Now, according to logic, there are different kinds of identities. Firstly, two terms can be identical because one is the obvious repetition of the other. This kind of identity is what is called a truism, i.e. a proposition of which each term is redundant, a hackneyed or self-evident truth—in short, a platitude which tells us nothing that is not already known.

Another kind of identity is the tautology. According to contemporary logic, a tautology is a necessary truth, i.e. a proposition that is true in every structure in which it is defined. Though logical truths, tautologies are not self-evident. They have to be proved, and once this has been done the result is an improvement in our knowledge. The third and last category we are concerned with refers to identities which have to be logically established from a given set of axiomatic propositions. Unlike tautologies, these identities are not necessary truths, yet, within a given framework, they cannot be rejected. Moreover, and like the tautologies, they are not mere platitudes and their determination is not meaningless.

Let us take two examples, one from mathematics and one from economics, to illustrate how this logical classification works. In mathematics it has been proved that $x^2 - 1 \equiv (x + 1)(x - 1)$. This identity is a tautology since, given certain logical axioms, it is always true that $x^2 - 1$ equals $(x + 1)(x - 1)$. In a similar way every mathematical theorem deduced from logical axioms can be considered a tautology. Once it has been proved that T necessarily follows from a set of logical axioms, A, T is recognised to be a tautology. This certainly does not mean that T is self-evident or useless. Even if T is necessarily implied in A its formulation is a discovery with a positive heuristic value.

Now, what about the following proposition? Given two agents A and B, any purchase by A is a sale by B, and vice versa. Does this identity need to be proved? Of course not. In fact, it is indisputable that in this two-sided relation, purchases by A and sales by B are immediately interchangeable expressions which leave our knowledge unaltered. Thus, its contents being essentially a self-evident truth, sales of $B \equiv$ purchases of A is nothing but a truism, a trivial platitude.

According to our classification, in which category should we put Keynes's identities? Consider, for example, $I \equiv S$. Saving and investment being always equal *by definition*, should we not consider their identity purely nominal? If so, Keynes's contribution would appear rather insignificant. In fact, the choice of a nominal definition is completely open, if not arbitrary, and in this respect terminological definitions are truisms: whatever term we use to describe an object, our knowledge of it remains unchanged. This conclusion seems to be supported by Keynes himself. 'We have defined income as equal to the sum of investment and of consumption; and we have defined saving as equal to the excess of income over consumption. It follows that, for the community as a whole, investment and saving are necessarily, and by definition, equal.'[76] Saving and investment appear to be different names for the same object, the excess of income over consumption, and, in this respect, their identity is a nominal one. Analogously, we could sustain that the identity of $C' + I'$ and $C + I$ is also terminological, since total cost of production, $C' + I'$, and final expenditure, $C + I$, are only different ways of describing the same object.

In reality, this analysis would hold *if, and only if*, Keynes's identities were a matter of nominal definition. Now, neither $Y - C = S = I$ nor $Y = C + I = C' + I'$ are the result of a purely terminological definition. On the contrary, S and I as well as $C + I$ and $C' + I'$ are different concepts whose relation has to be determined analytically. For instance, nothing allows us to write $I = S$ before we have proved that both concepts are always equal to the excess of income over consumption. $S = Y - C$ is not directly deducible from $Y = C + I$ but has to be established separately as a positive result, and it is only after this has been done that we can infer $I = S$. Undoubtedly, this is the path followed by Keynes. First, he proved that all saving is necessarily spent, and from this he deduced $S = H - C$ and therefore $S = I$. Saving and investment are thus recognised to be two different aspects of the same reality, and not two of its possible terminological definitions. 'In the previous chapter saving and investment have been so defined that they are necessarily equal in amount, being, for the community as a whole, merely different aspects of the same thing.'[77]

Income analysis is even more explicit. Definition of income as total cost of production, $Y \equiv C' + I'$, is certainly not a matter of terminological choice. What has to be understood under Y is not arbitrarily given, but results from a whole process of understanding that eventually ends in the formulation of an axiomatic proposition. Similarly, identity of income and final expenditures, $Y \equiv C + I$, is an analytical result which cannot be known *a priori* but must be induced from a set of axiomatic propositions. Both definitions of income are logically interconnected and their consequent identity is not a truism but positive information. Thus, income is not identified as a twofold object unless it has been proved that its definition implies the identity of $C' + I'$, and $C + I$.

Finally Keynes's identities are fundamentally new information whose ontological status is essential to the development of economics. In particular, they tell us that saving and investment, as well as production costs and final expenditures, are always necessarily equal whatever the level of income. $S \equiv I$ and $C' + I' \equiv C + I$ are not submitted to any conditional restriction, and that is why they are conceptual definitions and not simple descriptive hypotheses. Keynes himself was perfectly aware of the revolutionary significance of his theory. In a letter to G. B. Shaw, dated 1 January 1935, he writes: 'To understand *my* state of mind, however, you have to know that I believe myself to be writing a book on economic theory which will largely revolutionise—not, I suppose, at once but in the course of the next ten years—the way the world thinks about economic problems.'[78] Unfortunately, Keynes's prediction was an underestimate: ten years were not sufficient to discover the revolutionary importance of his contribution.

In this respect, it is interesting to look at Lipsey's point of view about the role which identities play in the determination of national income. In his article, 'The foundations of the theory of national income: an analysis of some fundamental errors', he starts by pointing out the confusion which is often made between identities and conditions of equilibrium.

In this paper I wish to argue that current teaching of macroeconomic theory, as evidenced by the great majority of elementary and intermediate macro textbooks published in the English language, contains a series of basic errors, all traceable to fundamental confusions over the nature of behavioural relations and identities.[79]

His analysis stresses the importance of empirical laws as against nominal identities.

Not only do we continue to introduce macro theory with a series of identities which we ourselves generally accept to be uninformative statements which add '. . . nothing . . . to our understanding of the working of the economic system', but we are led by this practice to make specific errors of analysis.[80]

Let us firstly note that Lipsey's concept of identity does not apply to Keynes's logical definition of national income. What Lipsey does not see is that there are identities which are not mere truisms adding nothing to our understanding of the working of the economic system. It is correct, of course, to say that terminological identities are purely tautological. This does not, however, mean that every identity is necessarily a terminological one. On the contrary, there are identities which can only be established as a result of a logical analysis. These identities are highly informative and correspond to the logical definition of their corresponding concepts. Thus, the identity between national income and the expenditures on consumption and investment goods is the result of the logical (and not of the terminological) definition of income. The discarding of this fundamental distinction is the main reason for Lipsey's rejection of $Y \equiv C + I$ as a tautological identity incapable of explaining the determination of income.

Klappholz and Mishan, in their brilliantly argued paper 'Identities in economic models', share the same point of view as Lipsey.

One need not labour the logical status of an identity. Its nature has been indicated by a multitude of writers . . . We may accept it, then, that an identity is necessarily true by virtue of the meaning we give to certain words: $Y \equiv C + I$ is an identity which defines the *magnitude* of Y as being that of the sum of the *magnitudes* of C and I, once these latter symbols have been defined.[81]

According to Klappholz and Mishan there are only two categories of identities, namely those defining what the philosophers call logical truths and those which are the result of terminological definitions. Economic identities are said to pertain to this second category. $Y \equiv C + I$ is therefore considered an empty statement since 'it is clear that equations commonly designed as identities, true by virtue of the meaning of language, are intended to be, and are in fact, empty statements. They tell us nothing at all about the universe, and are necessarily irrefutable.'[82] Now, this conclusion would be unavoidable if the definition of income as the sum of C and I were merely terminological. This is, however, not the case. In fact, there are identities which are neither logical truths nor terminological tautologies. $Y \equiv C + I$ is one of these logical identities with empirical content. It is therefore not true that empirical laws cannot be expressed in the form of identities, since it is not true that identities are necessarily 'uninformative statements which add nothing to our understanding of the working of the economic system'.[83] On the contrary, identities such as Keynes's are highly informative statements which can only *result from* our analysis of the economic system. Ultimately, the logical definition of income can only be established through a logical analysis whose empirical content is evident.

Our authors, unaware of this third possibility, affirm that $Y \equiv C + I$ can only be a tautology or a condition of equilibrium, and claim that to avoid the former we must necessarily accept the latter.

To avoid the identity, I must be defined independently of C and Y, in which case we can write $Y \equiv C + I$. Since, however, these three terms are defined independently of each other, this equation does not necessarily hold for all conceivable values of these variables as it does necessarily in the identity. The new equation requires a new interpretation. The proper one, in this context, is that the equation is a hypothesis, one stating the conditions (necessary and sufficient) for equilibrium in the goods market'.[84]

This false conclusion is entirely supported by Lipsey. Yet, his analysis is still very interesting.

In particular, he is certainly right to claim that the 'faulty interpretation of an identity as putting restrictions on what can happen in the world has led to a series of characteristic errors found almost universally in the literature'.[85] An identity, whether logical or terminological, should never be confused with a behavioural equation, and it should therefore never be claimed that individual behaviour must necessarily conform to the identity of Y and $C + I$. This clear-cut distinction between identities and behavioural equations does not, however, allow us to infer that an identity cannot have an empirical content. If it is true that a definitional identity cannot rule out certain imaginable events,[86] it is also true that these events could never be known and measured without a definitional identity. In other words, a logical identity is a definition which allows the understanding of events, and whose validity is unaltered by any change in behaviour. In the case of national income, identity $Y \equiv C + I$ corresponds to the logical definition of income and is true whatever the amounts of C and I. Contrary to what Lipsey believes, this identity does not introduce any restriction on what happens in the real world, but gives us the key to its understanding. Without this identity, income would remain an empty concept, and any attempt to determine it through empirical observation would lead to failure.

According to Lipsey and to many other well-known authors, definitional identities can only be tautological. He holds, therefore, what philosophers call a 'nominalist' view of definitions. This view is opposed to the 'essentialist' claim that definitions can have the force of logical necessities. Without any pretence of solving this centuries-long dispute between these two schools of thought, we claim that Keynes's identities are not a matter of terminological definition, but represent a necessary condition of the understanding of economics.

Despite this fundamental difference in his analysis, Lipsey's observations are very stimulating, in particular those referring to the traditional attempt at explaining the dynamic change of income through the identity of saving and investment. Criticising the attempts of Samuelson, Nevin, Benham and Shackle to prove that the equality of saving and investment is assured by changes in the size of national income, Lipsey correctly points out that: 'Every one of these passages is saying that there exists a *real world mechanism* that works (sometimes very hard for the task is clearly a difficult one) to ensure the realisation of a definitional identity.'[87] It is, in fact, obvious that an identity is a particular form of relation which is always realised, independently of any working mechanism. $I \equiv S$ means that S is always necessarily equal to I, and Lipsey is perfectly right in drawing a sharp distinction between this identity and the conditional equality of S and I.

Now, contrary to his view, the identity of S and I is not an 'identity which follows from our use of words and is compatible with any state of the universe'.[88] As we have already shown, $I \equiv S$ can only be determined through the logical identity of total demand and total supply. Lipsey is therefore missing the point when he says that: 'Our decision to use E and Y to mean the same magnitude has *no operational significance in any way*.'[89] In fact, E (total expenditures) and Y (income) are not two different names for the same object, and their identity is not a matter of nominal definition. On the contrary, total expenditures (E or $C + I$) are the logical definition of income: identity $Y \equiv C + I$ is the result of a logical analysis and not its arbitrary point of departure. Again, Lipsey is certainly right in rejecting 'the nonsensical idea that a mechanism is needed to ensure the realisation of an identity'.[90] However, the determination of a logical identity is not a matter of arbitrary choice. Income is not simply an alternative name for total expenditures, since $C + I$ is the logical content of Y. Thus, it is not correct to say, with Lipsey, that: 'An exact parallel to the S and I identity is the statement that three feet equals one yard.'[91] Whilst three feet and one yard are two different names for the same magnitude, saving and investment are two aspects of an object implying their identity, as are Y and $C + I$. Identities between Y, $C + I$ and $C' + I'$, as well as between S and I, are not mere accounting identities but result from a fundamental analysis of income which leads to its logical definition—a definition with empirical content since, let us repeat, a logical identity is a meaningful empirical statement whose determination is necessary for the understanding of the real world.

Like Klappholz and Mishan, Lipsey is not aware of the existence of these identities and claims, erroneously, that empirical statements can only represent behavioural relations, institutional facts, technical relations or equilibrium conditions and can, therefore, not 'be established with certainty'.[92,93]

Keynes's identities are the best counter-example of this claim. The relation between Y and $C + I$ can be established with certainty, and represents the empirical statement that income is logically defined by the identity of total demand and total supply.

Unfortunately, the true significance of Keynes's identities has not yet been completely understood. As Davidson tells us, this is partly due to the traditional, neoclassical misinterpretation of Keynes's work.

> By the fifties the mutant 'Keynesian' neoclassical synthesis was sufficiently entrenched in the orthodox macroeconomic literature for some economists to begin to warn that what had been propagated as the Keynesian theory of money and employment was a perversion of Keynes' own views about the real sector. These warnings went practically unnoticed and unheeded.[94]

With Davidson, we think that Keynes's widely misunderstood message has still to be rediscovered in its full originality.[95]

6. Autonomous expenditures

Our point of departure was income and its definition as a flow of expenditures. Analysis has proved that such a definition implies a circular explanation of income earning, and must, therefore, be substituted by a new theory in which income is not self-generated. Now, if income is not formed through its own expenditure, there has to be a process capable of explaining its creation. Once again, Keynes shows us the way out. Identity between income and cost of production does in fact tell us that Y is created and measured by the earnings of the factors of production, $C' + I'$. Money income, thus, is generated through what we shall call an autonomous expenditure, i.e. an expenditure which does not rely upon any pre-existing income.

$C' + I'$ corresponds to new production and to new income, independently of any past or future production. Though it is an identity and will therefore hold through time, $Y \equiv C' + I'$ is related to a given period and will not interfere with any identity referring to any other period. To put it another way, each production is defined by a particular income corresponding to its social cost and therefore requires its own specific autonomous expenditure.

Yet, this result seems to be partially inconsistent with a significant part of Keynes's analysis: the multiplier theory. Given an initial autonomous expenditure, is it not true that its spending will have an effect on some of the succeeding productions? Even if we reject the 'earning by spending' theory of income, is it not true that successive incomes influence each other through their expenditures?

The framework of our second chapter is thus well defined. Its main purpose is to analyse critically the multiplier theory and to determine what kind of costs correspond to a social definition of production.

APPENDIX

Keynes turned upside down: a short critical appraisal of Kalecki's income analysis

In his *Essays on the Theory of Economic Fluctuations*, Kalecki's second essay analyses the problem of investment and income in a way which seems to confirm our analysis of Keynes. In fact, Kalecki wants to prove that the relation between saving and investment is far from being a mere truism. Now, even if we could not agree more with his purpose, we are convinced that his procedure is dangerously misleading. Our belief is based on the consideration that Keynes's fundamental identities are either considered self-evident truths or reduced to simple conditions of equilibrium by Kelecki. Let us try to prove this.

Kalecki's point of departure is national income and its definition as

sales of investment goods + sales of consumption goods.

Keynes's basic identity seems to be accepted. In reality, the two definitions are completely different, since each of our two authors gives a different meaning to the identity between Y and $C + I$.

Kalecki considers definition of national income a platitude which can be rescued only by what he calls the 'exchange equation'.

Thus we have *by definition*:

National income = Sales of investment goods +
Sales of consumption goods,

where both national income and investment are gross concepts . . . Further, we shall call saving the difference between the national income defined above and the expenditure on consumption. Thus we have, again *by definition*:

Sales of investment goods + Sales of consumption goods = Saving + Expenditure by consumers,

saving again being a gross concept. We have now the further equation:

Sales of consumption goods = Expenditure by consumers,

which, however, is *not* a tautology since it represents the exchange process on the market of consumption goods (though it is an identity in the sense that it is fulfilled in all circumstances). Thus the equation derived from this exchange equation and the proceding tautology:

Sales of investment goods = Saving,

is also not a tautology.[96,97]

The difference between Kalecki and Keynes could not be wider. As we have already pointed out,[98] Keynes's identity cannot be considered a purely nominal one. $Y \equiv C + I$, on the contrary, is a statement which teaches us that total supply, Y, is always equal to total demand, $C + I$, at every instant in real time. This information is important and its consequences are fundamental for our science. Far from being self-evident, definition of national income is the result of long and painful research, as can easily be seen if we think of the difficulties caused for Keynes by the problem of profit.

Kalecki's reasoning, then, appears as an attempt to turn Keynes's theory upside down. The logical definition of *The General Theory* is considered a simple truism, while the only significant relation seems to be the exchange equation, that is:

sales of consumption goods = expenditure by consumers.

Yet, this equation is nothing other than a triviality, since each of its two terms is the simple repetition of the other: sales of consumption goods by firms is, redundantly, purchase of these same commodities by consumers. Kalecki's exchange equation is nothing but a repetition of the same idea in different words. If A is a seller and B a buyer of the same commodity, it is pleonastic to say that purchases of B are equal to sales of A. Such an equation does not increase our knowledge of the object, it simply recalls for us that the same transaction is a sale at one pole and a purchase at the other. So, Kalecki's analysis is mistaken from two points of view: firstly, it transforms

Keynes's message into a self-evident hackneyed truth and secondly, it assumes a platitude as its central feature.

Despite the procedure adopted, Kalecki's result is not inconsistent with Keynes's analysis. In particular, it is interesting to note that the relation between saving and investment is considered, at least in the first paragraph, an identity, since it is the result of a tautology (which, doubtless, is an identity) and the exchange equation which, according to Kalecki, 'is an identity in the sense that it is fulfilled in all circumstances'. Thus, any variation in one of the two terms necessarily implies the same variation in the other: if investment increases, saving increases for the same amount, and vice versa. Moreover, both variations are simultaneous as is shown by the following analysis in which Kalecki proves that saving and investment adjust themselves within one period.

> It is useful to show how an increase in expenditure on investment by ΔI causes—by means of the exchange process on the market of investment and consumption goods—saving S to increase by an amount ΔS equal to ΔI.
>
> If in a certain period the expenditure on investment is I and in the next $I + \Delta I$, sales of investment goods must increase by ΔI. If the output of them was not changed, the total amount ΔI is an addition to income of capitalists (entrepreneurs and rentiers), but if output and employment also increase a part of ΔI is received by workers. Out of the addition to income ΔI following to the investment goods industries a part S_1 is saved while another part $I - S_1$ is consumed. This last amount makes for an additional expenditure on consumption goods.
>
> Consider now the consumption goods industries: a part of the total sales of consumption goods is bought by the capitalists and workers in consumption goods industries, the rest is purchased by the capitalist and workers in investment goods industries. And it is the value of this latter which is equal to the savings 'in consumption goods industries' S, for it is equal to the difference between the total sales of consumption goods and the expenditure on consumption by the capitalists and workers drawing income from their production. Thus an additional expenditure on consumption by the capitalists and workers in the investment goods industries creates an equal additional saving S_2. We have:
>
> $$\Delta I - \Delta S_1 = \Delta S_2$$
>
> or
>
> $$\Delta I = \Delta S_1 + \Delta S_2 = \Delta S,$$

and we see how an additional expenditure on investment creates an equal addition to saving ΔS.[99]

Kalecki's proof is perfectly valid and meaningful if we consider expenditure on investment as its cost of production. In this case, the necessary correspondence between saving and investment signifies that all investment goods newly produced are inevitably financed by current saving: $I' \equiv S$. On the other hand, if we consider expenditure on investment as the income spent to purchase investment goods, our relation $S = I$ becomes useless. It is in fact trivial to say that, given

$$\text{sales of investment goods} = \text{saving} \tag{1.6}$$

and

$$\text{expenditure on investment} = \text{sales of investment goods}, \tag{1.7}$$

we have

$$\text{expenditure on investment} = \text{saving}. \tag{1.8}$$

Equation (1.8) is not new information, since it is already fully included in (1.6) and (1.7). Moreover, equation (1.7), assuming that expenditure on investment is equivalent to purchase of investment goods, is a very good example of a self-evident truth. Now, equation (1.7) becomes a positive source of information as soon as expenditure on investment is identified with I', the cost of production of investment goods. In this case, Kalecki's three equations must be represented as follows:

$$S = I, \tag{1.9}$$

$$I' = I, \tag{1.10}$$

$$I' = S, \tag{1.11}$$

where equation (1.10) corresponds to Keynes's identity between income created by the production of investment goods and income spent for their final purchase. Once it has been proved[100] that (1.9) and (1.10) are identities, (1.11) just follows, and Kalecki's argument can be adopted.

Let us suppose that investment is increased by $\Delta I'$. Income is then also increased by the same amount. Of the additional income $\Delta I'$, a part, ΔS_1, is saved while another part, $\Delta I' - \Delta S_1$, is consumed. Consider now the consumption goods industries.

A part, $\Delta I' - \Delta S_1$, of their production is bought by income holders from the investment goods industries. Therefore, income holders belonging to the consumption goods industries can only spend a part of their income within their own sector; the rest ($= \Delta I' - \Delta S_1$) is necessarily saved (ΔS_2). We have:

$$\Delta I' - \Delta S_1 = \Delta S_2$$

or

$$\Delta I' = \Delta S_1 + \Delta S_2 = \Delta S,$$

'and we see how an additional expenditure on investment ΔI creates an equal addition to saving ΔS'.

The same result can be obtained directly from a simple analysis of national income identity, $C' + I' \equiv C + I$. Just suppose that production of investment goods in period t_0 is nil. In this case, income created in t_0 is equal to C', production of consumption goods. On the other side, final demand for goods is C, so that Keynes's identity is reduced to the form $C' \equiv C$. When no investment goods are produced, total supply of consumption goods is necessarily equal to total demand for the same goods. Now, the identity of saving and investment follows directly. From

$$C' + I' \equiv C + I \text{ and} \tag{1.12}$$

$$C' \equiv C, \tag{1.13}$$

we have

$$I' \equiv I \tag{1.14}$$

and, given that saving is 'the excess of income over consumption', $S = C' + I' - C$, the final result is

$$I' \equiv S. \tag{1.15}$$

Provided we accept Keynes's definition of saving, any increase in expenditure on investment $\Delta I'$ causes saving to increase by an amount ΔS equal to ΔI.

Let us go back to Kalecki. What we have proved is that Kalecki has confused logical and tautological identities and that his demonstration of the identity between saving and investment is therefore meaningless. We have still to prove that his analysis can lead only to a transformation of Keynes's identity

$Y \equiv C + I$ into a condition of equilibrium. Our starting point is, once again, Kalecki's definition of national income, namely:

'National income = Sales of investment goods + Sales of consumption goods'. (1.16)

According to Kalecki this definition is a tautology. Now, if that is true, both terms of the equation must represent exactly the same concept: each of them must be the repetition of the other. In other words, if $Y = C + I$ is a tautology, Y and $C + I$ are simply two different names for the same transaction. Since the process of production and the process of circulation represent two different *concepts*, Kalecki's definition of national income cannot be concerned with both of them. In fact, only the process of circulation is taken into account by Kalecki. His equation is a description of what happens on the commodity market between firms who sell consumption and investment goods and income holders who buy them: the same transaction is observed from its two poles. Our interpretation is confirmed by the fact that equation (1.16) is considered by Kalecki to be equivalent to

sales of investment goods + sales of consumption goods = saving + expenditure by consumers, (1.17)

which, if we bear in mind that saving is 'the difference between the national income as defined above and the expenditure on consumption', is nothing other than:

sales of investment goods + sales of consumption goods = expenditure on investment + expenditure by consumers. (1.18)

Equation (1.18), doubtless, is a tautology and so are the following equations:

sales of consumption goods = expenditure by consumers, (1.19)

and

sales of investment goods = expenditure on investment. (1.20)

The equation

$$\text{expenditure on investment} = \text{saving}, \tag{1.21}$$

then, is also tautological so that, finally, all the equations introduced by Kalecki are pure truisms. Thus, Kalecki's identities do not introduce any relation between production and consumption, either for consumption goods or for investment goods. Since they are completely independent of each other, production and consumption can thereafter give different results, so that only their equality would be a matter of equilibrium. From Kalecki's point of view, production of consumption and investment goods $(C' + I')$ and final purchase of the same goods $(C + I)$ are only equal at equilibrium. Except at that point, total supply and total demand are different, even though sales and purchases are always tautologically equal. The same result is valid for the saving–investment relation: the identity between the supply side, represented by production of investment goods I', and the demand side, represented by their final purchase I $(= S)$, is conditional, while indentity between industries' sales and investors' purchase of investment goods is always true.

NOTES

1. I. Fisher, *Nature of Capital and Income*, London, Macmillan, 1912, p. 51.
2. A. P. Lerner, *Economics of Employment*, New York, McGraw-Hill, 1951, p. 58.
3. Fisher, op. cit., p. 52.
4. Lerner, op. cit., p. 59.
5. J. R. Hicks, 'Maintaining capital intact: a further suggestion', in *Readings in the Concepts and Measurement of Income*, eds R. H. Parker and G. C. Harcourt, Cambridge, Cambridge University Press, 1969, p. 133.
6. Lerner, op. cit., p. 64.
7. A. P. Lerner, 'Saving equals investment', *Quarterly Journal of Economics*, Vol. 52, 1938, p. 298.
8. Lerner, *Economics of Employment*, op. cit., p. 66.
9. A. P. Lerner, 'Mr. Keynes' *General Theory of Employment, Interest and Money'*, *International Labour Review*, October 1936, p. 210.
10. Lerner, *Economics of Employment*, op. cit., pp. 68–9.
11. J. M. Keynes, *The General Theory of Employment, Interest and Money*, London, Macmillan, 1973, p. 63.
12. P. A. Samuelson 'The simple mathematics of income determination', in *The Collected Scientific Papers of Paul A. Samuelson*, ed. J. E. Stiglitz, Boston, MIT Press, Vol. II, 1966, p. 1138.
13. A simple pedagogic expedient, this does not imply our acceptance of a causal chain of incomes through time.
14. Keynes, op. cit., p. 62.
15. The distinction between schedules and observables will be dealt with in

Chapter 4, but it is nevertheless possible to anticipate that the results obtained there are perfectly consistent with the present analysis: the saving-investment controversy cannot be dismissed by introducing virtual or imaginary quantities.

16. L. R. Klein, *The Keynesian Revolution*, London, Macmillan, 1968, p. 113.
17. This assumption is only made in order to simplify the analysis and does not modify its results. In fact, on the one hand, the argument based on the existence of lags is logically insufficient to explain any disequilibrium of the flow of income: if a real disequilibrium can exist it must be shown within a given income, whatever the lags between its successive expenditures. On the other hand, if other injections and withdrawals existed besides investment and saving, our analysis could also be applied to them.
18. R. G. Lipsey, 'The foundations of the theory of national income: an analysis of some fundamental errors', in *Essays in Honour of Lord Robbins*, eds M. Preston and B. Corry, London, Weidenfeld and Nicolson, 1972, p. 29.
19. Ibid., p. 31.
20. Ibid., p. 32.
21. A. P. Lerner, '*The General Theory*', in *The New Economics*, ed. S. E. Harris, London, Dennis Dobson & Co., 1948, p. 212.
22. D. H. Robertson, in his famous article 'Saving and hoarding' (*Economic Journal*, September 1933), does not include hoarding in saving. 'Thus Saving does not necessarily involve Hoarding. But neither does Hoarding necessarily involve Saving. For suppose our man on day 1 spends £10 on consumption but adds to his money stock by selling a tool or a security worth £2. In this case also he will be taking steps to raise the proportion specified above from 1 to 1 1/5, and will therefore be hoarding: but he will not be saving' (p. 400). Yet this analysis is not absolutely correct. Robertson, in fact, forgets that in selling a tool or a security worth £2, our man is dis-saving: he recovers the income previously saved in purchasing the same tool or security. 'If on day 1 he spends £8 on consumption goods and £2 on a tool or a security, he is saving but not hoarding.' If now our man leaves unspent the recovered income, he is hoarding *and* saving £2. 'If he spends £8 on consumption goods and leaves £2 unspent, he is hoarding as well as saving.' Finally, Robertson should have concluded that hoarding necessarily involves saving though saving does not necessarily involve hoarding.
23. Lerner, 'Saving equals investment', op. cit., p. 299.
24. D. H. Robertson, *Money*, Cambridge, Cambridge Economic Handbooks, 1970, p. 179.
25. Lerner, 'Saving equals investment', op. cit., pp. 298–9.
26. Lerner, *Economics of Employment*, op. cit., p. 64.
27. Lerner, 'Mr. Keynes' *General Theory*', op. cit., pp. 210–11.
28. Keynes, op. cit., p. 74.
29. Lerner, *Economics of Employment*, op. cit., p. 74.
30. Robertson, *Money*, op. cit., p. 174. Robertson is quoting Joan Robinson's *Introduction to the Theory of Employment*, London, Macmillan, 1969, p. 8.
31. Robertson, *Money*, op. cit., p. 174.
32. *Quarterly Journal of Economics*, August 1937.
33. Robertson, 'Saving and hoarding', op. cit., p. 411.
34. Klein, op. cit., pp. 112–13.
35. P. A. Samuelson, 'The *General Theory*', in Stiglitz (ed.), *The Collected Scientific Papers*, op. cit., Vol. II, p. 1529.
36. R. G. D. Allen, *Macro-Economic Theory*, London, Macmillan, 1968, p. 16.
37. Ibid., p. 17.
38. Ibid., pp. 17–18.

39. Ibid., p. 23.
40. Lerner, *Economics of Employment*, op. cit., p. 64.
41. J. R. Hicks, 'Some questions of time in economics', in *Evolution, Welfare and Time in Economics*, ed. Tang, Lexington, 1976.
42. J. M. Keynes, *A Treatise on Money*, Vol. I, *The Pure Theory of Money*, London, Macmillan, 1971, p. 111.
43. Ibid., p. 111.
44. Ibid., p. xvii.
45. Ibid., pp. 113–14.
46. Ibid., p. 124.
47. Ibid., p. 136.
48. Ibid., p. 137.
49. J. M. Keynes, *The Collected Writings of*, ed. D. Moggridge, Vol. XIII, *The General Theory and After,* Part I, *Preparation*, London, Macmillan, 1973, p. 251.
50. Keynes, *A Treatise on Money*, Vol. I, op. cit., p. xxiii.
51. Keynes, *The General Theory*, op. cit., p. xxxii.
52. Keynes, *The Collected Writings of*, Vol. XIII, op. cit., p. 275.
53. Keynes, *The General Theory*, op. cit., pp. 60–1.
54. Keynes, *A Treatise on Money*, Vol. I, op. cit., p. 141.
55. Ibid., p. 140.
56. Ibid., p. 125.
57. The distinction between *internal* and *external* profits has been introduced by Bernard Schmitt (*Monetary Expenditures and Quantum Time*, Albeuve, Switzerland, Castella/Presses Universitaires de Dijon, forthcoming) and is briefly analysed in the third chapter of this book.
58. Keynes, *A Treatise on Money*, Vol. I, op. cit., p. 112.
59. Keynes, *The Collected Writings of*, Vol. XIII, op. cit., p. 476.
60. Ibid., p. 235.
61. Ibid., p. 275.
62. Keynes, *The General Theory*, op. cit., pp. 81–2.
63. Keynes, *The Collected Writings of,* Vol. XIII, op. cit., p. 327.
64. Keynes, *The General Theory,* op. cit., pp. 83–4.
65. Keynes, *The Collected Writings of,* Vol. XIV, op. cit., p. 427.
66. Keynes, *The General Theory*, op. cit., p. 84
67. Ibid., p. 84.
68. Keynes, *A Treatise on Money*, Vol. I, op. cit., p. 121.
69. Ibid., p. 111.
70. Keynes, *The General Theory*, op. cit., pp. 81–5.
71. Ibid., p. 63.
72. Ibid., p. 184.
73. Klein, op. cit., p. 111.
74. Ibid., p. 113.
75. Keynes, *The Collected Writings of,* Vol. XIV, op. cit., p. 427.
76. Keynes, *The Collected Writings of,* Vol. XIII, op. cit., p. 476.
77. Keynes, *The General Theory*, op. cit., p. 74.
78. Keynes, *The Collected Writings of*, Vol. XIII, op. cit., p. 492.
79. Lipsey, op. cit., p. 3.
80. Ibid., p. 3.
81. K. Klappholz and E. J. Mishan, 'Identities in economic models', *Economica*, May 1962, p. 118.
82. Ibid., p. 119.
83. Ibid., p. 117.
84. Ibid., p. 124.

85. Lipsey, op. cit., p. 9.
86. Ibid.
87. Ibid., p. 21.
88. Ibid.
89. Ibid., p. 22.
90. Ibid.
91. Ibid., p. 23.
92. Ibid., p. 33.
93. Some authors seem to be unaware of the fact that 'empirical' does not mean 'hypothetical'. Even if some hypotheses about the real world can be considered as empirical statements, this does not imply that every empirical statement must necessarily represent a falsifiable hypothesis.
94. P. Davidson, 'Why money matters: lessons from a half-century of monetary theory', *Journal of Post Keynesian Economics*, Autumn, 1978, pp. 49–50.
95. Professor B. Schmitt is the first to have opened the way towards this rediscovery. See *La Formation du pouvoir d'achat*, Paris, Sirey, 1960; *Monnaie, salaires et profits*, Paris, Presses Universitaires de France, 1966; *Macroeconomic Theory: A Fundamental Revision*, Albeuve, Switzerland, Castella, 1972.
96. M. Kalecki, *Essays in the Theory of Economic Fluctuations*, London, Allen & Unwin, 1939, pp. 42–3.
97. The term tautology is used here as a synonym of truism. In fact, Kalecki considers as tautological the identities which, in his opinion, result only from a nominal definition.
98. See also B. Schmitt's works on this subject (see Bibliography).
99. Kalecki, op. cit., pp. 44–5.
100. Unfortunately, Kalecki does not prove either (1.9) or (1.10). Instead, he gives us a redundant demonstration of $S = I$ and considers expenditure on investment equivalent to expenditure by investors on the commodity market, so that the equation

    sales of investment goods = expenditure on investment

    is substantially equal to his exchange equation for the market of consumption goods:

    sales of consumption goods = expenditure by consumers.

2 The Multiplier Analysis

PART I: THE DYNAMIC MULTIPLIER

1. The traditional theory

Lord Keynes did not discover the multiplier; that honour belongs to Mr. R. F. Kahn. But he gave it the rôle it plays today, by transforming it from an instrument for the analysis of road building into one for the analysis of income building. From his own and subsequent work we now have a theory, or at least its sound beginnings, of income generation and propagation, which has magnificent sweep and simplicity. It set a fresh wind blowing through the structure of economic thought.[1]

This quotation from R. Goodwin is representative of the way the multiplier theory has been looked at by hundreds of economists since Keynes transferred Kahn's dynamic effect from employment to income analysis. The infinite sequence of secondary employments generated by an increase in public work expenditures led on to the infinite series of secondary incomes induced from an autonomous increment of public investment.

Let us call this autonomous income-generating expenditure injection. The theory tells us that any positive injection is submitted to a process of induction caused by its own expenditure. It is currently said that a new income is only partly consumed depending on the value of the marginal propensity to consume. In other words, it is assumed that consumption is a function of income whose particular form is determined socially. Whatever this form may be, the consumption function establishes a functional relation between the total income increase, ΔY, and the initial injection, ΔI, where $Y = k\Delta I$. This can easily be verified by introducing the consumption function into the definition of income. From

$$Y = C + I \tag{2.1}$$

and

$$C = C(Y), \tag{2.2}$$

and assuming $I = \bar{I}$, we have in fact what Samuelson calls one of the three seminal equations of economic theory:

$$Y = C(Y) + I. \tag{2.3}$$

'Equation [2.3] is crucially important for the history of economic thought. It is the nucleus of the Keynesian reasoning. If it *in no way* gives insight into the analysis of employment, then the Keynesian system is sterile and misleading.'[2]

The importance of Kahn–Keynes's discovery cannot be overlooked, but its consequence is even more striking: the multiplier establishes once and for all the existence of an objective link between successive incomes and represents the decisive and so desperately needed corroboration of the 'earning through spending' theory of income. Given the significance of the subject, we shall develop our critical appraisal very carefully, starting with a systematic analysis of what is logically inherent to the theory.

Didactically, we distinguish between two kinds of multiplier, the *horizontal multiplier*, which analyses the effects of a unique injection, and the *vertical multiplier*, where injections are repeated from period to period. Where a single injection is concerned, the sum of induced incomes can be calculated only through time, horizontally, whereas in the case of a repeated injection this sum can be measured in a single period, vertically.

As has been proved by P. Samuelson and by B. Schmitt, the horizontal and vertical multipliers are identical: they are merely two alternative ways of describing the same process.

> Two alternative definitions of the multiplier are met with in dynamic sequence analysis. The first measures the multiplier by the increased level of income finally reached as the result of a *continual* stream of a unit expenditure, repeated in every period. The second, which may be called the cumulated multiplier, is measured by summing throughout all the time the increments in income resulting from a unit, non-repeated, impulse of expenditure.[3]

Let us take firstly the horizontal multiplier. At the initial period p_0 a new injection of 100 is created. As already suggested by Wicksell, this initial injection will generate further increases in expenditure, which in turn will increase production and thus further income and expenditures, the process going on *ad infinitum* if nothing intervenes to stop it or slow it down.

Kahn's great contribution was to introduce the notion of *leakages* so that the multiplier effect is limited in time, the flow of inductions being counterbalanced by a growing loss of income. As Patinkin so clearly put it:

> . . . the question was, if it [the multiplier] is so good, why does it not go on to infinity? If you spend an additional pound, why does it not just keep on being spent by successive recipients until it employs everybody? Thus the real contribution of Kahn was less in demonstrating that the multiplier was greater than unity, than in defining and analysing the notion of leakages, and then demonstrating rigorously that as a result of these leakages the expansionary process converges to a finite limit.[4]

Unfortunately, the exact nature of such leakages remains quite mysterious. Two main possibilities seem to exist:

1. leakages are a loss of income due to its expenditure; and
2. leakages are a non-expenditure of income.

In the first case, income expenditure would be the cause of leakages: final expenditures destroy income instead of creating it. In the second case, on the contrary, expenditures maintain income, whose flow is assumed to be the same as the flow of expenditures. Leakages are therefore decreasing income by decreasing its expenditure; they represent that part of income which is lost so far as expenditures are concerned. Economists seem to have accepted almost unanimously this second broad definition of hoarding. Let us therefore analyse its implications when income is suddenly increased by a single injection.

The theory says that this unique injection will induce new incomes from period to period according to the value of c, the marginal propensity to consume. If, for exmaple, the newly injected income is totally spent for the purchase of consumption goods and services $c = 1$, the process of induction will go on and on without a limit, and k, the multiplier, will be infinity (see Figure 2.1). On the contrary, if $c = 0$, i.e. if the initial injection is totally saved, k is said to be equal to 1, and in this case no flow of induced incomes can be observed (see Figure 2.2).

Leakages are therefore defined here as the part of income which is not spent on consumption and which is held as idle balances or used to repay debt at banks.[5] Now, since the marginal propensity to consume is generally assumed to be less

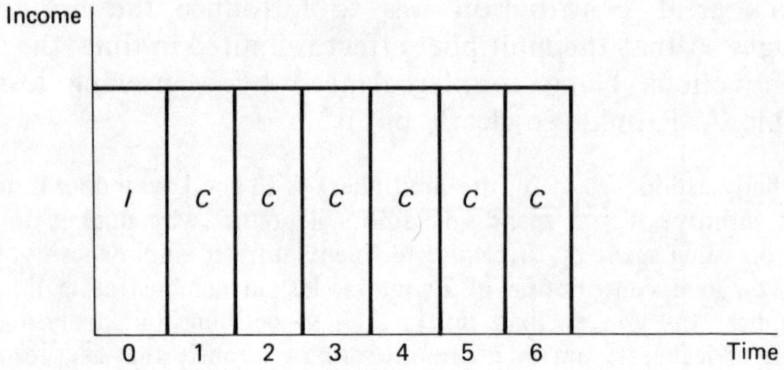

Fig. 2.1.

Fig. 2.2.

than unity, the dynamical horizontal multiplier can be represented as in Figure 2.3. The initial injection of 100 is decreasing from period to period according to the value of the marginal propensity to save. Conversely, the value of leakages, whose coefficient is $1 - c$, is increasing in each period, the limit of these two opposite movements being reached when all the initial increment is reduced to leakages. At each period following p_0 the induced income is less than the initial injection, so that the multiplier process is correctly defined as the representation of an ever-greater decrease of income through time.

> Because the marginal propensity to consume is less than unity, and there is no additional investment forthcoming, the national income decreases in geometric progression, in each period being only a fraction of that of the previous period, until finally the effect of the initial impulse of expenditure is completely dissipated.[6]

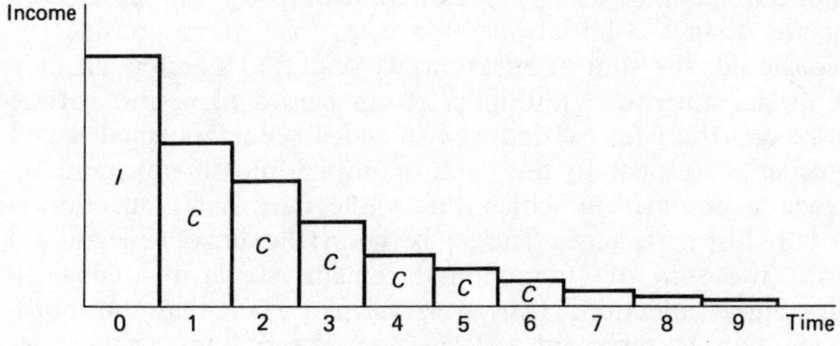

Fig. 2.3.

What has been said concerning a single, unrepeated injection is also valid in the case of a periodically repeated injection. The resulting vertical multiplier is represented in Figure 2.4. Even from a superficial observation of this diagram it is immediately apparent that the final result can either be read vertically, in a single period, or horizontally, for the infinite series of periods $p_0 \ldots p_n$. Obviously, when the injection is repeated the sum of

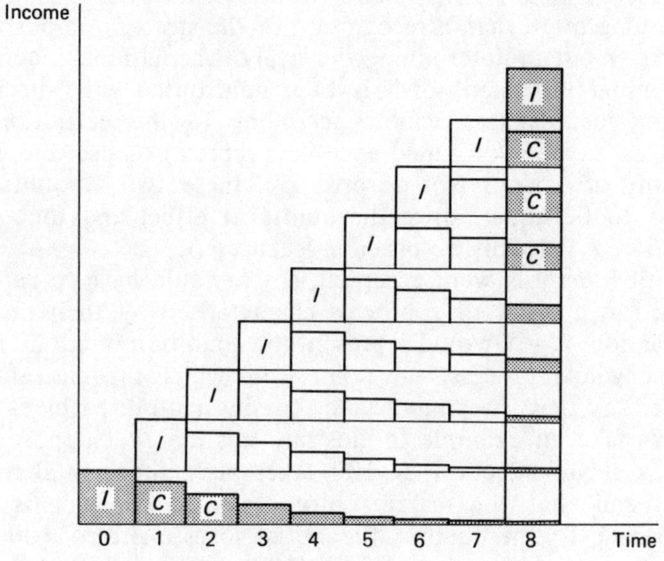

Fig. 2.4.

induced incomes at any period following p_0 will usually be greater than the initial injection of p_0. Yet, if we consider, as we should, the sum of injections we shall find a perfect analogy with the horizontal multiplier: from period to period as time goes on (the sum of) induced incomes become(s) smaller and smaller in respect to the (sum of) initial injection(s), until we reach a point from which the whole (any new) injection is totally lost in leakages. The gap between (the sum of) injection(s) and (the sum of) induction(s) remains stable and equal to the initial injection. Thus it is verified again that the multiplier aims to represent a *decreasing* flow of induced incomes through time.

2. The multiplier and the identity of *S* and *I*

A simple and powerful way of determining income, the multiplier seems also capable of resolving the apparently hopeless inconsistency between the identity of saving and investment, and their conditional equality.

Symptomatically, the initial injection is identified with an increment in investment, *I*, and the multiplier is thus represented as a relation between this increment and the following increase of income, $Y = k\Delta I$. 'The doctrine of the Multiplier is nothing more than a recognition of the strategic importance of investment in determining the level of the national income.'[7] The initial increment of *I* is then confronted with the final amount of leakages which, according to the definition of leakages as non-consumed incomes, represents also the final amount of saving. Not surprisingly, these two amounts are found to be equal, since the multiplier effect ends once the injection, *I*, is totally absorbed in leakages, *S*.

If this analysis were accepted, $I = S$ would have to be considered as a result of a process characterised by their mutual interaction. $I = S$ would represent the condition of equilibrium of the whole process, the point from which income remains stable, any new investment being totally neutralised by saving. Let us take an example to illustrate this theory. Suppose that only a single injection of 100 takes place (horizontal multiplier) and that the marginal propensity to consume is 4/5. According to the theory, the initial investment of 100 will induce a successive income of 4/5 (100), which will itself induce an income of 4/5 (80), and so on while the marginal propensity to consume can be applied to a positive income. Correspondingly, the part of income which is not consumed can be calculated by applying the marginal propensity to save (which is obviously equal to 1 minus the marginal propensity to consume) to the amount of available income. Thus saving will be equal to 1/5 (100) in p_1, 1/5 (80) in p_2, and so on until its sum equals the initial investment. In fact, at the end of the process we have

$$S = 1/5\,(100) + 1/5\,(80) + 1/5\,(64) + \ldots = 100 = I,$$

this result being also obtainable by applying s (marginal propensity to save) to the total increase of income ΔY, where $Y = k\Delta I = 5\Delta I = 500$. Graphically this can be represented as in Figure 2.5, where the sum of 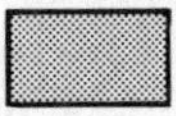 equals the first investment 

.

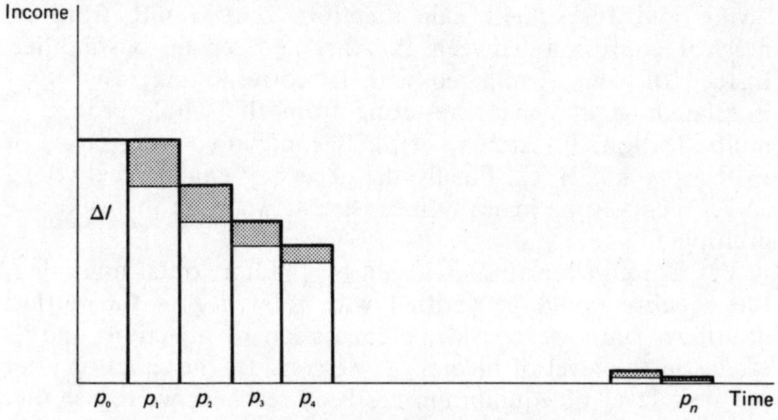

Fig. 2.5.

Equality of saving and investment seems to have been definitively transformed into a condition of equilibrium.

Savings and investment will only be equal for a constant level of income. When investment exceeds saving, income must be increasing. When saving exceeds investment, income must be decreasing. It is precisely these differences which cause income to increase or decrease, and it is the gradual equating of the two that determines the level that income gradually approaches.[8]

As we have seen in the case of a unique injection, equality of S and I is reached when the aggregate of savings in the successive periods $p_1 \ldots p_n$ equals the initial investment ΔI. In fact, this limit coincides with the point from which income will remain stable, all the initial investment having been neutralised by saving.

Were this analysis successful, it would realise the old dream of reconciling the necessary equality of S and I with the 'flow of expenditures' definition of income. Unfortunately, this attempt does not achieve its aim. In particular, saving and investment cannot be made equal by the aggregation of saving. Only two logical possibilities exist. Either:

1. we compare I and S at every distinct period, or
2. we compare the sum of I to the sum of S.

In both cases the equality of S and I cannot be verified. At each period $p_1 \ldots p_n$, I is smaller or greater than S. The equality of saving and investment can therefore only result from an illogical confusion between the first and second possibilities. Instead of being compared with its corresponding saving, ΔI is related to the saving resulting from the whole process of multiplication: investment of p_0 is confronted with saving of $p_1 + p_2 + \ldots + p_n$. Finally the necessary equality between I and S seems to be logically inconsistent with the theory of the multiplier.

Yet a doubt remains. Rejected by the horizontal multiplier, the equality could be verified with reference to the vertical multiplier once we consider a succession of injections and its effect on the level of income. If we consider the situation after the new level of equilibrium has been reached, we realise that at each period following p_n the amount of ΔI is exactly equal to the amount of S (see Figure 2.6). While apparently satisfactory, this analysis does not stand a critical examination. The repeated injection ΔI should in fact be compared with its own saving within the period considered. If, on the contrary, we take into account the whole amount saved in the period, we have to compare it with the total amount of investment of this same period and not only with the new investment, ΔI. Thus, if this logical constraint is respected, saving and investment appear to be different, either before or after p_n.

Another way of criticising this attempt to establish $S = I$ as a

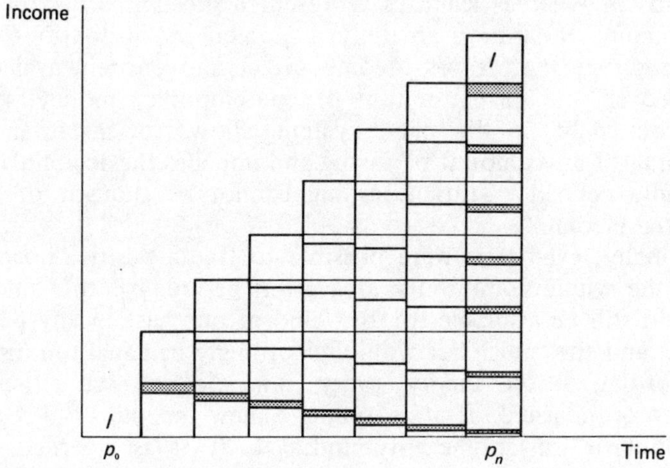

Fig. 2.6.

condition of equilibrium is by considering the concept of leakages. As we have seen earlier, most economists agree in defining leakages as a non-spent income which can therefore be identified with that part of saving which is hoarded. 'Savings, moreover, which assumed the form of hoarded currency or idle bank deposits would likewise run to waste so far as expenditures are concerned.'[9] Now, by definition, the multiplier effect stops once the initial investment has totally 'run to waste', i.e. once ΔI = leakages, or, identically, when no more residual income can be spent. Would this mean that once the equilibrium has been reached investment and leakages are necessarily equal, and therefore that, from that point on, saving and investment are also necessarily equal? Of course not, since it is obvious that the amount of savings is greater than the amount of hoarded currency and idle bank deposits. Even if it could be proved that at the end of the process investment and hoarded savings are equal, that would not imply the equality of S and I. Let us suppose, however, that saving and hoarding are one and the same thing. Once again, like Tantalus, our effort is in vain. In fact, savings and leakages cannot be identical, even at equilibrium, since it is not true that 'hoarded currency or idle bank deposits would likewise run to waste so far as expenditures are concerned'. Hoarding and leakages should not be confused. Whereas leakages represent a substantial destruction of income, hoardings are only a momentary abstention from expenditure that leaves income intact and entirely available. Moreover, the proper nature of contemporary money, spontaneous debt of the bank system, allows for instantaneous lending of any amount of saving and impedes the accumulation of idle deposits. Thus, hoarding cannot be thought of as a wasted income.

Finally, even if it were possible to find a positive hoarding for the whole community at a given period, p_x, this amount would still be available for any kind of purchase in any period p_{x+y}, and the multiplier would accordingly be equal to infinity. According to the theory, every new injection can either be spent or hoarded. If it is spent, a new income of the same amount is instantaneously induced; if it is hoarded, the induction is simply postponed and the income reaches its previous level as soon as the momentarily unspent income is dishoarded. Thus, the process of multiplication never comes to an end, every income reproducing sooner or later an equivalent income, and so on indefinitely. For the multiplier to be less than infinity, it is therefore necessary that at least part of the injected income be literally destroyed. As Kahn correctly pointed out, the notion of leakages is essential for the expansionary process to converge to a finite limit, and should not be deprived of its originality and confused with concepts of hoarding and saving, which do not imply the idea of income destruction.

Despite these discouraging results, economists do not surrender but try obstinately to find a way of expressing $S = I$ as a condition of equilibrium. Another example of such an attempt is given by Hansen. In his article, 'A note on savings and investment', he introduces a distinction between actual and normal which should allow the conciliation of the necessary equality of S and I with their conditional equilibrium.

Evidently there are two concepts with respect to the relation of actual savings to investment:

1. that they are always identically equal, and
2. that actual savings equal investment when the 'multiplier' process has raised income to a level sufficiently to induce that much saving.

These two concepts are, however, not contradictory or inconsistent.

What is true is that *actual* savings may or may not be at a point corresponding to the *normal* relation of savings to income.[10]

Thus, according to Hansen, though actual saving and actual investment are always equal, their identity does not necessarily correspond to the normal value of the propensity to consume. Therefore, if actual and normal value do not correspond, the level of income will vary until the identity $I = S$ reaches its level of equilibrium, i.e. a level where actual saving = normal saving = actual investment = normal investment.

But all this does not mean that income has to rise by the 'full' or 'normal' multiplier before actual savings equal investment. Actual savings always equal investment whatever the momentary marginal propensity to consume and whatever the income level. But actual savings will not hold a normal relation to income until income has risen by an amount which permits a normal propensity to consume.[11]

As the careful reader will immediately notice, Hansen's distinction between actual and normal values sounds very similar to the one between ex-ante and ex-post, or virtual and realised quantities. Yet, it seems possible to avoid the imaginary world and speak of actual and normal values within the theory of realised income. What Hansen is suggesting is that there are different levels of stability corresponding to each identity of S and I. Thus identity $I = S$ will change until its implied marginal propensity to consume corresponds to the normal one. But if it is true that actual saving and actual investment are always equal, how can we determine their normal level? Moreover, were it possible to determine it, which forces would be available to make income move towards this normal level? Certainly neither S and I, which are always equal to each other, nor supply and demand, whose difference depends upon S and I, can do so. In reality, every level of the marginal propensity to consume is as 'normal' as any other, and no forces are available, within a given income, to make it grow or decrease in order to fulfil the main requirement of the multiplier theory. Distinction between actual and normal is purely terminological, and logically inadequate for proving the coexistence of identities and conditions of equilibrium within any realised income. Once we admit, like Hansen, that actual saving is necessarily always equal to actual investment, we lose any chance of explaining the variation of income in terms of S and I and we reduce the multiplier either to unity or to a mere truism. Let us try to prove this last point.

3. The multiplier and the identity of Y and $C+I$

The multiplier is usually defined in terms of marginal propensity to consume. Given an initial injection ΔI, it is said that the level of income will increase according to the value of k, the multiplier coefficient, which is equal to $1/(1-c)$ where c represents the marginal propensity to consume: $Y = k\Delta I$. Now, as Keynes puts it, the marginal propensity to consume 'is of considerable importance, because it tells us how the next increment of output will have to be divided between consumption and investment'.[12] But, in this case, $1/(1-c)$ is not really a multiplier. It simply means that, if $C = cY$, and given the identity $Y \equiv C + I$, the national income can also be represented by $Y = \{1/(1-c)\}\, I$, and that this equation is necessarily true for any realised income. In fact, it is equivalent to saying either that $Y = C + I$ or that $Y = cY + I$, where $C = cY$ and $cY = Y - I$. The main point is that C and I are complementary in the definition of income, so that if we know one of them and the proportion according to which they enter in the measurement of Y (Keynes's marginal propensity to consume), we also know Y. This result is also valid in the case in which we distinguished between short and long run. C, instead of being simply expressed by cY, would take the form of

$$C = \beta_0 + \beta_1\, Y + (1 + \beta_2)\, C_{-1} - (\beta_1 + a\beta_2)\, Y_{-1},$$

where β_0 is a constant, β_1 the marginal propensity to consume in the short run, and a the marginal propensity to consume in the long run, and where β_2, the coefficient of error correction, is > 0. According to this formula, the proportion (x) that C enters in the measurement of Y is

$$\frac{C}{Y} = x = \frac{\beta_0}{Y} + \beta_1 + \frac{(1 + \beta_2)\, C_{-1}}{Y} - \frac{(\beta_1 + a\beta_2)\, Y_{-1}}{Y}.$$

Thus, knowing x and I we also know Y, since $Y = C + I$. It is then obvious that the multiplier loses all its significance once we identify the initial injection with $\Delta I + \Delta C$ and the coefficient of induction with the marginal propensity to consume.

As a matter of fact, when Keynes maintains that the marginal propensity to consume 'tells us how the next increment of output will have to be divided between consumption and investment', he is implicitly assuming that ΔI is only part of the net increase of income, the total net increment being equal to $\Delta C + \Delta I$. Thus, it is not surprising that the two expressions $Y = C + I$ and $Y = \{(1/1 - c)\}I$ are perfectly equivalent and independent of any dynamic determination of income.

Yet, it must be recognised that the definition of autonomous expenditure, our initial injection, is sometimes difficult to understand, confusion being caused by Keynes's definition of the marginal propensity to consume and of the logical multiplier based upon it, the initial injection corresponds to any expenditure for the production of consumption or investment goods, so that the term 'investment', when referring to autonomous expenditure, accounts for the total amount of income created by the production of C and I. In fact, if a multiplier theory is to exist, it must apply to any kind of income injection. Whether a new income is created by producing consumption goods or investment goods should not matter, for the theory states the existence of a causal chain of induced incomes resulting from the expenditure of any new income, whatever its origin. Once it has been understood that that injection, correctly defined, is not confined to the production of investment goods, it also becomes evident that the relation between saving and investment has nothing to do with the relation between injection and leakages. The result of our previous chapter seems thus to be confirmed: identity $I = S$ holds good for any level of realised income and independently of the marginal propensity to consume. As Hansen puts it, '. . . actual savings always equal investment whatever the momentary marginal propensity to consume and whatever the income level'.[13]

Despite all of this, would it not be possible to consider the marginal propensity to consume as a driving force which, given a certain amount of investment, pushes C to a kind of predetermined level where $Y = cY + I$? In this case it would be possible to say that the marginal propensity to consume transforms any increase in I or C into a final increase of Y, which is a multiple of the initial increase. Now, this analysis would be correct only if $Y = C + I$ were a condition of equilibrium, fulfilled only when $Y = cY$ for a given c, and not an identity, satisfied whatever the level of c. As we know, Keynes is categorical:

$Y = C + I$ is an identity applying to any level of realised income. Thus, the marginal propensity to consume is effectively only observable once production has already taken place. If the community shares its purchases between 10 units of investment goods and 40 units of consumption goods we can then say that the marginal propensity to consume is 4/5 or, equivalently, that the net increment of output is divided between consumption and investment in the proportion of 4 to 1. Were $C = 30$ and $I = 20$, the marginal propensity to consume would be 3/5, and so on, the value of c varying according to the proportion of C and I in the identity $Y \equiv C + I$.

From what has been said it follows that the true multiplier must be derived from the total expenditure of income and not from its division into C and I. In other words, if any link between successive incomes can be found to exist it must result from the *marginal propensity to spend* and not simply to consume. Represented by a flow of expenditures through time, the multiplier is an attempt at establishing a causal relation between any given income and the result of its expenditure. It would therefore be mistaken to restrict this influence to consumption only. Expenditures on investment goods are as effective, from the multiplier point of view, as expenditures on consumption goods. Thus, we have now to analyse what kind of influence can be exerted by the marginal propensity to *spend* on incomes created by the production of consumption and investment goods.

Firstly, we must determine the value(s) of the marginal propensity to spend. Apparently this problem is too wide to be tackled within the restricted limits of economics. Yet, social and psychological considerations can be laid aside if we limit our analysis to the problems of leakage. As has already been pointed out, the multiplier would be equal to infinity if there were no leakages due to the expenditure of income. It is important to notice that, according to Keynes, leakages can only be caused by income spending and that they are, therefore, not that part of income 'run to waste so far as expenditures are concerned'. In fact, leakages must be related to expenditures for the very simple reason that every income is necessarily and totally spent:

$$C' + I' \equiv C + I \equiv Y.$$

By definition, income corresponds to the final purchase of consumption and investment goods. Final expenditure being the measure of income, a non-spent income is a *contradictio in adjecto*. Any income which is lost before its final expenditure is an income which has never existed since, as Keynes proved, income creation, $C' + I'$, and final expenditure, $C + I$, are one and the same thing. Thereafter, leakages must be explained within the expenditure of income: they must result from it and can no longer be considered as wasted income. Thus, if we do not support the absurd idea of a multiplier equal to infinity, we have to accept the fact that income expenditures do imply its destruction: $k \equiv 1$. Let us give another proof that the coefficient of multiplication can only be equal to one.

4. The multiplier is always and necessarily equal to 1

$k \equiv 1$ can also be established autonomously, without referring to the Keynesian identity between total demand and total supply. The proof that we propose here has been elaborated by B. Schmitt in his 1971 book *L'Analyse macroéconomique des revenus.*[14]

Let us consider a process of multiplication characterised by a repeated injection ΔY of 50 and a marginal propensity to spend of 5/6. The theory tells us that income will grow from 0 to 300, at which level it will remain stable, the value of leakages being equal to the value of ΔY. This situation is represented in Table 2.1.

Table 2.1

Day	0	1	2	*n*
Injections	300	50	50	50
Inductions	0	250	250	250
Leakages	0	50	50	50
Income	300	300	300	300

If we start from the new equilibrium, this will be maintained at the same level as long as the daily injection is equal to 50. For example, at day 1 income available is 300 (one-day lag) so that the induced income is (5/6)(300) = 250; adding the injection to this income we obtain 300, the amount corresponding to equilibrium and which will become available at day 2.

Now, what we want to know is whether or not *leakages* can be construed as *hoarding*. The determining point here is that hoarding does not represent a destroyed income, i.e. an income which will never again be available in the future. On the contrary, hoarding is an income which is only momentarily subtracted from consumption and which will again be available the following day. Accordingly, our representation, once hoardings are substituted for leakages, becomes that shown in Table 2.2.

Table 2.2

Day	0	1	2	n
Injections	300	50	50	50
Inductions	0	250	(5/6)(350)	$(5/6)\{300 + (n-1)50\}$
Hoarding	0	50	(1/6)(350)	$(1/6)\{300 + (n-1)50\}$
Income	300	300	(5/6)(350) +50	$(5/6)\{300 + (n-1)50\}$ +50

Given that hoardings do not destroy incomes, from the second day onwards inductions no longer respect their equilibrium level of 250. In fact, 5/6, the coefficient of induction, must be applied to every disposable income, hoarding included. In our numerical example, at day 2 the coefficient of induction must be applied to 300, the income created in day 1, plus 50, the income which was hoarded in day 1 and is still available. As a consequence, the equilibrium level of income cannot be maintained unless we drop all ideas of identifying leakage with hoarding. Thus, the theory of the multiplier requires leakages to be strictly defined as *destroyed incomes*. Moreover, from the exclusion of hoarding from the definition of leakages it follows that macroeconomic hoardings are always equal to zero; once a new injection, ΔY, has been shared betweeen induction, $i(\Delta Y)$, and leakage, $(1 - i)(\Delta Y)$, nothing is left to feed a positive hoarding which, by definition, is neither an expenditure nor a leakage.

The consequence of $H = 0$ is invaluable for the analysis of income. From it we learn firstly that it is logically impossible for an income not to be spent. In fact, hoarding defines the non-expenditure of income, and since macroeconomic hoarding is always nil it follows that every new available income is necessarily spent for the purchase of consumption and investment goods. Hence our coefficient of induction can only be equal to 1 or 0, all conceivable intermediate values being excluded by the fact that the expenditure of income cannot be avoided. Thus, either we adopt an 'earning by spending' theory of income, in which case every expenditure induces a corresponding income, $i = 1$, leakages being inevitably equal to zero, $1 - i = 0$, or we claim that income is destroyed by its final expenditure, leakages being therefore equal to 1 and inductions equal to zero. In the first case the coefficient of multiplication is infinite, $k = \infty$, in the second it is one, $k = 1$.

First case	*Second case*
$i = 1$	$i = 0$
$1 - i = 0$	$1 - i = 1$
$k = \infty$	$k = 1$

The choice between these two possibilities is not arbitrary. Acceptance of the first possibility, $k = \infty$, implies an inescapable pitfall for the multiplier theory: if $i = 1$ income never reaches an equilibrium, since the initial impulse has endless repercussions. It thus follows that 1 is the only acceptable value of k: 'the propensity to spend incomes is equal to one, but purchases do not induce income. Created income leaks out in final purchases. Incomes feed purchases, and purchases do not feed back incomes.'[15]

As we shall see in the following chapter, this implies a new conception of time. Income is, in fact, the instantaneous result of an event, called an *emssion*, which takes place in *quantum time*. The traditional, functional relation between successive incomes is definitively dismissed by quantum analysis, which defines income as a creation, and which establishes the rigorous identity of income creation and income destruction.

PART II: THE INSTANTANEOUS MULTIPLIER

In this second part we shall start from Keynes's analysis of the multiplier and show that, of the two alternative solutions offered to us, only one is consistent with his fundamental identities. Accordingly, we shall then claim that, although apparently transformed into a mere truism, the multiplier remains a central concept in economics provided the stress is put upon the *multiplicand* and not upon the coefficient of multiplication, which is necessarily always equal to one. Having proved this point, we shall explain the autonomous expenditures in terms of their relation with money and with the factors of production. We shall then also establish that the true multiplier does not imply any static or dynamic analysis and that, although logically instantaneous, it is absolutely 'in time'.

1. The multiplier and the multiplicand

Our normal psychological law that, when the real income of the community increases or decreases, its consumption will increase or decrease but not so fast, can, therefore, be translated—not, indeed, with absolute accuracy but subject to qualifications which are obvious and can easily be stated in a formally complete fashion—into the proposition that ΔCw and ΔYw have the same sign, but $\Delta Yw > \Delta Cw$, where Cw is the consumption in terms of wage-units. This is merely a repetition of the proposition already established [earlier]. Let us define, then, dCw/dYw as the *marginal propensity to consume.*

This quantity is of considerable importance, because it tells us how the next increment of output will have to be divided between consumption and investment. For $\Delta Yw = \Delta Cw + \Delta Iw$, where ΔCw and ΔIw are the increments of consumption and investment; so that we can write $\Delta Yw = k\Delta Iw$, where $1 - (1/k)$ is equal to the marginal propensity to consume.

Let us call k the *investment multiplier.* It tells us that, when there is an increment of aggregate investment, income will increase by an amount which is k times the increment of investment.[16]

The first part of this quotation refers to the relation between income and what Keynes calls his normal psychological law, which states that the marginal propensity to consume is usually less than one. Obviously, this psychological law cannot interfere with the identities defining national income. Whatever the propensity to consume, income will always be measured by the total amount of final expenditures. Thus, the marginal propensity to consume can be easily introduced into Keynes's identities. For example, a marginal propensity to consume of 1/2 will tell us that the total production has to be equally divided between consumption and investment. This information does not modify the amount of income created: it simply suggests the proportion of C and I within $Y \equiv C + I$.

It is true that, as with any other psychological law, the marginal propensity to consume is an empirical law which can be verified or invalidated by facts. Nevertheless, the total amount of income will remain unchanged, since it depends on the total cost of production regardless of its subsequent division between consumption and investment. It then follows that the marginal propensity to consume represents the reverse of the marginal propensity to invest. In other words, it is exactly the same to affirm that a certain amount, x, of income will not be consumed, as to affirm that the final purchase of investment goods will be equal to x. Thus a propensity to consume of less than 1 implies a positive production of investment goods: agents devote part of their energy to producing investment goods instead of consumption goods. Knowing the propensity to consume, we also know how much of national income is made up of investment, that is, we know the division of income between consumption and investment.

Hitherto, identity of saving and investment is respected. Keynes's normal psychological law is not opposed to the identity, which is verified for any level of the marginal propensity to consume. By reducing consumption, the community increases investment and saving at the same time and by the same amount. This is because C and I are complementary in the measure of national income and, by definition, saving is 'the excess of income over consumption', and investment is 'that part of the income of the period which has not passed into consumption'.[17]

According to this conception of the marginal propensity to consume, the multiplier becomes instantaneous in the sense that, whatever the initial injection and whatever the consumers' behaviour, it will always be instantaneously true that $Y = \Delta C + \Delta I$ or, equivalently, that $Y = (\Delta C/\Delta Y)\ \Delta Y + \Delta I$. Is such a multiplier something more than a tautology? Hansen seems to have no doubt about the answer.

> Suppose, instead of speaking about a 'propensity' (i.e., a behaviour pattern) we simply use an arithmetic ratio $\Delta C/\Delta Y$. The coefficient relating the increment of investment to an increment of income is indeed

$$\frac{1}{1-(\Delta C)/(\Delta Y)},$$

but in this context the coefficient is not based on a true propensity, i.e. either a 'short-run normal' or a 'long-run normal' relation of consumption to income. Such a coefficient is a mere *arithmetic* multiplier (i.e., a truism) and not a true *behaviour* multiplier based on a *behaviour* pattern which establishes a verifiable relation between consumption and income. A mere arithmetic multiplier,

$$\frac{1}{1-(\Delta C)/(\Delta Y)},$$

is tautological.[18]

Shall we then share Haberler's drastic judgement and conclude that Keynes's approach to the multiplier is inadequate and fruitless?

We have now to ask, what is gained by this procedure? In reality nothing more than that a new name is given to the multiplier. The multiplier is defined in terms of marginal propensity to consume. Instead of the multiplier we can always say

$$\frac{1}{1-(\Delta C)/(\Delta Y)}$$

and for marginal propensity to consume we can always substitute $1-(1/k)$. One and the same thing has got two names.

Now, I do not question that sometimes it may serve a useful purpose to have two names for the same thing, but it seems that Mr. Keynes has fallen into the trap of treating such a relationship by definition as a causal or empirical relationship between investment and income and that thereby a large part of what he says about the multiplier and its probable magnitude is vitiated. By assuming something about the marginal propensity to consume he assumes something about the multiplier, but this is no more an explanation of the multiplier than *pauvreté* is an explanation of poverty.[19]

If by multiplier we mean a functional relation between income expenditure and income earning, such that an initial injection will be followed by a finite chain of induced incomes, it is certainly true that Keynes's definition of the marginal propensity to consume does not support the concept in any decisive way. Yet, this obviously does not imply the falsity of Keynes's point of view. On the contrary, the arithmetical multiplier seems the only logical way of avoiding a contradiction between the necessary equalities $I = S$, $Y = C + I$, total supply = total demand, and the psychological law represented by the marginal propensity to consume.

Before reaching any conclusion, let us analyse the last paragraph of this section's initial extract from Keynes. 'Let us call k the *investment multiplier*. It tells us that, when there is an increment of aggregate investment, income will increase by an amount which is k times the increment of investment.'

What Keynes is asserting here corresponds to the traditional theory of the multiplier, according to which a flow of induced incomes following an initial increase of I will push ΔY to a level $k - 1$ times greater than ΔI (where the coefficient k is determined by the marginal propensity to consume which is assumed to be desired by the community).

Thus their effort to consume a part of their increased incomes will stimulate output until the new level (and distribution) of incomes provides a margin of saving sufficient to correspond to the increased investment. The multiplier tells us by how much their employment has to be increased to yield an increase in real income sufficient to induce them to do the necessary extra saving, and is a function of their psychological propensities.[20]

Psychological behaviour, as represented by the marginal propensity to consume, is therefore introduced to justify a possible, though temporary, discrepancy between saving and investment or, equivalently, between total demand and total supply. Now, Keynes is perfectly aware of the contradiction to which this kind of analysis could lead. Having previously proved that saving and investment, as well as total demand and total supply, are necessarily always equal, how is it possible to sustain their conditional equality without falling into an apparently unavoidable contradiction? As Hansen points out, Keynes's solution is based on the distinction he introduces between actual and desired values of the marginal propensity to consume. Keynes claims that although savings and investment are always identical at their actual value, this identity can be a 'moving' one if it does not correspond to the equilibrium value of the marginal propensity to consume. In this case, saving and investment will move together towards a new level, where their identity is associated with an amount of realised income which guarantees the return to a normal value of c.

Yet, variation through time of the marginal propensity to

consume is not sufficient to explain the constant fulfilment of $I = S$. In fact, given an initial investment of x in p_0, saving would be equal to x only if the marginal propensity to consume were equal to zero, in which case there would be no multiplier effect at all.

I have found, however, in discussion that this obvious fact often gives rise to some confusion between the logical theory of the multiplier, which holds good continuously, without time-lag, at all moments of time, and the consequences of an expansion in the capital-goods industries which take gradual effect, subject to time-lag and only after an interval.[21]

To avoid this problem, Keynes assumes a gradual variation of aggregate investment such that at any period the increase in demand is equal to the product of actual investment and the actual multiplier.

The central point here is the relation of equivalence between total demand and total supply, which 'holds good continuously, without time-lag, at all moments of time'. To satisfy this logical requirement of the theory, Keynes adapts the level of investment and the marginal propensity to consume. Now, what are the consequences of this exercise for the traditional analysis of the multiplier? Does the constant equality of saving and investment allow for a sequence of induced incomes through time?

Let us consider Keynes's argument once again. What he is trying to prove is that the constant equality of total supply and total demand is perfectly consistent with the multiplier effect, even where the time-lagged expansion in capital goods industries is concerned. In order to prove this, Keynes starts his analysis by comparing the situation created by an unforeseen increase in output of the capital goods industries with the situation where the multiplier exerts its effect instantaneously, the increase in production being perfectly foreseen. First of all, we have to understand the real meaning of Keynes's logical theory of the multiplier. A numerical example would be useful. Suppose that at period p_0 an initial injection of 100 takes place within an economy characterised by a marginal propensity to consume of 1/2. According to Keynes, the logical theory of the multiplier implies an instantaneous adjustment between the increment of aggregate demand and 'the product of the increment of aggregate investment and the multiplier as determined by the marginal propensity to consume'.[22] Although it appears obvious, this statement could be interpreted in two different and mutually exclusive ways.

1. It could be assumed that Keynes's equality is referring to the total increase in income due to the initial injection in investment. In this case, we should conclude that the logical multiplier requires the instantaneous fulfilment of $\Delta Y = k\Delta I$ which means, in our numerical example, that income will instantaneously increase by an amount equal to $k(100) = \{1/(1 - 1/2)\}(100) = 200$. As we have already seen in the previous chapter, this analysis could be used to prove that the multiplier leads to a new identity between saving and investment and is therefore not inconsistent with Keynes's fundamental identities.

In fact, it could be argued that the logical multiplier is in constant agreement with $S = I$ since, $\Delta Y = k\Delta I$ holding good continuously, and k being the reciprocal of the marginal propensity to save, $\Delta S = (1/k)\Delta Y = (1/K)k\Delta I = \Delta I$. Without repeating what has already been said, a new critique can be raised here against this last attempt at reconciling identities and conditions of equilibrium. As we know, identity of saving and investment can also be considered as an equivalent way of expressing the necessary equality of total supply and total demand. Therefore, $\Delta Y = k\Delta I$ must be consistent with Δ supply $= \Delta$ demand. Now, in Keynes's own words, ΔY is the increment of aggregate demand. Thus, ΔY must correspond to an equivalent increase on the supply side.

A problem arises here: what is the increase in total supply due to an unrepeated injection and an instantaneous multiplier?

Following traditional thought, we are tempted to answer that Δ supply $= k\Delta I$, which would definitely prove the compatibility of Δ supply $= \Delta$ demand and the multiplier. Yet, after careful consideration, we should be forced to admit that the increase in supply is only equal to ΔI. In fact, supply stands for the total output of a given period and ΔI represents the total increase in production which can be accounted for at the very instant that the new injection takes place. With the logical multiplier, everything must be verified instantaneously. This means that the instantaneous increase in demand, equal to $k\Delta I$, must be immediately equal to the instantaneous increase in supply, ΔI. But, how could it be possible for $k\Delta I$ to be equal to ΔI once we define k as $1/(1 - c)$ and we assume that $0 < c < 1$?

Before concluding that k must necessarily be equal to 1, let us analyse the second possible way of interpreting Keynes's logical multiplier.

2. According to the necessary equality of income created, $C' + I'$, and income's final expenditure, $C + I$, it could be said that the instantaneous multiplier corresponds to an operation which allows the continuous equivalence of these two terms. In other words, the logical multiplier requires the constant identity of total supply, $C' + I'$, and total demand, $C + I$, whatever the level of income or the amount of its increase, i.e. the amount of any new injection. Thus, any time that a new income is injected it will instantaneously define an identity, demand ≡ supply. If we now bear in mind that the theory of the multiplier, logically defined, necessarily applies to any kind of produced income, and that inductions, if any, must be derived from expenditures, it follows that any income resulting from the production of investment or consumption goods is an injection. It also follows that the marginal propensity to consume must be replaced by the marginal propensity to spend. Hence $\Delta Y = k\Delta I$ becomes

$$\Delta(C + I) = k\Delta(C' + I'),$$

where k is the multiplier, as determined by the marginal propensity to spend. This last identity can also be written as follows:

$$\Delta \text{ total demand} = \Delta \text{ total supply},$$

and it is immediately evident that k is necessarily equal to one. Both interpretations of Keynes's logical multiplier lead, thus, to the same conclusion. But, if all newly created income is necessarily spent (marginal propensity to spend equal to 1, and $k = 1$), the coefficient of induction can only be equal to zero: no income is ever induced by expenditure of income. Every income is totally spent, $s = 1$, and by this process it is also totally destroyed, $k = 1$.

This apparently odd and uneasy conclusion is nevertheless logically implied in Keynes's definition of the instantaneous multiplier. To reject it would also imply the rejection of Keynes's fundamental identities and, with them, of any possibility of defining national income. Yet, its acceptance seems to involve a series of unpleasant consequences. Its coefficient being always equal to one, is the multiplier still meaningful? From the rejection of any objective link between successive incomes, does it not inevitably follow that income analysis is necessarily static?

Let us deal here with the first of these two problems, the importance of $k \equiv 1$. Once it has been proved, this identity has an indisputable heuristic importance since it tells us that every income created by the production of consumption and investment goods (and services) is necessarily destroyed by the final purchase of these same goods (and services). The lack of any true effect of multiplication implied in $k \equiv 1$ represents a positive piece of information about the relation between production and final purchase. In fact, it is an additional proof of the inadequacy implied in the definition of income as a flow of expenditures. Resulting from a confusion between psychological and logical laws, the positive multiplication of income through time is nothing more than a skilful piece of magic that would find a more suitable place in alchemy than in economics.

The multiplication aspect having been rejected, the importance of the multiplier must rest in the definition of *the multiplicand*. In fact, in Δ total demand $= k\Delta$ total supply, when $k \equiv 1$ all the emphasis is put on the supply side. From $k \equiv 1$ we know that all income will be spent and destroyed, but what we still have to determine is the source of any new income. In other words, we have to find the real definition of autonomous expenditures, or injections.

2. The autonomous expenditures

In order to have a better understanding of this problem it is useful to go back to the traditional multiplier theory. This theory, when correctly interpreted, requires the equilibrium of saving and autonomous expenditures for Y to be constant. But saving equals investment. Therefore, from saving = autonomous expenditures it follows that autonomous expenditures $= I$, and in this case income does not remain constant: Y, which by definition is the sum of C and I, increases when I (or C or both) increases. Thus it seems unavoidable to conclude that if autonomous expenditures correspond to an investment, then income $(C + I)$ is necessarily increased by their total amount: the multiplier is either one or infinity. This result can also be obtained immediately once we remember that, according to Keynes, savings represent an income which is necessarily spent on the financial market and thus do not 'run to waste so far as expenditures are concerned'. Obviously, if we want to support the traditional theory, we have to consider saving and leakages as two separate and independent concepts. At equilibrium, then, the increase in autonomous expenditures is totally neutralised by a corresponding increase in leakages: income is instantaneously increased and decreased for the same amount, i.e. it remains at its previous level. Now, we face two possibilities. Either we maintain that

1. autonomous expenditures and leakages are the result of the same operation; or that
2. autonomous expenditures and leakages are the result of two distinct operations.

In the first case, income could remain constant but it would be impossible to explain the formation of any new income, since any attempt to do so would lead to a contradiction. The same object, income, would be simultaneously submitted to two opposite requirements: instantaneously created and destroyed, income could never positively exist. This inconsistency is fortunately avoided once autonomous expenditures and leakages are no longer related to the same operation. In this second case, autonomous expenditures create an income which is destroyed by its final expenditure. Although strictly correlated, these two operations are not simultaneous, so that income can positively exist in time; it is created and subsequently destroyed, and not destroyed as soon as it is created.

From this short analysis we can obtain interesting information concerning the concept we are investigating, namely that autonomous expenditures must not be identified with final expenditures, i.e. with the final purchase of consumption and investment goods and services. We already know that autonomous expenditures denote the creation of income, and that this creation precedes, and must therefore be kept separate from, its final expenditure. We also know that it would be erroneous to refer autonomous expenditures to investment only. 'Thus the multiplier process operates equally potently whether income is raised in the first instance by an increase in investment or by an increase in consumption.'[23] Production of consumption goods is as good as any other from the income creation point of view. Thereafter, it is clear that autonomous expenditures and production of goods and services are in reality one and the same concept. Every time that a production takes place, a new income is created whose magnitude corresponds to the monetary factor's cost. Consequently, autonomous expenditures and money cost of production are fundamentally equivalent. In perfect agreement with Keynes's analysis, income creation is thus related to the monetary remuneration of the factors of production.

Before any further consideration of the role of money, let us briefly remark that the multiplicand, $C' + I'$, is in fact independent of the distinction between consumption and investment goods. Identity $Y \equiv C' + I'$ simply means that the creation of income corresponds to the total remuneration of the factors of production whatever their activity. The distinction between consumption and investment goods is somehow artificial, and usually difficult to establish in an indisputable way. Yet, this dichotomy does not influence our definition of autonomous expenditures, which are determined only by the total activity of production, independently of its subsequent repartition. Finally, division of products between C and I is determined both by process of production and by final purchase, whereas the multiplicand is related only to production.

3. Static, dynamic and $k \equiv 1$

> A static position is a time-less concept. The variables, indeed, may be stocks or flows, but they are all dated at the same moment or period of time, and there are no conditions imposed that relate to different points of time. In *static equilibrium*, we require that the variables balance out, without surplus or deficit, in some specified way, very much as the forces operating in a body at rest balance each other. The position is time-less in the sense that there are no links with the past or with the future; we are not interested in how it got there or in what will happen to it later . . . A system becomes dynamic as soon as the dated variables relate to different moments or periods of time and have links with the past and future.[24]

According to this widely accepted definition, the absence of links between past and future should be regarded as characteristic of a situation of static equilibrium, i.e. of a situation whose analysis is necessarily static. Thus, it is essential to know the exact nature of the assumed links. Our conclusion may, in fact, vary considerably according to whether or not we regard these links as a functional relation between successive incomes. In the first case, the possibility of having a dynamic analysis of income would depend upon the possibility of considering income as a flow of expenditures. As is well known, the theory of the multiplier purports to establish a dynamic chain of production processes. According to this theory, any production has a precise influence on the next production by means of the marginal propensity to consume. Yet, we have shown that the multiplier coefficient is logically equal to 1, which means that consumption does not recreate income at all. Instead of reproducing it through time, consumption destroys the produced income, so that any production is a completely new process. In this sense, production is synonymous with creation and not with transmission and, as such, it does not allow any functional relation between successive incomes. Hence, in default of any functional relation, the comparison of different productions cannot be dynamised. All we can do is try to find, *a posteriori*, the factors that influence the passage from today's production to tomorrow's, bearing in mind that these reasons and their mutual interaction vary continuously, and that any attempt to place them in a functional relation is impossible. Thus, starting from a given situation, say production p_0, we can only presume what the next production, p_1, will be, without being able to *determine* any 'path' or 'traverse' at all, because such a determination would be possible only if successive productions were linked by some objective law.

Must we, therefore, conclude that income analysis is necessarily static? This conclusion, which is the logical consequence of an 'equilibrium' conception, would lead to the absurd situation in which income were timeless. A timeless income, considered literally, would be represented by an empty production, since it would refer to a production with a time dimension equal to zero. Yet, if 'timeless' is considered merely as a synonym for static equilibrium, it seems to be possible to refer income to a finite period of time.

> *Statical* then refers to the form and structure of the postulated laws determining the behaviour of the system. An equilibrium defined as the intersection of a pair of curves would be statical. Ordinarily, it is 'timeless' in that nothing is specified concerning the duration of the process, but it may very well be defined as holding over time.[25]

A very important point must be underlined here, namely the logical distinction between *an instantaneous determination of income* and the *determination of an instantaneous income*. Whereas the first statement refers to any production defining a finite period of time, the second is related to the production of a mere instant. Now, the traditional static analysis of income is based upon the assumption that income can be defined as a continuous or discontinuous function of time, which means that the amount of production can be continuously determined at every instant in real time. The maintenance over time of a static equilibrium does not modify this situation, in particular it does not contradict the assumption that income is a function of time: the shift in time of a static equilibrium is clearly based upon the possibility of a positive determination of an instantaneous income. Hence, production in a finite period of time is determined by the infinite addition of instantaneous productions (the integral of income over time).

But, how can an instantaneous production be positive? The static analysis of income is seriously challenged and, as we shall see in the next chapter, will have to be replaced by a new conception of the relation between income and time. Logically opposed to the functional determination of income, this new conception defines production as an *instantaneous event relating to a finite period of time*. Therefore, although income is instantaneously determined it does not define the product of a mere instant: production is a creation whose result defines a positive quantum of time.

Before proving this, let us discuss very briefly one of the points which has proved to be essential for any theory that aims to provide a correct definition of income: the integration of money.

4. The integration of money: a short appraisal

Let us discuss here the way income can be related to the past and the future even when production is a creation referring to a finite period of time. The central idea is to be found, once again, in Keynes's work. In fact, income is, from the beginning, correctly identified with the payment of wages. Thus, money plays a central role in the determination of income.

An economy which uses money but uses it merely as a neutral link between transactions in real things and real assets and does not allow it to enter into motives or decisions might be called—for want of a better name—*a real exchange economy*. The theory which I desiderate would deal . . . with an economy in which money plays a part of its own and affects motives and decisions and is, in short, one of the operative factors in the situation, so that the course of events cannot be predicted either in the long period or in the short, without a knowledge of the behaviour of money between the first state and the last. And it is this which we ought to mean when we speak of a monetary economy.[26]

An example of motives and decisions that money allows for can be found in the relation between production and final expenditure. Although they are always necessarily equal, Y and $C + I$ can be moved through time according to the decisions taken by income holders, since money guarantees their objective link. Income created by a given production in t_0, while not determining subsequent productions in $t_1, t_2, \ldots t_n$, can be shifted in time, since money is a perfect vehicle for allowing income to be spent at any moment in time. Some readers may disagree with our definition of money as an objective link in time. It is true, they will argue, that money carries income through time, but this is not enough to justify such a definition for, if shifting consumption or final expenditure of income does not affect future productions, money becomes a mere link between production and consumption. This argument is correct. However, it does not contradict our definition, since money is precisely what secures a perfect correspondence between Y and $C + I$ through time. Identity $Y \equiv C + I$ means that income associated with a given production always has the necessary and sufficient power for its final purchase independently of when this power is exerted. Every income is permanently linked to the production which created it, and yet this relation can be shifted from the initial to subsequent periods owing to the particular nature of money. As Arrow and Hahn put it:

Keynes wrote that 'the importance of money essentially flows from it being a link between the present and the future' to which we add that it is important also because it is a link between the past and the present. If a *serious monetary theory* comes to be written, the fact that contracts are indeed made in terms of money will be of considerable importance.[27]

Keynes's determination of national income is undoubtedly monetary. Explicitly in the *Treatise*, and implicitly in his analysis of purchasing power, Keynes emphasises the particular relation existing between money and production. Before his contribution, the dichotomy between the real and monetary aspects of economics was fundamental to almost all the foremost theories.[28] If we take, for example, the works of Wicksell, we can easily verify that he does not reject the dichotomous view of the economy. On the contrary, his analysis is based on a rigid separation between the two sectors. The existence, in Wicksell's theory, of two sorts of prices, relative prices and money prices, is symptomatic of the rigid distinction drawn between real and monetary forces. On the commodity market, money plays no role at all, so that relative prices are due only to the action of real factors. The intervention of natural and banking rates of interest does not modify this basic assumption.

It is easy to see that the solution to the dichotomy coincides with the determination of purchasing power which, by definition, expresses the fundamental relation between commodities and money. Now, where can the relation between commodities and money be observed, if not in exchange? From this simple consideration, some economists deduce that the purchasing power of money is determined by the commodity price level. The higher the prices, the lower is purchasing power, and vice versa. Thus, the problem has slipped from one level to another, from purchasing power to the price level. However, the relation between the two is *not* a causal one: purchasing power being, by definition, equal to the reverse of price level, their relation is nothing other than an identity whose value has to be independently determined. Clearly, this means that the determination of purchasing power must precede the exchange in which this power is exerted.

Does this conclusion fit with Wicksell's theory of money? In other words, does Wicksell determine money prices before any transaction takes place in the commodity market? No clear answer to these questions can be found. The difference between the bank rate of interest and the natural rate of interest does not explain the formation of prices but only their variation relative to a given level. Now, since the prices we are looking for are money prices, it is useless to refer to relative prices.

Purchasing power introduces a concept of money which cannot be determined in a barter economy. Nevertheless, the confusion between the two sorts of prices (money and relative prices) is firmly fixed in many theories of money, as can be easily verified with reference to the quantity theory. According to this theory, the purchasing power of money can be determined by the price level. As we know already, this determination is in reality an identity, so that the problem remains open: how do we determine the price level? The answer given by the quantity theorists is clearly influenced by the theory of relative prices. In fact, the price level is determined on the commodity market because, according to the neoclassical theory of value, realised exchange is the only equivalence available. The result is not very encouraging, and it can be neatly summarised as follows: the purchasing power of money is . . . what it is! That is, we can only observe it when it is used. Surely this cannot be a satisfactory analysis, since it ends in a simple truism. We all know that the purchasing power exists: the problem is, how is it determined? Exchanges can be observed, and doubtless they are financed by money, but how has money acquired this purchasing power?

To answer these questions is to explain the integration of money. Does Friedman's restatement of the quantity theory represents a positive step toward this? According to the Chicago school, 'the Quantity Theory is, in the first instance, a theory of the *demand* for money'. The variable to be determined by the equation is, therefore, the quantity of money demanded by the system at a given point in time. In that context, the price level is one of the forces which influence the quantity of money (the demand for money is a function of the price level). It follows that the theory is no longer interested in determining purchasing power, which is taken as given by some sort of *deus ex machina*.

The question remains unresolved: how can the demand for money be determined if it depends on a price level whose measure implies the explanation of the purchasing power of money? If the price level cannot be explained by the demand for money, why could it not be determined by the joint action of the demand for and the supply of money? As in the case of relative prices, it is possible that the solution could be the result of an equilibrium in which all the variables are simultaneously determined. Thus, it would appear that everything were going to be for the best in the best of all possible theories. In fact, all we have to do is to put the money equation into the general equilibrium system and look for a simultaneous solution. This is, for instance, the approach adopted by Hicks. Having proved that Wicksell's theory leaves money prices completely undetermined, Hicks tries to overcome the dichotomy by introducing into his general equilibrium model the supply of and the demand for money.

> Suppose that there are *n* kinds of exchangeable goods and services; then there are in all *n* prices to be determined. For among the 'goods' must be reckoned that good which is taken as a standard of value (money). This leaves us $n - 1$ prices of the other goods and services in terms of the standard, and one rate of interest (here the rate on loans for one week). This makes *n* prices in all. To determine the *n* prices, we have $n - 1$ equations of supply and demand for $n - 1$ commodities (excluding money), one equation of supply and demand for loans, and one for money. This makes $n + 1$ in all. However, as in the Walrasian systems with which we are previously acquainted, one of these $n + 1$ equations follows from the rest. This leaves us *n* equations to determine the *n* prices. The system is neither over- nor under-determined.[29]

In reality, the problem is not simply a matter of equations and variables. The integration of money and commodities is not the result of an act of faith; the desire to integrate money is not a sufficient explanation. The money equation can at most be the result of the integration process: it can never be its cause. Thus, supply of and demand for money depend on the integration, and not the reverse.

Now, that difficulty seems to be irrelevant here, since all the variables are determined simultaneously. There is no direct causal link between prices on one side and demand and supply on the other. But, even if we accept simultaneity, integration has still to be explained because prices, as well as supply and demand, require the previous integration of money into the real world. In other words, we are confronted with the following question: what is the principle that guarantees the homogeneity of commodities and money?

Two logical possibilities are available. We could answer that the principle we are seeking is exchange; in so doing we are approaching the neoclassical point of view, according to which money is basically nothing other than a commodity.[30] The complication of such a theory, however, is that the whole system is reduced to a simple barter economy. Furthermore, in this theoretical context the equation of demand for and supply of money becomes redundant because, according to Walras's law, it is always necessarily included in the supplies and demand for all other commodities. However, if the money equation is dropped, the system can only determine relative prices and the real rate of interest: Wicksell and the dichotomy triumph.

> But it must be observed that the argument merely enables us to eliminate *one* out of the $n + 1$ equations; it does not matter in the least which equation we choose to eliminate. If we decide to eliminate the money equation, then we can think of prices and interest being determined on the markets for goods and services, and the market for loans; the money equation becomes completely otiose, having nothing to tell us.[31]

Keynes, being aware of the inconsistency inherent in the general equilibrium analysis of money, tries to overcome it by starting from the determination of income. This leads to the second logical possibility. In fact, national income is defined and measured directly in terms of money. Thus, no income could ever exist independently of the monetary remuneration of factor cost: physical products and money are understood to be in a relation of equivalence which defines national income. This conclusion is consistent with the only possible solution to the integration problem. Income and money are necessarily interrelated in such a way that the economic value of a product is nothing other than the numerical expression of its social value.

The consequences of this monetary definition of production are invaluable. In particular, Keynes's analysis allows for an entirely new approach to the relation between production and time. The traditional *functional* relation is thus seriously challenged by the *quantum* definition of income. The next chapter will be devoted to this question.

NOTES

1. R. Goodwin, 'The multiplier', in *The New Economics,* ed. S. E. Harris, London, Dennis Dobson & Co., 1947, p. 482.
2. P. A. Samuelson, *The Collected Scientific Papers of Paul A. Samuelson*, ed. J. E. Stiglitz, Boston, MIT Press, 1966, p. 1198.
3. Ibid., p. 1191.
4. D. Patinkin, 'The process of writing *The General Theory*: a critical survey', in *Keynes, Cambridge and 'The General Theory*', eds D. Patinkin and J. C. Leith, London, Macmillan, 1977, p. 19.
5. See A. H. Hansen, *A Guide to Keynes*, New York, McGraw-Hill, 1953, pp. 93–4.

6. Samuelson, op. cit., pp. 1132–3.
7. Ibid., p. 1131.
8. Goodwin, op. cit., p. 492.
9. Hansen, op. cit., p. 90.
10. A. H. Hansen, 'A note on savings and investment', *Review of Economics and Statistics*, Vol. 30, 1948, pp. 30–1.
11. Ibid., p. 31.
12. J. M. Keynes, *The General Theory of Employment, Interest and Money*, London, Macmillan, 1973, p. 115.
13. Hansen, 'A note on savings and investment', op cit., p. 31.
14. B. Schmitt, *L'Analyse macroéconomique des revenus*, Paris, Dalloz, 1971.
15. B. Schmitt, *Macroeconomic Theory: A Fundamental Revision*, Albeuve (Switzerland), Castella, 1972, p. 137.
16. Keynes, op. cit., pp. 114–5.
17. Ibid., p. 62.
18. Hansen, *A Guide to Keynes*, op. cit., pp. 110–1.
19. G. Haberler, 'Mr. Keynes' theory of the "multiplier": a methodological criticism', in American Economic Association, *Readings in Business Cycle Theory*, London, Allen & Unwin, 1950, p. 195.
20. Keynes, op. cit., p. 117.
21. Ibid., pp. 122–3.
22. Ibid., p. 123.
23. A. H. Hansen, *Business Cycles and National Income*, London, Allen & Unwin, 1964, p. 192.
24. R. G. D. Allen, *Macro-Economic Theory*, London, Macmillan, 1968, p. 76.
25. P. A. Samuelson, 'Dynamic, statics, and the stationary state', in Stiglitz (ed.), *The Collected Scientific Papers*, op. cit., Vol. I, p. 202.
26. J. M. Keynes, *The Collected Writings of*, ed. D. Moggridge, Vol. XIII, *The General Theory and After*, Part II, London, Macmillan, 1973, pp. 408–9.
27. K. J. Arrow and F. H. Hahn, *General Competitive Analysis*, Amsterdam, North-Holland, 1971, pp. 356–7.
28. The main exception being Marx's work on the general equivalent.
29. J. R. Hicks, *Value and Capital*, London, Oxford University Press, 1978, p. 155.
30. If, alternatively, we do not include money in the commodity set, then our analysis must be consistent with the law of the circuit proposed by Bernard Schmitt. One of the consequences of that law is the impossibility of deducing integration from exchange on the commodity market.
31. Hicks, op. cit., p. 158.

3 The Theory of Emissions

PART I: THE TRADITIONAL ANALYSIS OF TIME

1. Continuous versus period analysis

Although statics and dynamics are both related to time, it is widely admitted that a static position is timeless. 'The variables, indeed, may be stocks or flows, but they are all dated at the same moment or period of time, and there are no conditions imposed that relate to different points of time.'[1]

Because we are particularly interested in the problem of time, we shall therefore limit our analysis to the study of economic dynamics. It is well known that economic dynamics is concerned with the variation in the values of some, or all, endogenous variables over time. Now, since Newton's discovery of the calculus, economic variables have been regarded as continuous or discontinuous functions of time. Two kinds of dynamic analysis have been developed on this basis, according to whether changes intervene continuously or periodically.

> Changes may be continuous or discontinuous, and still time may be regarded as the order of succession of events. Every entity in the system may be continuously in a process of becoming another entity, in which case we may say that change is continuous. Or some entities may be conceived, at least, as persisting and changing discretely; in this case we say that change for such entities is discontinuous.[2]

Both analyses are concerned with changes, and consider time as the relation between successive events. It is also admitted that the flow of time is irreversible or, as Joan Robinson puts it, 'in time the strictest possible rule of one-way traffic is always in force'.[3]

Now, the difference between period and continuous analysis is that 'in *period analysis*, the flow of time is divided into successive periods of constant length, taken as the time-unit', while 'in *continuous analysis*, time flows continuously and each variable is taken as a continuous and differentiable function of time'.[4] This difference in capturing the flow of time has a direct consequence for the mathematical determination of the variables. In the case of continuous analysis, 'the conditions of a dynamic model then reduce to an equation that is essentially a *differential equation*'.[5] On the contrary, in period analysis 'the conditions of the model reduce to an equation, in a selected variable, that is essentially a *difference equation*'.[6]

The choice between these two kinds of analysis depends on economic considerations. In fact, we are taught that for many purposes it is preferable to assume that the variables change discontinuously while, for others, it is better to treat the economic process as continuous through time. Yet, the choice remains open, and, as Allen says, it is often a matter of taste. This is, of course, not the case as far as mathematics are concerned. In fact, 'the continuous form is almost invariably the easier to handle and the solution of the differential equation is obtained more quickly and in simpler form than that of the difference equation'.[7]

Despite any nominal distinction between difference and differential equations, it can be proved that an ordinary difference equation which 'relates to a function $Y = Y(x)$ considered for a series of equally-spaced values of x'[8] allows for a continuous solution. In fact, 'although difference equations relate to a function $Y = Y(x)$ of a variable x which is not changed continuously but which jumps over successive terms in a series of equally-spaced values',[9] it is also true that 'the series of equally spaced values can start from any value x whatever, and the starting value can be varied, and varied continuously'.[10]

> A difference equation in Y_x relates to any series of equally-spaced values of the independent variable x. The discrete solutions considered so far apply to one particular series of values of x denoted by $x = 0, 1, 2, 3, \ldots$ The difference equation, however, is not limited in this way; the starting point for x can be any value whatsoever. If $x = 0$ is the starting point, the difference equation generates the discrete solution $y_0, y_1, y_2, \ldots$ If $x = \frac{1}{2}$ is selected, then a completely different discrete solution is obtained and involves $Y_{\frac{1}{2}}, Y, Y, \ldots$ There is evidently no limit to the number of different discrete solutions which can be written. Any value of x between 0 and 1 can serve as the starting point, and x can be made to vary continuously.[11]

Finally, as Samuelson points out:

> If we deal with analytic functions possessing Taylor's expansions, a difference equation could be written as an infinite series of differential equations.

Conversely, in finding the actual solutions of differential equations, as in exterior ballistics, the usual methods of numerical approximation involve using difference equations to achieve any desired degree of accuracy. So it would seem that there is not much to choose between the two devices. Either or both will often do. And, as will be seen, each is but a special case of the more general use of 'functionals', in which the position of a system now and forever depends upon all its past behaviour.[12]

The possibility of a continuous solution of difference equations is a very important result of traditional analysis. Accordingly, every dependent variable can be analysed as a continuous function of time. In other words, even within a period analysis, the dependent variable is continuously related to time (the independent variable) since time can be made to vary continuously.

Not surprisingly, this conclusion is perfectly consistent with Frisch's formulation of a quantitative economic theory.

Formulating a determinate and quantitative economic theory means that we first define a set of variables to be explained $x, y, z, \ldots$ Let these be n in number. We then define n independent *structural relations* between these variables. I shall in particular consider the case where at least one of these relations is *dynamic*. This means that it contains at least one of the variables as related to *different points of time*. This may be either in the form that the equation involves both a certain variable and its rate of change with respect to time (possibly also higher derivatives), or by the fact that it contains this variable and its integral over time (possibly a weighted integral), or that it contains both lagged and unlagged values of the variable. The magnitude of any given variable x at the point of time t—denoted x_t—will be called the *instantaneous (principal) form* of this variable.[13]

The significant point here is the existence of instantaneous values of a given variable. This means that at every instant a relation can be established between this variable and time: for every point on the axis of time there is a corresponding value for the variable Y on the vertical axis (see Figure 3.1). Therefore, whatever analysis is chosen, period or continuous, it will always be true that the dependent variable acquires a distinct value at every point in time. More precisely, what we are saying is not that the value of the variable is necessarily known at every moment in time, but that it does exist even when the system determines the values of the variable only at the end (or beginning) of a particular period. Once again, every instant

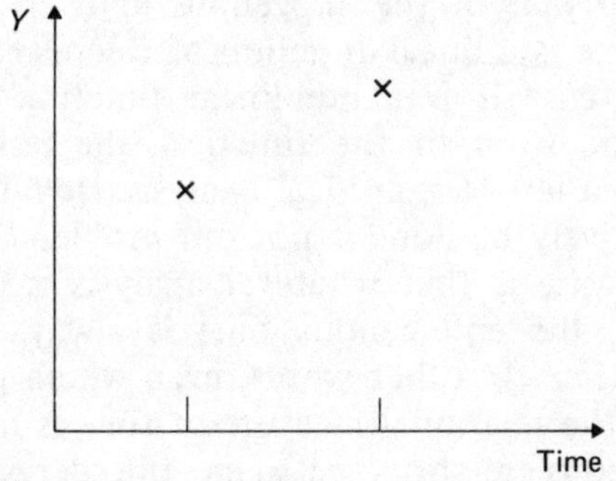

Fig. 3.1

within the period corresponds to a given value of the variable, since the relation between the variable and time is supposed to hold continuously.

Let us very briefly introduce the problem of measurement of time. The traditional method that economists use to deal with this problem leads to the *relational* measure of time, where time is merely considered as the order of succession of events. 'The key to the measurement of time given by the relational theory is, then, that events date each other and that time is measured in terms of events. It follows that there will be as many measures of time as there are events in terms of which time can be measured.'[14] Taking into account that the flow of time is irreversible and that changes can occur either continuously or discontinuously, it follows that 'in the economist's concept of time four attributes are essential: time is to be viewed as the order of succession of physical events, it is to be measurable in terms of such events, it is to be assigned both a continuous and a discrete character since change displays these two characteristics, and it is to be regarded as irreversible'.[15]

Now, once the concept of relational time has been accepted, it becomes essential to find a functional relation allowing for the passage from this 'endogenous' time to the chronological or 'exogenous' time. The interesting point here is that this transformation is not influenced by the distinction between period and continuous analysis. In both cases the endogenous time units of economic models must be translated into calendar time units. Two possibilities are conceivable according to whether or not the length of the endogenous unit is always proportional to that of the exogenous unit. In the first case, endogenous time is a linear function of calendar time, whereas in the second case it is a non-linear function of exogenous time. Given the form of the function, the task of its determination is then left to empirical analysis. How this determination can effectively be done is not our problem here. What we want to emphasise is that whatever analysis is chosen, period or continuous, the endogenous time is always a function of chronological time. In other words, even where period analysis is concerned, the relational measure of time is not opposed to the instantaneous relation between the dependent variable and real time. Since time flows continuously, every variable which is a function of time has a specific value at every point within the interval considered.

2. The determination of national income in continuous and period analysis

Although the mathematician's preference for continuous analysis can be opposed to the economist's preference for period analysis, we know that every variable can usually be analysed both continuously and discontinuously. In particular, income is sometimes regarded as a continuous function of time and sometimes as a discontinuous function of time. Our purpose is to show that in both cases income is assumed to be continuously related to time. Let us start with the traditional representation of income in continuous analysis.

Continuous analysis. If time is considered in its continuous flow, then income is taken to be functionally related to it in such a way that every point on the axis of time corresponds to a determinate value of income on the vertical axis (see Figure 3.2). The definition of income as a continuous function of time is based upon the assumption that income can be continuously known in time.

Now, since income is the result of production, its determination is said to depend on the level of production. The greater this level and the period of time to which it is applied, the greater is the income produced. The level of production, which is also defined as the rate of income per unit of time, is assumed to represent the economic evaluation of the factors at work at a given point in time.

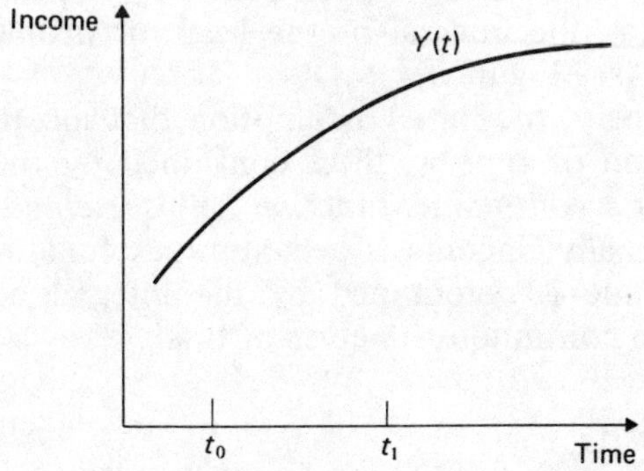

Fig. 3.2

As will have been noted, we do not distinguish between national income and national product, nor between the level of income and the level of production. In fact, since national product is measured by the expenditure corresponding to the payment of the cost of production, income and product (as well as their respective levels) are necessarily equivalent. Thus, the level of income represents both the measure of the flow of income per unit of time and the measure of the flow of production per unit of time. Now, according to traditional analysis, this level is assumed to be continuously known in time: as income, its level is said to be a continuous function of time. Thus, the instantaneous levels of income at t_0, t_1, t_2, . . . t_n are assumed to give the magnitude of the flow of income at instants t_0, t_1, . . . t_n (see Figure 3.3). The amount

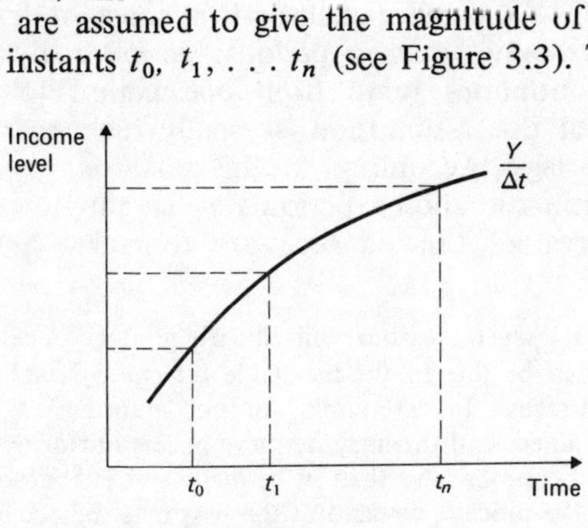

Fig. 3.3

of income produced during a given period $t_0 - t_1$ can therefore be calculated as the integral of the level of income over the interval $t_0 - t_1$ (see Figure 3.4).

Not surprisingly, the initial assumption that income is a continuous function of time is, thus, confirmed by the fact that '*the integral of a continuous function* f(x) *is itself a continuous function*'.[16] Finally, income is a continuous function of time whose magnitude is determined by the integral of its level, which is itself a continuous function of time.

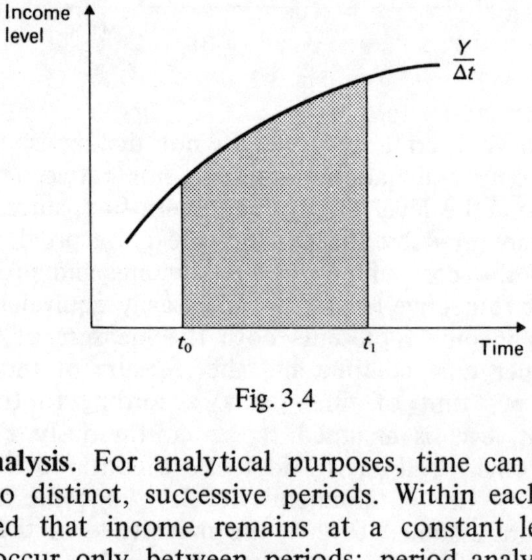

Fig. 3.4

Period analysis. For analytical purposes, time can be broken down into distinct, successive periods. Within each period it is assumed that income remains at a constant level. Thus, changes occur only between periods: period analysis presupposes a discontinuous jump from one period to the next. The reason for this assumption is usually reckoned to be the existence of lags. According to this analysis, income does not vary within the chosen period for the simple reason that a finite interval of time is necessary to realise a change in production.

A lag can arise for several reasons, conveniently grouped under two heads. First, the lag can be due to the inevitable *interval of time* involved in the economic process. In determining output, information on demand needs to be obtained, and this may be more or less out of date when the records are in. Decisions have then to be made and put into effect, with more delay. In the process, demand of the past must be projected ahead, so that expectations are involved. So, when demand is changing, there can be a considerable interval before output is changed to match. Secondly, for *technical reasons*, output changes generated by varying demand may involve some spreading or averaging over time. For example, if the decision is to raise output, then it may be possible or at least convenient to reach the higher level only in stages. Meanwhile, there can be adjustment of plans in response to further changes in demand and some averaging of demand over time so that output can match it, not at one time, but over a period. Hence, actual output at a given time can be the result of a complicated process of averaging out past changes in demand.[17]

The periodic variation of income can be represented as shown in Figure 3.5. Income is still a function of time, but a discontinuous function since it changes only by sudden jumps from period to period. The link between time and income within each period is nevertheless a relational one. In other words, even when it does not vary, income remains constantly related to time. At every instant of every period, income is said to exist, even though its value is only measured at some points in time.

In period analysis, the level of income is also assumed to be a discontinuous function of time. This means that within each period the level of income is supposed to represent the average level of income. The implementation of this constant level during a finite period of time gives the amount of income produced. At every instant the rate of flow of income is known (by its average level) and its multiplication by the time factor gives the corresponding value of income (see Figure 3.6). Hence, even in period analysis, income is assumed to be a function of

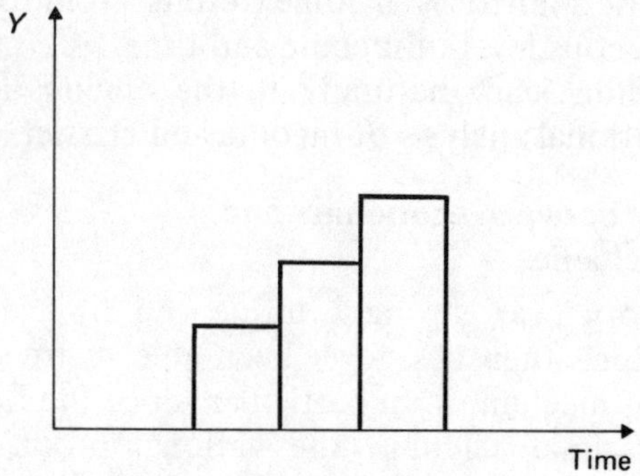

Fig. 3.5

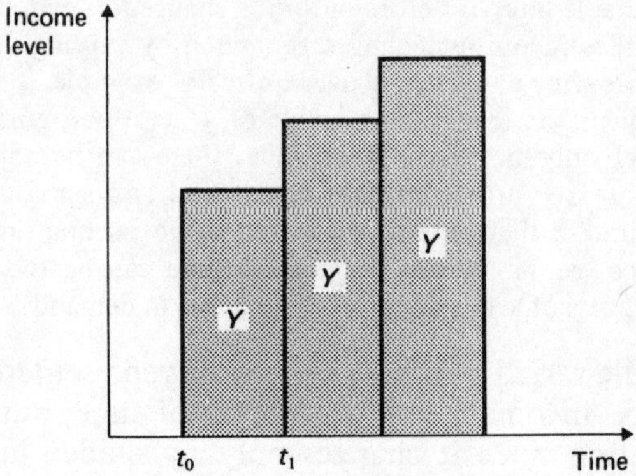

Fig. 3.6

time and is determined by the implementation of its level over a finite interval of time.

In summary, in both continuous and period analysis time is assumed to flow continuously and income is defined as a flow,[18] so that in both cases income is continuously related to time. The difference between the two analyses is that in continuous analysis the rate of income per unit of time is said to be known continuously, while in period analysis the rate of income can only be known through its average level. Moreover, in both cases the amount of income produced is determined by the implementation of the instantaneous level of income over a finite period of time. But, while in continuous analysis this amount is given by the integral of the level of income, in period analysis income results from the product of the instantaneous level of income and time.

This conclusion leads naturally to the obvious analogy between the traditional analysis of income and classical mechanics.

3. The analogy between economics and classical mechanics

Economic theory was strongly influenced by Newton's discoveries and since then has never been able to free itself from the concepts of mechanics. In particular, since the final elaboration of infinitesimal calculus, the national product has been considered as the economic equivalent of the distance covered by a moving body. In the same way as this space is determined by the integral of velocity over time, income is said to be determined by the integral of its level over time. Before developing this false analogy, let us briefly introduce some considerations about the relation which exists in mechanics between motion, time and space.

Classical mechanics. Since Aristotle's work on kinematics, motion has been determined by the relation between space and time. Accordingly, velocity is defined as the distance covered per unit of time:

$$v = \frac{D}{\Delta t},$$

thus

$$D = v\Delta t.$$

With Barrow, Newton's predecessor at Cambridge, the spatial representation of motion was defined on the assumption that: 'The study of curves by kinematic methods rests, in the first instance, on an intuitive idea of a quantity continuously varying with time'.[19] Time is itself considered a continuous flow 'made up either of the simple addition of rising moments, or of the continual flux of one moment',[20] and the distance covered during motion is represented by the space enclosed between the line representing velocity and the line representing time.

Later, Newton developed infinitesimal calculus and was able to determine distance by the integral of the velocity over time, the velocity itself being conversely determined by the differential of the distance at a point in time, and being represented by the tangent to the curve at that point.

For our purpose, it is enough to stress two important assumptions of the kinematic analysis of motion. Firstly, the concept of a quantity continuously varying with time 'implies the idea of time as an independent parameter',[21] which means that, according to mechanics, motion is assumed to be a function of time:

$$\text{velocity} = f(t).$$

Consequently, distance is also assumed to be a function of time, since it is the product of a function of time (motion or velocity) and time:

$$\text{distance} = f(t).$$

Consistent with infinitesimal calculus, the variations of the distance covered are therefore known at every instant.

The second assumption is that time is made up of instants representing 'infinitely small parts of time in which infinitely small spaces are moved through'.[22] This means that velocity can be instantaneously determined by a non-infinitesimal amount. In other words, velocity does not tend towards zero when Δt tends towards zero. What tends towards zero when $\Delta t \to 0$ is the distance covered, and not the velocity, which remains positive and finite even if the two terms of the relation $D/\Delta t$ become infinitely small. If, for example, a uniformly moving body is covering a distance of 80 kilometres in 1 hour, its velocity is equal to 80 kilometres per hour at every instant within the period considered. Kilometres can be reduced to metres, metres to centimetres, and so on, while hours are *pari passu* reduced to minutes, seconds, and so on, without modifying the value of their relation.

Another implication of this second assumption is that the only definition of an instant consistent with the traditional analysis of motion is such that an instant is an infinitesimal part of time. In other words, the time dimension of an instant is not zero. An instant is assumed to be a positive, though infinitesimal part of time, since only in this case can instantaneous motion be considered to be positive. If an instant were timeless or durationless, instantaneous motion could only be zero, since no displacement is ever possible in a period of time equal to zero. Let us now return to economics and to its assumed analogy with mechanics.

Neoclassical economics. By analogy with classical mechanics, income, whether considered as factor payments, value of production or final expenditure, is defined as a flow of expenditures determined by its implementation in time. Accordingly, income is either represented by the product of expenditure and time or by the integral of its level over time. In this analogy with mechanics, expenditure is regarded as a velocity or a motion, and income as the distance covered:

$$\text{income} = \text{expenditure}\ \Delta t.$$

As in the case of distance, variations of income are assumed to be known at every instant. Expenditure, as well as income, is therefore assumed to be a function of time.

Now, if we apply to this analysis the second assumption introduced in the case of the kinematic determination of motion, we are bound to conclude that expenditure, like motion, does not tend towards zero when Δt tends towards zero. Expenditure, as well as production, is considered an activity whose instantaneous value is not infinitesimal even though the result of its instantaneous implementation in time is obviously infinitesimal: income (the product) tends towards zero when Δt tends towards zero.

Thus, on the basis of this assumed analogy, income is determined mathematically and infinitesimal calculus, already introduced into economic analysis through the theory of value, seems to be definitively established as the principle governing 'every part of political economy'.

> Modern investigations in the theory of value have led to the setting up of a principle—or rather to the generalization and establishment of a principle already known and applied—called the *marginal principle*, whose application extends far beyond the actual province of the exchange of goods into the fields of production, distribution, and capital. In other words, it governs every part of political economy.
>
> This so-called marginal principle is, in reality, only an adaptation of the fundamental idea from which higher mathematics and mathematical physics have developed; namely, the idea of regarding given magnitudes as variable (as a rule *continuously* variable) quantities, and of regarding their rates of change as new quantities (the Newtonian fluxions, the differential coefficients of Leibniz).[23]

Since then it has therefore been widely assumed that income can be functionally expressed and mathematically determined either as the product of expenditure and time, or as the integral of expenditure over time (continuous or period analysis).

This traditional analysis of income determination stands as long as the analogy between classical mechanics and economics holds good. Now, if it were true, this analogy would confirm the hidden assumption of the traditional analysis of income: the production of income would be, in reality, the mere reproduction of an already pre-existing income. This result is readily understood as soon as we bear in mind that the space covered by a moving body in a given interval of time is not created by this same movement. The space is defined before the moving body covers it or, in other words, space is not created by the displacement of the body but is pre-existent to it. This is proved by the fact that the velocity of a mobile body is determined by relating a *given* distance to the time the mobile body needs *to cover* that distance. In

$$\text{distance} = \text{velocity } \Delta t,$$

distance refers to a given portion of space and to its being covered by a moving body. 'We must entirely reject the notion of a *state* of motion. Motion consists *merely* in the occupation of different places at different times, subject to continuity.'[24] It is clear that the 'different places' are pre-existing parts of space successively occupied. In multiplying velocity by the time of displacement we merely measure a distance previously existing. Applied to economics, this would mean that income pre-exists the expenditure from whose implementation in time it is assumed to be determined. It is correct to state that physical space exists independently of motion.[25] However, this cannot be transposed into economics, where income and expenditure are simultaneously determined as equivalent quantities. In other words, what is instantaneously spent is not the result of a continuous activity. It is obvious, in fact, that every expenditure has an instantaneous result. It is true that expenditure is an event and income its result, but 'cause' and 'effect' are equivalent. The important point here is that the result of expenditure is not the product of time. As soon as an expenditure takes place, income is a finite number, and

$$\text{income} = \text{expenditure}$$

whatever the length of the period to which expenditure refers. At the very instant that money is received, the sum credited is effectively and tautologically equal to the expenditure.

The logical equivalence between the activity of spending and its result precludes any functional determination of expenditures. In particular, it is not true that

$$\text{income} = \text{expenditure } \Delta t,$$

where Δt is an infinitely divisible period of time. This equation can be accepted if, and only if, Δt is the second number in the set of natural integers. For every individual expenditure considered, this number defines an indivisible period of time. This indivisible and finite period of time is a *quantum*.

Thus, a quantum of time is 'a *finite and indivisible* period of time equal to the number one in the series of natural positive numbers'.[26] The reason why time is indivisible is to be found in the very nature of expenditure. The fact that every monetary payment is an instantaneous event defining a positive income means that every expenditure is instantaneously endowed with a positive time dimension. In other words, an expenditure instantaneously covers a positive length of time: its velocity of displacement in time is infinite. The quantum of time is thus given as a whole by an instantaneous event, i.e. by an operation whose extension is zero. As Schmitt points out: 'Since Δt is covered in zero time—by the expenditure—it would be illogical to maintain the divisibility of Δt, because this would amount to the division of the number zero'.[27]

Once again, the traditional link between classical physics and economics is seriously challenged. Income is not the result of a continuous stream of expenditures through time, and therefore cannot be determined by the same relation which determines the distance covered by a moving body in a given period of time.

Two main differences can therefore be found between the classical determination of distance and the analysis of economic expenditures. The first is that the distance covered by a moving body is determined in continuous (or discontinuous) time, whereas expenditure is not. The reason for this difference is that the result of every expenditure is instantaneous, while in classical physics a finite period of time must elapse for the activity to produce a positive result.

The distance covered by a moving body is determined not instantaneously, but by the product of velocity and time. In economics, on the contrary, the sum expended is not the product of expenditure and time, since the economic activity of spending and its result are simultaneously determined as equivalent. The very nature of monetary payments is such that, instead of being the product of a continuously determinable variable and time, income is the instantaneous result of an instantaneous event. Yet, this instantaneous event defines a finite period of time. This leads us to the second difference between distance and income.

Although both velocity and expenditure can be instantaneously determined, velocity does not refer to a quantum of space or of time. An instantaneous velocity can undoubtedly be positive, but it does not determine a positive and finite distance. In fact, a finite distance can only be covered if velocity is applied for a finite period of time. In economics, however, expenditure is not only an instantaneous event, but is also an event which defines a positive amount of money spent. Thus, expenditure instantaneously refers to a non-zero receipt and, therefore, defines the product of a non-zero period of time. Expenditure is an event which has a finite time dimension, whereas the time dimension of instantaneous velocity is always infinitesimal. It also appears that, as far as expenditures are concerned, the concept of instant is not restricted to its definition as an infinitesimal part of time. In economics an instant is indeed a time of zero duration, while in classical physics it is an infinitely small period of time.

The analogy between mechanics and economics should be rejected in favour of a new analysis of income determination based on the concept of quantum time. Before developing this in some detail, let us introduce a short appraisal of the intuitive perception of expenditures as events which are instantaneously endowed with a positive time dimension.

4. Expenditures are instantaneous events related to a finite period of time

Macrophysical events are usually identified with processes of change whose duration is necessarily positive. 'While we do have experience of events which last for some time and have some non-zero duration, we do not have direct experience of anything whatsoever that has no duration.'[28] Newton-Smith's pessimistic conclusion is, in fact, already implicit in his definition of an event: 'An event involves a change, and hence involves at least a pair of times and some difference between what is the case at the respective times'.[29] Now, his conclusion rests on a restrictive definition of an event, and does not really explain the difference between duration and instant. However, as Newton-Smith himself points out: 'We expect any viable theory of time to provide an account of what temporal items such as instants and durations are'.[30]

Russell's attempt to construct instants by reducing events

of non-zero duration cannot be used here. If instantaneous events do exist, they must exhaustively take place instantaneously. Every instantaneous event must be complete and independent. Foley's suggestion sounds interesting: 'The proper method of modelling transactions would presumably be to allow time to flow continuously and to view transactions as discrete events of zero duration, like the "arrivals" in a Poisson process.'[31] Thus, according to Foley, expenditures are instantaneous events comparable to 'at random' events described in a Poisson process. Let us define this briefly.

Statisticians tell us that: 'One important process is the *Poisson process*, used to describe a wide variety of phenomena that share certain characteristics, phenomena in which some kind of "happening" takes place sporadically over a period of time in a manner that is commonly thought of as "at random".'[32] Now, a random process is defined as follows: 'An experiment of chance that continues in time (or in space) and is observed as it unfolds is sometimes called a *stochastic process*, or a *random process* (or, simply a *process*). A snapshot or observation at each instant of time (or at each point in space) is an experiment of chance.'[33] Thus, 'happenings' are instantaneous events whose probability is determined within non-overlapping intervals of time. 'Examples of happenings for which the model is found useful include arrivals at a service counter, flows in a long manufactured tape or wire, clicks or counts recorded by a piece of equipment or a component (when failures are corrected as they occur and equipment is put back into operation).'[34]

Conveniently called 'failures', these events take place at some point in time without it being possible to determine a finite period during which the event starts, develops and ends. For example, an arrival at a service counter is an instantaneous event in the exact sense that before a person reaches the counter, the arrival is only a potential event. Just after the person has reached it, the arrival is already in the past. The event takes places at the precise instant the counter is reached: its duration is zero.

As Foley points out, economic transactions are one of the best examples of such durationless events. An expenditure is, in fact, an instantaneous event, since it becomes effective at the precise instant that money reaches the payee and leaves the payer. No positive slice of time can ever be found between the moment money leaves the payer and the moment it reaches the payee. The nature of expenditure is such that these two events take place at one and the same moment in time. As for the arrivals at a counter, just before the transaction takes place the payment is merely announced, and just afterwards it is already accomplished. It seems, therefore, perfectly correct to consider monetary expenditures as discrete events of zero duration like the 'happenings' in a Poisson process.

There is, however, at least one major difference between expenditures and the random variable of a Poisson process. The random variable of the latter is not, in fact, connected to a finite period of time. 'Arrivals' and 'failures' are durationless events which are confined to the instant of their happening: they are events which, taking place in continuous time, fail to quantise it, and whose quantum dimension is therefore zero. It is true that these stochastic events are instantaneous, but when they happen at a given point in time they necessarily refer to this same point, and not to a finite period of time. Their happening binds them to a particular instant of chronological time. Expenditures, on the other hand, are events which quantise time, since their time dimension is finite. Thus, the fundamental difference between Poisson's arrivals and expenditures is the same as the difference between events which are merely instantaneous and events which, though instantaneous, are also endowed with a positive time dimension.

As we already know, this conclusion merely states the fact that the result of every expenditure is instantaneously positive. Thus, if Y defines the expenditure of income for the period Δt, the result of Y in period Δt is Y and not $Y\Delta t$: in $Y = Y\Delta t$, Δt is necessarily equal to number one. This conception of expenditure as an instantaneous event related to a quantum of time seems to have been intuitively perceived by some economists. For example, in an essay published in 1933, Knight says that:

> Purchase and sale are almost never continous, but rather take place as 'events' at a point in time. What enters into exchange and gets measured is, therefore, not a flow as such, but an absolute quantity, in fact the 'value' of a right to some stream of service of some magnitude *over some time period.*[35]

What Knight does not see is that if expenditures are instantaneous events as he claims, the absolute quantity they measure, i.e. wealth, must also be determined as the result of an instantaneous event. From this it follows that income must also be defined by this same instantaneous event since wealth is, finally, a quantity of income, which is itself the result of an expenditure. Once we admit, as Knight does, that wealth is given through an instantaneous expenditure, then we have to admit that wealth is not a function of continuous or discontinuous time, although its time dimension is certainly positive since, as we shall see, it defines a finite and indivisible period of time.

5. A recent dispute on time analysis

In his paper 'Period analysis and continuous analysis in Patinkin's macroeconomic model' published in 1970, J. May sets out to prove that the use of

> the continuous approach is preferable—for two reasons. The principle reason is that period analysis may be misleading: if the time interval used is too long, the state of the economy at given moments within the interval can differ significantly from its state at the beginning or at the end of the interval. A second reason is that in period analysis, all quantity variables have the dimension of stocks, whereas in continuous analysis one is forced to distinguish between stocks and flows.[36]

Subsequently elaborated by Foley in 1975, May's analysis suggests that 'sometimes the additional information gained from continuous analysis leads to conclusions that differ from those derived from period analysis'.[37] Both May and Foley agree that in reality economic transactions do not take place continuously. However, they are also convinced that both continuous analysis and period analysis are abstract approximations to the real situation. Period analysis is an artificial way of modelling economics, and so is continuous analysis. Yet, according to May and Foley, continuous analysis is more comprehensive since: '*No substantive prediction or explanation in a well-defined macroeconomic period model should depend on the real time length of the period.*'[38] In fact,

> If the results of a period model do not depend in any important way on the period, the model can be formulated as a continuous model. The method used to accomplish this is to retain the length of the period as an explicit variable in the mathematical formulation of a period model

and to make sure that it is possible to find meaningful limiting forms of the equation as the period goes to zero.[39]

Finally, the asset equilibrium approach of macroeconomics aims to prove that: 'The proper method of modelling transactions would presumably be to allow time to flow continuously and to view transactions as discrete events of zero duration, like the "arrivals" in a Poisson process.'[40]

This study of the relation between period and continuous analysis has been criticised by E. A. Kuska in his paper 'On the fundamental flaw in the portfolio-balance or asset approach to modelling economic systems'. Kuska's main argument is related to the concept of instant and the logical impossibility of assuming the existence of an instantaneous adjustment. In particular, he criticises May's assumption that individuals are able to rearrange completely their portfolios at each point in time. 'The economic meaning of the last constraint is that at a given moment, an individual can control only the composition of his financial wealth (between money and bonds), but he has no control over the total of his financial wealth.'[41] According to Kuska, his adjustment of financial wealth

> requires some physical movement, but then such an assumption implies that the parts of their anatomies these agents use to effect the exchanges are capable of being moved an *infinite distance over any finite period of time*, just as could any other body in the universe if the same assumption were made concerning it.[42]

Based on Einstein's principle that no entity travels in space faster than the speed of light, Kuska's critique is intended to show the absurdity of any theory assuming instantaneous movement.

> Physical bodies from snails to electrons and phenomena such as light and electricity may be supposed to have an 'instantaneous speed', defined as the derivative of the relevant distance function. None of these entities are assumed to be able to move at a point in time, however, for to do so would entail the ability to move an infinite distance over any finite period of time, no matter how small. This implication is, of course, so contrary to experience that such an assumption is never made.
>
> The abstract mathematical formulations of the above situations are identical. May's area of enquiry is also an instance of this general mathematical problem, and, if in economics one makes the equivalent assumption to those presented above which led to such absurd implications, one should prepare for analogous results.[43]

On this basis, Kuska can then conclude that the asset approach analysis does not essentially modify the traditional general equilibrium type of analysis, whose 'most fundamental properties are not altered by letting the period contract and ultimately vanish'.[44] However, Kuska does not reject continuous analysis, but seems to regard it as a particular case of period analysis. 'Period analysis includes period length spanning the whole of the set of positive real numbers, and *this includes numbers indefinitely* close to zero. Continuous analysis considers one case only, that when the length of period vanishes.'[45]

Both Foley's and Kuska's analyses are, thus, compatible with the traditional definition of income. They both assume the existence of a functional relation between divisible time and expenditure so that, finally, their dispute concerns the choice between alternative versions of the same theory.

Let us discuss this further, starting from Kuska's critique. Referring to physics, Kuska proves that within an instant no adjustment between real physical forces can occur. 'The assumption of movement at a point in time by any entity in the universe has the immediate consequence that the entity is able to travel an infinite distance over any finite period, however small.'[46] This argument is undoubtedly correct as far as displacement in space is concerned. However, from the point of view of classical mechanics, the velocity (or displacement) in space cannot be infinite. Assuming that transactions are physical activities requiring some physical displacement in space, Kuska rejects the asset equilibrium approach to macroeconomics.

Kuska's critique, which refers to the impossibility of the instantaneous rearrangement of portfolio balances, can be extended to include all kinds of transactions. In particular, it would be interesting to show that monetary expenditures are non-instantaneous (trans)actions. This seems possible if we consider expenditure as a set of physical activities. It is quite obvious that, from a physical point of view, the act of spending requires some positive physical outlay. Thus, physical expenditure requires time, a mere instant being insufficient if any finite result is to be obtained. According to this particular concept of expenditure, income is determined in the same way as the distance covered in classical mechanics, i.e. through the implementation of an instantaneous velocity during a finite period of time.

On the basis of purely physical considerations, Kuska's analysis could be considered as an attempt to prove that income is a function of time. In order to prove that transactions cannot take place instantaneously he does actually refer to an argument derived from physics. After stating correctly that 'physical bodies may . . . be supposed to have a positive instantaneous speed' although they are not 'assumed to be able to move at a point in time', he introduces a strict analogy between economic transactions and physical displacement. In so doing, he considers expenditure as a displacement in space and identifies it with a velocity. In other words, he assumes that instantaneous expenditure (speed) can be positive even though its instantaneous result is zero.

By introducing so strict an analogy between economics and physics Kuska fails to see that *monetary expenditures are conceptually different from the physical activity of spending*. In economics an expenditure cannot be considered as a set of physical movements, for it is an instantaneous event defined by the simultaneous gain and loss of a given sum of money. Thus Foley is right when he defines the economic transaction as a discrete event of zero duration. From an economic point of view, monetary transactions are events which do take place instantaneously. This result obviously does not confirm Kuska's optimistic conclusion about the validity of traditional general equilibrium analysis.

> It is disturbing when a long-established uniformity seems to disintegrate either in general or in important special cases. This is what the asset-approach theorists seemed to be saying about traditional general-equilibrium analysis. It is, therefore, consoling to realise that their stance was not well taken. There is essentially one general equilibrium type of analysis. It has been with us now for a considerable period of time. Its most fundamental properties are not altered by letting the period contract and ultimately vanish.[47]

In reality, the consequences of an expenditure being an instantaneous event are far more important than the simple alteration of some properties of traditional analysis. In fact, a concept of time is entailed which is totally absent from both continuous and period analysis.

As we already know, expenditure is an instantaneous event whose velocity of displacement *in time* is infinite: the period of time instantaneously covered by the expenditure is a quantum of time. Let us now return to Foley: 'The proper method of modelling transactions would presumably be to allow time to flow continuously and to view transactions as discrete events of zero duration.'[48] This statement is only partially correct. In fact, monetary transactions are discrete events of zero duration in continuous time, but of a positive duration in quantum time. What Foley lacks is the concept of infinite speed of displacement in time. His expenditure is not related to quantum time and remains a function of chronological time. In this respect, the analyses of Kuska and Foley are not fundamentally different: whether in period or continuous analysis, expenditures are posited as a function of time. Both authors remain within the theoretical framework of general equilibrium analysis, and both fail to understand income as the result of a quantum event.

6. Quantum time and the traditional theory

The 'week' and the 'day' as first approximation of quantum time. The claim that expenditure is an instantaneous event is not really new in economics. Since Walras it has, in fact, been suggested that market price determination occurs instantaneously at discrete points of time. Thus, it seems possible to refer the instantaneous determination of income to the traditional neoclassical framework. Let us analyse this possibility, with particular reference to Hicks's concept of the *week*.

Hicks introduced this concept as a pedagogical device for a better understanding of his temporary equilibrium analysis. Leaving aside consideration of the unrealistic aspect of Hicks's assumptions, let us consider the week as a finite interval of time chosen as the period unit. According to Hicks,

> . . . there is only one day in the week (say Monday) when markets are open, so that it is only on Mondays that contracts can be made. Contracts can, indeed, be carried out during the week (goods can be delivered, and so on); but no new contracts can be made until Monday week. Monday's prices will therefore rule during the week, and they will govern the dispostion of resources during the week.[49]

Hicks's main concern is the determination of the process established on Monday, as well as the determination of 'the system of plans which will govern the distribution of resources during the following week'.[50] If we focus our attention on the problem of expenditure it seems possible to assume that income is instantaneously determined on Monday for the whole of the following week, which could thus be considered as an indivisible unit of time. The determination of income would therefore correspond to the payment of the factors of production, which takes place on Monday.

This is not, of course, Hicks's point of view. Accordingly, the contracts which are made on Monday refer to *trading* plans and are, therefore, dimensionally *stocks*. At the same time, production as well as consumption is supposed to be a flow of activity occurring in real time, so that income cannot be determined instantaneously at the beginning of the week. Income, which is defined as a stream of expenditures, is determined as a function of time, that is, a process over time. Whether or not we 'are replacing the actual expected stream of receipts by a standard stream, whose distribution over time has some definite standard shape',[51] the determination of income is supposed to take place continuously during the week. In other words, even if the amount of income were measured at a discrete point in time on Monday, its determination would be proportional to (i.e. is a function of) the length of the period. Thus, if a transaction between firms and factors takes place on Monday, it is supposed to represent the result of a process over time. In fact, the distinction between stocks and flows involves

> . . . implicitly defining a 'flow' not as a quantity whose dimensions are $1/T$, but as a quantity whose magnitude is directly proportionate to h (the length of the market/planning period); similarly, the implicit definition of a 'stock' is that of a quantity whose magnitude is independent of h.[52]

If Hicks had had the intuition that expenditures are not a function of time, then he might have been aware of the instantaneous determination of income on Monday. Thus, the week could have been considered as a quantum, being instantaneously related, as a whole, to Monday's expenditure. As it is, the quantum concept of time is foreign to Hicks, whose attempt at defining income does not take into account the novelty of Keynes's identities.

Robertson's analysis also comes near to the discovery of quantum time. In his well-known article on saving and hoarding, Robertson assumes 'the existence of a period of time, to be called a "day" '[53] which in another paper is defined as 'a finite but indivisible atom of time'.[54] This could be read as an attempt to assume the existence of a finite and indivisible slice of time to which income must be related in order to explain its instantaneous determination.

Traditionally, however, the 'day' has been considered as a mere device to express the existence of a lag between income earning and income spending. Robertson himself sustains 'the successive existence of a short number of slices of time during each of which the money which appears as income for *A* cannot also appear as outlay by *A* (and therefore income for *B*)'.[55] The day is related here to the interval of time separating the earning of a given income by *A* from the spending of the same income by *A*, i.e., according to traditional analysis, from the earning of an equivalent income by *B*. The introduction of what is usually called a consumption lag does not modify the 'earning through spending' theory of income, which is basically accepted by Robertson.[56] Considered as an interval of time between formation and expenditure of the same income, the day does not introduce any substantial change in the traditional analysis of income. It is true that Robertson's day is a quantum, but this quantum is not defined by the emission of income. The 'day' is not the positive time dimension of an instantaneous event, but the indivisible period of time separating the emission of income from its final expenditure. Thus, Robertson fails to recognise income as the result of a quantum event and continues to define it in terms of flows. He also fails to see that this event (expenditure) and its result are logically equivalent. Obviously, this does not mean that income is spent as soon as it is earned since, as we shall see in the following pages, the expenditure which creates income (first emission) is logically and chronologically distinct from the expenditure which destroys it (second emission), even though the results of these two expenditures necessarily coincide in quantum time.

The problem of indivisibilities. Another example of quantum variables can be found in microeconomics. Authors are well aware of the theoretical difficulties which arise when the concept of indivisibilities is introduced into microeconomics to denote factors, processes or products which cannot be continuously divided. As Arrow and Hahn acknowledge, the indivisibility of commodities and the indivisibility of activities are the sources of two major problems. In fact, whereas 'non-convexity arises only because of indivisibility of commodities',[57] the indivisibility of production activities can oppose feasibility.

> Even if the divisibility of commodities is accepted, at least as an approximation, that of divisibility of production activities does not follow as a logical truth. Rather it is an empirical generalization that, for the great majority of ordinary production processes, a uniform reduction in scale preserves feasibility.[58]

The existence of commodities or processes which are not continuously divisible is a serious challenge for the traditional analysis of production. By attempting to reduce its importance, many authors seem to recognise the logical impossibility of overcoming it within the traditional theoretical framework.

> Clearly its economic significance is relatively less when the number of units is larger. Thus, the difference between one stamping mill and none is important, but if the relevant choice is between 100 and 101 shovels, the assumption of divisibility is unlikely to be seriously misleading.[59]

Now, this attempt to avoid the problem is far from satisfactory. The mere multiplication of an 'indivisibility' obviously does not alter its specific nature: one shovel is neither less nor more divisible than 100. Unresolved by traditional analysis, the problem of indivisibilities leads us to the quantum theory approach to economics.

In a paper significantly called 'A quantum-theory model of economics' Samuelson seems to recognise the importance of such an analysis. In this paper he proves that under certain conditions the marginal product is of a 'finite quantum type'.[60] The analysis is based on the existence of a co-ordinating entrepreneur whose activity is defined as a quantum and whose remuneration corresponds to the quantum marginal product.

> Often, tacitly or explicitly, economists assume that the 'firm' needs a co-ordinating manager (or management), whose time and attention devoted to it involves some indivisible, minimum quantum of time and energy.[61]

> Thanks to the writings of such Cambridge economists as Joan Robinson, students of competitive price have realized that the lumpy entrepreneur usually gets his lumpy marginal productivity just as a divisible factor gets its smooth marginal productivity. But this has never been properly demonstrated.[62]

Samuelson sets out to prove this, and argues that

> . . . if a firm is selling at a competitive price equal to its marginal cost and that marginal cost is competitively above the average cost outlay to hired factors, then the profit doled out to it as a residual rent is equal to its opportunity cost and, more interestingly, is asymptotically for large enough scale precisely equal to its marginal product, even though that marginal product is of *finite* quantum type rather than of smooth-partial-derivative type.[63]

Leaving aside any consideration of the quantum of energy, it would be interesting to know what Samuelson really meant by marginal quantum product. Although his paper does not provide an answer, Samuelson seems very near to the quantum theory of income. If followed up, his idea of a 'lumpy' product could have shown him that production itself, and not only the activity of a co-ordinating entrepreneur, 'can change only in integral steps'.[64] The definition of production as a quantum jump, i.e. an event which instantaneously quantises time, would then have been within easy reach, and Samuelson would have been able to define time as a 'granular variable'. The crucial role played by quantum time would have emerged in full light, opening the way towards a solution of the uncomfortable problem of indivisibilities. The attempt to replace the traditional analogy between economics and classical mechanics by a new analogy between economics and quantum mechanics, an attempt strongly supported by Qadir in his paper 'Quantum economics', could thus have found its theoretical justification and it would have been possible to specify the conditions under which economics can undergo a quantum formalisation. 'We need to find the *economic* assumptions which should lead to the use of the quantum formalism to derive a genuine economic theory of quantum economics as has been done for deriving a physical theory of quantum mechanics'.[65]

PART II: TIME AS QUANTUM

> The energy in a beam of light emanating from a point source is not distributed continuously over larger and larger volumes of space but consists of a finite number of energy quanta localized at points of space, which move without subdividing and which are absorbed and emitted only as units. [Einstein]

1. The link between expenditures and production

As we have shown, expenditures are defined in quantum time: experience shows that expenditures are determined as absolute magnitudes, since the expended sum (income) and expenditure are instantaneously determined as equivalent quantities. Thus, expenditures are defined relative to a period of time which is necessarily finite and indivisible. This is confirmed by Schmitt's analysis, which states that 'if expenditures are defined in continuous or discontinuous time, reasoning tells us that the arithmetic value of every expenditure is zero'.[66]

If expenditures were defined in continuous or discontinuous time their value would tend towards zero as time tends towards zero, since the measure of the action, expenditure, cannot be distinguished from its result, the expended sum (income). In

$$\text{income} = \text{expenditure}\ \Delta t,$$

every division of Δt is a division of its corresponding expenditure. Thus if, like Samuelson,[67] we consider expenditure as an infinite series of infinitesimal impulses, we must conclude that the value of every expenditure is zero, since by its infinite division expenditure is converted, at the limit, into a continuous series of instantaneous events equal to zero. For these instantaneous events to be positive in continuous or discontinuous time, expenditure should be identified with a velocity so that, as in the motion of a body, the division of time would not equal its own division. In this case, expenditure would be assumed to have no time dimension. Observation shows, however, that although they are instantaneous events, expenditures have a positive time dimension and can therefore only be defined in quantum time. 'In the analysis of the finite speed of a moving body, it is possible to consider time as either continuous or discontinuous, whereas in the analysis of expenditure, time is logically a quantum.'[68]

Let us now consider the relation between production and product. Is it possible to define the product as the result of the continuous or discontinuous implementation of production and time? In other words, is it possible to consider production as a velocity? Here again, the answer is negative. Production could, in fact, be identified with a velocity only if its result could be measured (and not merely described) in physical units, which is impossible because of the heterogeneity of physical products.[69] It then follows, as in the case of expenditures, that the action (production) and its result (product) are the two terms of an equivalence,

$$\text{product} \equiv \text{production},$$

which means that in

$$\text{product} = \text{production } \Delta t,$$

Δt is necessarily equal to number one: the time dimension of production is a quantum.

The existence of this quantum of time is confirmed by the fact that the output is itself emitted as a quantum. The production of every commodity is given as a whole: ' . . . at the very instant the product is achieved it is formed as a whole in only one "quantum leap" '.[70] Let us consider, for example, the transport by rail of a person from London to Paris. The service given by the railway is nil, inexistent, as long as the destination has not been reached. At the instant the train stops in Paris the journey is perceived in its indivisible unity, as a quantum, so that the time of the journey is itself an indivisible quantum. In classical mechanics, the distance travelled from London to Dover would be regarded as a part of the total distance from London to Paris and similarly the wheel would be regarded as a part of the bicycle. In economics, experimental reality is different: every product is nil in its non-accomplishment, 'the wheel being an achieved wheel and not an unachieved bicycle'.[71] A quantum event is an instantaneous creation whose result is given as a whole. Accordingly, the time dimension of this event is also a quantum, i.e. a finite and indivisible period of time. It is true, as we shall see, that a quantum event like production gives a result which is laid down in continuous time, but this does not imply any functional relation between production and continuous (or discontinuous) time. If we consider production as a process of becoming, we are bound to add that becoming is defined here as an instantaneous event endowed with a positive time dimension, or, as Whitehead puts it, that 'extensiveness becomes, but "becoming" is not itself extensive'.[72]

Having established that expenditure and production are quantum events, we have now to determine whether they stand in a mutual logical relation to each other. This is easily done by pointing out that, since physical objects are heterogeneous, production cannot be defined in physical terms. 'The problem of comparing one real output with another and of then calculating net output by setting off new items of equipment against the wastage of old items presents conundrums which permit, one can confidently say, of no solution.'[73] This leaves us with only one possibility: production must be defined in terms of money. 'It is my belief that much unnecessary perplexity can be avoided if we limit ourselves strictly to the two units, money and labour, when we are dealing with the behaviour of the economic system as a whole.'[74] As we shall see later in this chapter, every expenditure is the emission of the product as a given sum of money. The identity between expenditure and production is, thus, the fundamental reason for expenditure being a quantum event: '. . . expenditures are defined in quantum time because they define production'.[75] Before analysing this identity in some detail, let us return to the distinction between traditional and quantum definitions of production.

2. Creation versus transformation

The concept of production has always been a very controversial one. At least two main definitions have been proposed since the early stages of our science. The first definition states that production is essentially a physical process of transformation. According to the principle of conservation of matter and energy, production is seen as a process whose output is necessarily equivalent (or less if we take into account what has been wasted during the process, i.e. Marx's 'devil's dust') to its input. The result of production is a change in shape, colour, dimension, etc. The output, however, is physically equivalent ('devil's dust' = 0) to the input. The change is a simple transformation and not a creation, since according to physics nothing is created, nothing is destroyed, everything is transformed. The concept of production as an element of an uninterrupted chain of transformations is therefore strongly supported by the laws of thermodynamics. As a consequence of this physical way of looking at production, income has frequently been considered as the result of a process in which capital, land and labour are transformed into goods and services.

Shackle's analysis is a good example of the way the traditional concept of production as physical transformation has been used in economics. The link between this process of transformation and time is so clearly stated that the definition of production as a function of time seems to follow quite naturally.

Production is a change in the things themselves. It can be a change in location, shape, physical or chemical or biological constitution, arrangement in relation to other things, or date of availability. Any such change is inseparable from the notion of the passage of time. Any such change is *accompanied* by the passage of time. If a change of a given kind and degree occurs in a larger rather than a smaller quantity of stuff in a given lapse of time, we say that the measure of this production is greater. Or if a given kind and degree of change in a given quantity of stuff occupies a shorter rather than a longer time, again we say that the measure of production is greater. To measure production we have to consider the amount of change in relation to the amount of time.[76]

The logical conclusion of this analysis is to consider production as a flow of physical transformations.

In stating the measure of a flow we must say both how much change there has been (how much stuff has changed or how much change a given quantity has undergone) and also how long this change has taken. For the purpose of measuring it, production is a *flow.*[77]

Undoubtedly, physical changes take place in time. Thereafter, it seems plausible to say that the amount of these changes is a function of time. Thus, if we define production as a process of physical change, the conclusion should be that production is also a function of time.

The idea of a process of accumulation involves time both as measureable lapse and as extension, and the latter in two ways. Lapse of time must be present as the necessary condition, the vehicle or at least the reflection of a transformation, the carrying-up of the accumulating pile to a larger size. The amount which is added to the pile between two dates will be a function of the 'distance' between those dates, and this distance can evidently be conceived as measurable on an axis, the 'calendar axis'.[78]

Production functions are the best example of this method of determining national income. 'Until the laws of thermodynamics are repealed, I shall continue to relate outputs to inputs—i.e. to believe in production functions.'[79] Samuelson's faith in thermodynamics is not justified in the case of economics. From a physical point of view it is undoubtedly correct to say that production is not a creation since, as far as energy and matter are concerned, nothing is created nor destroyed by people. However, this physical principle is not adequate as an explanation of production.

As we have shown, production is an instantaneous event which instantaneously quantises lapses of time. From an economic point of view, therefore, production is an emission, a *creation*.

This concept of creation obviously does not apply to matter or energy, apart from the 'big bang' theory, which is irrelevant to this analysis. Economic value is not a substance. What is instantaneously created or produced is not a physical entity but the mere economic form of the goods. Money lends duration to this form. Thus, the definition of production requires the 'mediation' of money. In other words, the production-emission is defined by a monetary expenditure. The separation (dichotomy) of the two worlds, real and nominal, is thus repealed and replaced by the complete integration of monetary and real factors. The dichotomy can never finally be solved by traditional theory, but is overcome by the quantum analysis of production. To realise this it is essential to note that, although the costs of the output in terms of input are nil (since every production is a net creation), the act of creation has a positive social cost, the expenditure incurred in terms of labour. Social cost is thus defined in money or, identically, as labour spent. The following sections of this chapter are devoted to a more elaborate formulation of this analysis. For the time being, however, let us note that in defining income as 'the earnings of the factors of production',[80] Keynes is explicitly adopting the social determination of production. The whole of his analysis is expounded in monetary terms, where money is not a simple number arbitrarily referring to physical goods, but is the social expression and definition of production. Keynes's definition of income is therefore not physical. From his *Treatise* onwards, he points out that production must be considered from the 'community's earning or money income' point of view.

> I propose, therefore, to break away from the traditional method of setting out from the total quantity of money irrespective of the purposes on which it is employed, and to start instead—for reasons which will become clear as we proceed—with the flow of the community's earnings

or money income, and with its twofold division (1) into the parts which have been *earned* by the production of consumption goods and of investment goods respectively, and (2) into the parts which are *expended* on consumption goods and on savings respectively.[81]

It is possible to claim that thereafter Keynes took over the classical concept of production but as a new theory, closely akin to the quantum-theory approach.

The physical and economic concepts of production are not fundamentally opposed. Outputs can be consistently analysed from both points of view since they represent the physical as well as the economic results of production. However, these two results are substantially different. The purely physical product is the result of a process of transformation, whereas the specifically economic product is the outcome of an act of creation. The choice between these two concepts is therefore not arbitrary. In fact, the physical heterogeneity of products does not allow production to be expressed in physical terms: the logical impossibility of finding a homogeneous unit of measurement is an impassable obstacle. 'The community's output of goods and services is a non-homogeneous complex which cannot be measured.'[82] Moreover, even if it were possible to avoid this difficulty, physical measurement would never yield any net product. Output being always substantially equal to input, no difference can ever be found to explain the presence of a net product. In terms of matter and energy the output cannot be greater than the input, so that the equation

$$\text{output} = \text{input} + \text{net product} \tag{3.1}$$

only means that

$$\text{net product} \equiv 0. \tag{3.2}$$

Thus, it is confirmed that the monetary definition of production is not a mere device but a theoretical necessity.

Now, the expenditure corresponding to the payment of the social cost of production is a quantum, an emission, as is production. What we have to explain, therefore, is the process by which these two emissions, expenditure and production, enter into a relation of identity. In other words, we have to analyse more closely the relation between money expenditure and production in order to establish that the emission of income is the only definition of production and, therefore, that income *is* the product and not, as it is widely thought, its monetary counterpart.

3. The theory of 'integrated' money: a short account

Consider a bank, B, in its relation with the public and suppose that one of its clients, Smith, makes a deposit equal to x units of account. The deposit can either consist of cash or of a claim against another bank (a cheque drawn in favour of Smith), and increases the assets of the bank which is receiving it. Correspondingly, the liabilities of the bank are also increased by the same amount, since by 'paying in' x units of money Smith acquires a deposit of this amount, i.e. the bank incurs a debt to him to the amount of x. Although increased by the same amount, liabilities and assets are not related to the same person. Thus, when a client makes a cheque deposit, his bank is in debt to him and owns a claim against another bank.

A bank will also give a credit balance (i.e. incur a debt) to anybody who offers it a claim against another bank. This happens, for example, when Smith, who banks with Barclays, draws a cheque in favour of Jones, who pays it into his own account at the Midland. In that instance there has merely been a transfer of indebtedness between banks— no increase.[83]

Accordingly, the amount of money is not increased by this kind of operation: the deposit of cash or cheque does not create money. 'Passing cash across a bank's counter is essentially changing one kind of money for another—the proximate result is no change in the aggregate supply of money in the hands of the public.'[84] The balance sheet of the bank is then as shown in Table 3.1.

Table 3.1

Bank			
Liabilities		Assets	
Deposit of Smith	x	Cash in hand or claim against another bank	x

In a subsequent operation, the bank can lend to Jones the whole or part of the deposit made by Smith. If, for example, Jones borrows x from the bank, this loan becomes the asset of the bank whose balance sheet is thereafter as shown in Table 3.2.

Table 3.2

	Bank		
Liabilities		Assets	
Deposit of Smith	x	Loan to Jones	x

Other operations are conceivable in addition to this. Further study, however, lies outside the scope of the present analysis, which is devoted to the definition of money. What we want to stress by means of the preceding example is only that this class of operation (which corresponds to the principle that 'deposits make loans') requires the pre-existence of money as its necessary condition. It is obvious, in fact, that the economy at large, here represented by Smith, can deposit only money which exists prior to and independently of this operation. Before considering the deposits of the economy as a whole, we have thus to determine an operation defining the creation of money.

By general admission, money is created by any joint-stock bank which spontaneously incurs a debt to the public. In the previous example, the bank acted as a purely financial intermediary. In the case of creation, however, the bank's debt is not caused by the deposit of its client. The bank does not receive any money, but through its spontaneous indebtedness creates completely new money. This operation defines a bank deposit, i.e. a debt to the public, an IOU which is voluntarily entered in the books of the bank. Thus, this deposit is created by a spontaneous act of the bank, which means that the object of this deposit is the deposit itself. When it acts as a financial intermediary, the bank receives from its client a certain amount of cash, or claims against another bank. When it creates, the bank issues a deposit whose object is nothing other than the spontaneous debt of the bank: the newly created money and not a pre-existing sum.

Now, according to traditional analysis, the creation of money results from an exchange of claims: the bank gets into debt, which is a claim against the bank, in exchange for the assets offered by the public.

> The bank deposits—i.e. the debts of the bank to the public—are always covered by the assets people have offered to the bank in exchange for deposit claims against the bank. The process of 'creation' of bank deposits is essentially an exchange of claims. The member of the public offers a claim of some sort—such as legal tender State money, or a government bond, or a mere promise—and the bank offers a book debt called a bank deposit.[85]

Is this analysis quite correct? To answer this question, let us first establish the logical principle allowing an event to be defined as a creation. Metaphysical considerations apart, nothing can be created out of nothing. Thus, creation can only be defined as an operation which is simultaneously positive and negative. The object which is created must instantaneously be destroyed. Applied to the creation of money, this rule means that the only result of this operation can be its 'purely nominal' recording in the balance sheet of the bank. In other words, the creation of money is the simultaneous increase of assets and liabilities by the same amount, which is caused by the bank voluntarily entering into debt to the same client. By the same operation, the same person is credited and debited by the same amount: as is consistent with the established rule, the final result is nil (see Table 3.3).

Table 3.3

		Bank	
Liabilities		Assets	
Smith	x	Smith	x

In the light of what has just been said, let us now consider the claim that: 'The process of "creation" of bank deposits is essentially an exchange of claims.'[86] According to Sayers, one of the claims the public may offer in exchange for a bank deposit is securities.[87]

Another way in which a bank may add to its debts is by the purchase of securities, such as government bonds. The bank pays for the bonds by a cheque on itself, i.e. it gives a debt in exchange for the bonds that become part of its assets. The balance-sheet shows change on both sides:

Liabilities	£	*Assets*	£
Deposits (i.e. debts to clients)	1,000	Investments (Government bonds)	1,000

It appears that the assets of the bank are increased by securities of some sort, while its liabilities are increased by its deposits. But, how is it possible to have money on one side of the balance sheet and a security on the other, when the creation of money is defined as a twofold operation whose negative and positive aspects are simultaneously created out of nothing? The collateral of the bank deposit is an equivalent debt of the public, but these two opposite debts must be related to the same object: they result from the same operation. Surely, Sayers is mistaken when he writes that the claim against the bank 'is *money*, whereas the debt against which it was exchanged is not money'.[88] If this statement were correct, money could be created as a positive entity and consequently exchanged against any positive assets whatsoever. This positive creation, however, is more a metaphysical statement than a scientific assumption. In fact, no positive creation (net credit) can ever take place by the simple decision of the bank to enter into debt to the public. No bank is ever endowed with such a supernatural power. What the bank can create is money, that is a debt *and* a simultaneous credit. Thus conceived, money can be said to result from an exchange of claims related to the same object, the public owing the bank the very same thing which the bank owes the public. Like the claim against the bank, the claim against the public is a mere promise, and in this sense the overdraft and loan systems can be considered good examples of the creation of money. In the case of a loan:[89]

The bank at once places the sum of the loan to the credit of the client: its debts are increased by that amount, and, since its debts constitute money, the supply of money is increased by the same amount. At the same time the assets of the bank have increased by the amount of the loan. Its liabilities and its assets have increased by equal amounts. Were the amount £1,000 and were this the sole operation of the bank the balance-sheet would be:

Liabilities	£	*Assets*	£
Deposits (i.e. credit balances of clients)	1,000	Loans to clients	1,000

This example can be retained in its existing form only if the same money appears on both sides of the balance sheet, since the debt of the bank is inseparable from the debt of the public. The theory according to which 'loans make deposits' is therefore perfectly correct. On request from the borrower, the bank makes a deposit. Loan and deposit are determined by the same operation: the creation of money.

The creation of money being simultaneously negative and positive, it cannot result in an addition of purchasing power. How could it be true that 'the economic significance of this exchange of claims lies in the fact that the claim against the bank—a debt which did not previously exist—can be used as general purchasing power'?[90] Money results from a creation by the bank, and if it is not integrated it becomes neither a unit of account nor a unit of payment. In other words, the free incurring of a debt by the bank is an unfulfilled creation: the creation of money is an emission not yet completed. On the other hand, purchasing power is a positive income which cannot be created *ex nihilo*, but requires the intervention of production. The understanding of purchasing power requires, then, the creation of money in a quantum of action. To explain the functions of money as unit of account and unit of payment, we must integrate the theory of money creation and the theory of real production.

The banks are important not only because they create money but also because they distribute that money into particular channels. In some way or other, therefore, the actions of the banks have to be consistent with both the total and the composition of the country's production of goods and services. Just how this consistency is achieved must be the most fundamental question on which an analysis of the banking system should throw light.[91]

Sayers is right: money must be related to real production, otherwise its creation is inconceivable. This relation is the object of the next section.

For the time being, let us suppose that money and production are integrated by the payment of the borrowing client, whom we shall call *F*, to the workers, *W*. As *F* pays away the amount borrowed, the liabilities of the bank become liabilities to the payee, *W*. The balance sheet is as shown in Table 3.4.

Table 3.4

	Bank		
Liabilities		Assets	
(I) Deposits *F*	x	Loan to *F*	x
(II) Deposits *W*	x	Loan to *F*	x

(I) and (II) are not separate entries but define one and the same operation: the emission of money. In fact, taken on its own, (I) is a void operation whose existence can only be verified if it is instantaneously transformed into (II). The payment in favour of *W* is a necessary and sufficient condition for the emission of money.

The purpose of this short review of the theory of money is to stress the fact that money is created and destroyed by the same operation, and that this operation defines a triangular relation between bank, firms and workers. Accordingly, the circuit of money is given as a whole by the identity of the two opposite flows. Money is, therefore, identified with its circulation, or as Smith put it, money is 'the great wheel of circulation'. Moreover, and still in conformity with Smith's thought, money is logically distinct from income: it 'makes no part of the revenue of society to which it belongs; and though the metal pieces of which it is composed, in the course of their annual circulation, distribute to every man the revenue which properly belongs to him, they make themselves no part of that revenue'.[92] What Smith established long ago for coin is still perfectly valid today for credit money. What is created by the bank is just money and not money income, which is 'emitted' by the factors of production and not by banks. Correspondingly, production could never be accounted for without the aid of money. As we shall see in the following section, income integrates money and product.

4. Emissions

In this section we show that the creation of money, i.e. the spontaneous incurring of a debt by the bank, is related to production through the payment of wages. We are assuming, firstly, that money cannot be directly integrated on the commodity market and, secondly, that labour is the sole factor of production. The justification of these two assumptions is to be found within the analysis. In the case of labour, we shall prove that analysis does not allow for the existence of other categories of factors of production. With regard to the logical possibility of integrating money and products by exchanging them for one another, we shall simply observe that traditional analysis has never met the challenge. The dichotomy remains an unresolved problem as long as we try to integrate money on the commodity market. To find a solution we must refer to Keynes's identities, but, as Clower realised, this implies the eventual rejection of the category of 'relative exchange'.[93] 'If Keynes did add something new, the integration problem becomes explicable; but then we have to give up Walras' law as a fundamental principle of economic analysis.'[94] Thus, in 1984 the situation is still the same as when Samuelson wrote that 'we still lack in 1972 a really adequate theoretical structure that encompasses the foundations of a money economy'.[95] In order to avoid this impasse we shall follow Schmitt's analysis and show that the integration is possible, on the factor markets.

The first emission. Let us represent money by two equivalent spheres of negative and positive sign. When the bank voluntarily incurs a debt to the public it defines money which is simultaneously a debt, the sphere with the negative sign, and a credit, the sphere with the positive sign. As we have already shown, this is only the first aspect of an emission. The creation of money becomes meaningful only if its positive and negative aspects are not related to the same person. Let us see what happens when firms, *F*, pay the workers, *W*, with the newly created money.

The first result of this payment is the earning of positive money by *W*. The money received by *W* is not simultaneously negative and positive, since workers are not indebted to the bank. The payment of wages defines a positive credit of *W* which corresponds to an equivalent debt of *F* (see Figure 3.7).

Fig. 3.7

The negative situation in which *F* find themselves is due to the simultaneous creation of money as a positive and as a negative quantity. Firms cannot lose positive money, for the simple reason that they do not own any (i.e. the 'revolving fund' = 0).[96] In their initial relation with the bank, firms are neither net creditors nor net debtors. Their payment to *W* is not financed from positive money but it nevertheless results in the payment of positive wages. Workers gain money which they do not owe to the bank, and which defines their income. Thus, the payment of wages is not a displacement of income from *F* to *W*. The income earned by *W* is not lost by *F*, but is positively issued for the benefit of *W*, whose earnings are a net gain for society as a whole.

Now, this positive money earned by *W* is the very definition of an equivalent sum of negative money created for *F*. The twofold creation of money is therefore the first important result of the monetary payment of workers.

Another important result is the transformation of the nominal emission of the bank into a positive real emission. Since it is an expenditure, the payment of wages is necessarily a quantum event, i.e. an instantaneous event which quantises time. What has still to be determined, then, is the time dimension of this event. The answer to this question lies in the particular nature of the purchase financed by the payment of wages. What is purchased by *F* is not what is sold by *W*: workers sell their activity of producing, whereas firms acquire the result of this activity, i.e. the physical product. More precisely, the real product is neither sold by workers, who never possessed it as yet, nor purchased by firms, since this purchase requires the expenditure of positive money which *F* do not possess.[97] Thus, the real product is directly formed in *F*. The exchange between *F* and *W* is therefore characterised by:

1. the expenditure by *F* of a sum of nominal money and the gain by *W* of a sum of real money, a unit of payment; and
2. the formation of a product in *F* which has not been lost by *W*.

It is important to recall here that the real product is not the result of a continuous activity in time, but of an emission. What is created by the *real emission* is not a new substance but a new 'utility' form defining the product. This social utility must not be mistaken for the material product. Even if the result of a real emission is apparently the creation of a new stuff, it would be wrong to assert that an emission can create anything physical. It is true that the product takes the form of a physical object, but it is obviously not true that the creation of the product is the creation of the physical object. Defined as an emission, production is merely 'the realisation of a project'[98] which allows matter or energy to acquire a new form or utility. Thus, the real emission allows the transformation of matter and energy into a *product*. This emission is entirely due to the activity of labour. Workers are therefore the agents of this creation, which quantises time. Finally, the product is not physical, even though the result of the real emission exists in the utility of a physical object. Human work endows physical matter with a new utility, thus transforming it into a commodity.

Now, this 'value in use' is not produced in continuous time. Its creation results from an emission which does not locate it in continuous time. In other words, the time dimension of the 'value in exchange' is positive in quantum time and nil in continuous time. This means that what exists in continuous time is a physical object and not an economic value. Let us take the example of the production of a car. If the time necessary for its production is one month, the car is created as a product as soon as it is completed at the end of the month. Thus, the car results from an emission which defines the month as a quantum of time. As a product, the car exists only after completion of the 'work in progress', which takes a month. What is found in continuous time is not the car as a product, but the car as a physical object. The economic value of the car is created at the end of the month, at the precise moment when wages are paid out to its factors of production.

In a monetary economy, the real emission is given together with the emission of money. To the emission of positive money at *W* corresponds the emission of a real product at *F*.[99] The two emissions are the two sides of the same transaction, the time dimension of both being the time which elapsed during their *physical* production. In other words, the time defined by the two emissions is one and the same 'lump'.

Let us now analyse the situation as it appears at *F* and *W* after the payment of wages. While at *F* we find negative money (the debt to the bank) and a real product, at *W* we find positive money (the net credit of *W*) defining the same product. The negative money at *F* and the positive money at *W*, being the result of an emission, have a quantum dimension and can be called the *negative quantum deposit* and the *positive quantum deposit* respectively. When the real product is formed at *F* it is lodged in the negative quantum deposit, since real product and negative quantum deposit are simultaneously defined by the same operation. The real product literally disappears into the negative quantum deposit as into a trap (a 'liquidity trap'). This is shown in Figure 3.8, which represents the conjunction of negative quantum deposit and real product, as shown in Figure 3.9.

The situation at *F*, being simultaneously negative and positive,

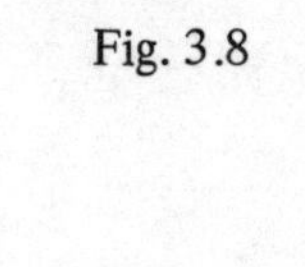

Fig. 3.8

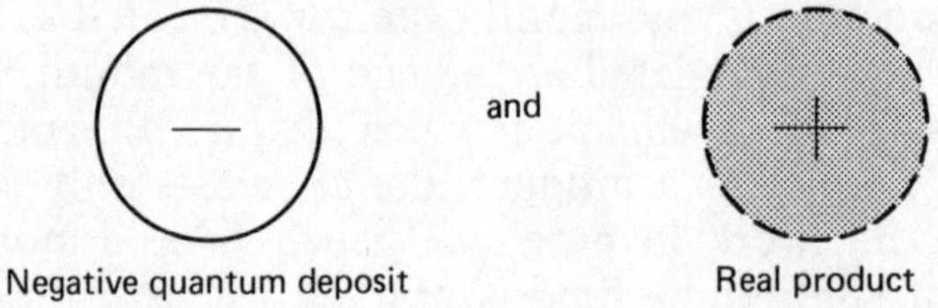

Fig. 3.9

is balanced and equal to zero: *F* owe the amount of wages paid out and hold a real product of the same value. On the other side, the situation at *W* is positive, since wages are the net gain of society as a whole. The positive money earned by *W* (defining their income) is also the result of a monetary emission, and its 'content' is the real product. Dissociated from real emission, the monetary emission would be an empty transaction, since it would create a positive and a negative quantum deposit with no substance in them. It is the real emission which defines the product as the real content of these two deposits. The positive quantum deposit of *W* is therefore the monetary form of the real product (see Figure 3.10).

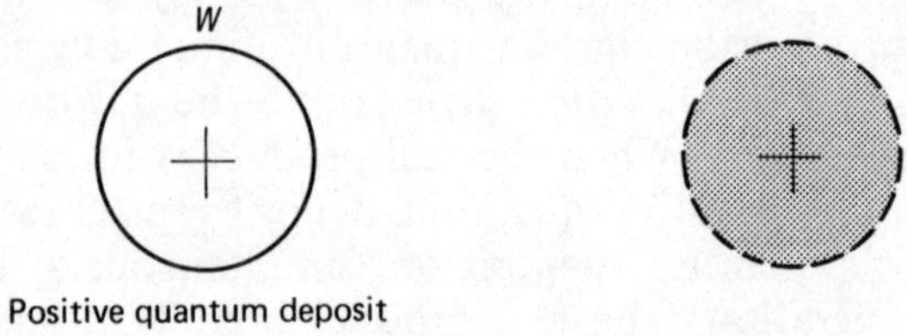

Fig. 3.10

The coexistence of real and monetary emissions in the payment of wages transforms the money issued by the bank into positive real money.

The creation of money results from the collaboration, in one single transaction of the bank and of the real sector. Banks create money which is negative and positive while the economy creates the product in the negative quantum deposit, and transforms, thus, the money issued by the bank (which amounts to nothing) into positive money. The coexistence of these three quantum deposits is necessary to the definition of the net positive money; banks create two of them by the monetary emission and the economy creates the third in the real emission.[100]

Now, if it is true that without a real emission the money

issued by the bank would amount to nothing, it is also true that in a monetary economy the emission of wages transforms the real product into money. As a result of the payment of wages, workers own the product in the form of money. As soon as the real and monetary emissions are given (in the payment of wages), the physical product disappears into the negative quantum deposit of F and is replaced by money. This *absolute* exchange signifies that the emission of money is identically the emission of the product. The product, which as a result of the real emission exists in the form of physical objects, is thus immediately replaced by *a set of numbers*. This operation coincides with the payment of W, so that the payment of wages literally creates the product. Workers are the agents of this creation, which defines the substance of their financial credit (positive quantum deposit). Thus, workers are both the emitters and the recipients of the economic product.

An important result of this analysis is that *wages are not the monetary counterpart of the product, but the product itself.* According to this analysis, in contradistinction to previous theories, money and product are one and the same thing. The integration problem is solved by the emission of the product in the form of money. 'The product of a monetary economy is by definition an amount of money.'[101] This means that the real product is immediately a 'dimensionless' *number*, the amount of nominal wages paid out to the workers. The result is twofold: real output is a set of numbers, the measurement of output is an exercise in pure accounting.

'The counting of the units of money produced by the economy is identically the *measurement* of the real (national) product.'[102] By identifying the product with a number, we avoid the logical impasse to which the classical theory of value leads.

Using classical terminology, we would say that labour creates value and that this value is the amount of wages paid, i.e. a mere number and not a substance. Accordingly, value is no longer conceived as a particular quality or predicate of the product, but as the product itself:

$$\text{value} = \text{product} = \text{amount of money (number)}.$$

Ultimately, the result is partially consistent with both classical and neoclassical analysis. In fact, it follows from classical analysis that products have to be measured before being exchanged on the commodity market. At the same time, adopting the neoclassical view, the unit of measurement is a pure number (the numéraire). The emission of wages fulfills these two requirements and in this respect the theory of emissions could be considered as a synthesis of classical and neoclassical theories.

The second emission. As we have already seen, through the payment of wages workers earn an income which is the substitute of the physical product deposited within the negative money issued by the banks. This income is a net social gain and corresponds to what is usually called the national product or national income. This income, although resulting from an emission, is positively 'deposited' in continuous time: the purchasing power earned by *W* has a positive existence in continuous time, a time duration. The income of *W* is in fact instantaneously recorded as a deposit of *W* (and a debt of *F*) in the bank.

Now, to the payment of wages corresponds a second emission which takes place when income is finally spent on the commodity market. Every emission creating a positive income is followed by an equivalent emission of a negative income. This second emission is, literally, a destruction of income. Creation and destruction are two aspects of the same real emission. Now, in the same way that the first part of the real emission is defined by the monetary emission of wages, its second and complementary part is defined by the monetary emission comprised in the final expenditure of wages. Let us start again from the payment of wages (see Figure 3.11). The final expenditure of the positive money by *W* allows firms to cancel out their debt to the bank. By the same operation, the physical product is freed from the negative quantum deposit where it had previously disappeared. Positive and negative quantum

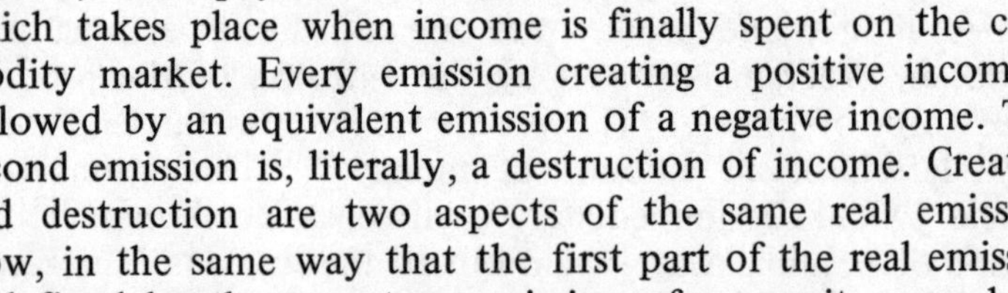

Fig. 3.11

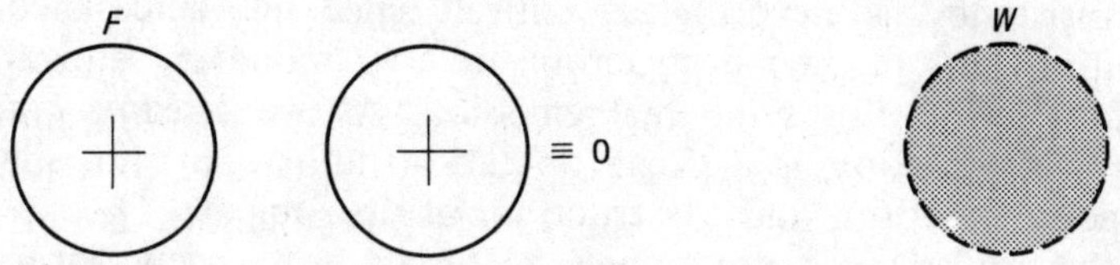

Fig. 3.12

deposits destroy each other and the final result is financially nil, both for *W* and for *F* (see Figure 3.12).

As was the case with the payment of wages, their expenditure is an emission which defines a positive and a negative quantum deposit at *F* and *W* respectively. This second monetary emission, which is subsequent to the payment of wages, does not define a new production. Accordingly, the two opposite quantum deposits created by this expenditure do not define a new net situation, either in *W* or in *F*. The second emission is necessarily related to the first: the positive quantum deposit of *F* is destroyed by the negative quantum deposit, and the negative quantum deposit of *W* is likewise destroyed by the positive quantum deposit. The expenditure from *W* to *F* does not create a new income in *F* since workers are not creating, but spending an income they already owned. Having totally spent their income, workers have destroyed their positive quantum deposit: their final position is financially nil (i.e. the 'revolving fund' = 0). The same is true for *F*. By selling the physical product firms acquire an income which, being comprised within their negative quantum deposit, is instantaneously destroyed and leaves *F* as it was before the first emission. At the same time, the physical product is transferred from *F* to *W*. In spending their income, workers free the physical product from the negative quantum deposit into which it had vanished and definitively destroy its economic value. The first emission, which defines the creation of income, has as its exact counterpart the second emission, which is its final destruction.

Now, the existence of income between the first (positive) and the second (negative) emission is something of a theoretical puzzle. The positive existence of income in continuous time seems inconsistent with the fact that the creation of anything real (like income) must logically define its simultaneous destruction. This inconsistency is nevertheless entirely specious, since income creation and income destruction are two monetary emissions which define the same real emission. As we already know, this real emission is a single operation defined by the simultaneous creation and destruction of its object. The result of this emission is not a new material, but a new form or utility. Thus, the real emission is an event which simultaneously creates and destroys what Schmitt calls 'the utility wrapper',[103] leaving the physical product with a new 'utility' form. Through the real emission, matter and energy are put into a mould from which they are simultaneously withdrawn, and which gives them their utility. The real emission is the simultaneous creation and destruction of this mould.

In a monetary economy, the payment of wages and the purchase of product are complementary aspects of the same real emission. Therefore, the presence of money does not alter the result of production. Whether the product is transformed into money or not, the real emission does not allow any positive creation (or destruction): what subsists in continuous time is a mere physical object and not a product. When money intervenes, the real emission is taken over by two monetary emissions which necessarily take place at the same instant. Since they define a single operation of creation–destruction (the real emission), the payment of wages and the final expenditure of income are simultaneous.

Far from being solved, the problem seems to have become even more intractable. If income is simultaneously created and destroyed, how can its existence still be positive in continuous time? And, if its existence in continuous time is also necessarily nil, is there any point in defining the product as a sum of money? The answer to these questions requires the intervention of quantum time. The simultaneity of the two monetary emissions is a result of their being identical quantum events, i.e. events which instantaneously quantise the same period of time.

Let us consider, for example, the production of day 1. Production is given by the payment of wages. This expenditure is an emission which quantises continuous time. Thus the corresponding output is defined in quantum time: the product has a positive time dimension (in quantum time) equal to one calendar day. Now, if we refer to the final purchase of this product we can see that it also corresponds to an instantaneous event defining a quantum of time equal to day 1. The two operations of creation and destruction are positive emissions, in quantum time. It then follows that, being related to the same finite and indivisible period of time (day 1), these two events can be arbitrarily parted in continuous time, but they necessarily coincide in quantum time. In our example, if we suppose that wages paid at the end of day 1 are totally spent at the end of day 2, we can say that:

1. in chronological time, income creation and income destruction happen at two different points in time, at the end of day 1 and day 2 respectively, whereas
2. in quantum time, creation and destruction are *simultaneous*: they define the same quantum of time.

The second emission, which implies the same quantum of time, is simply the repetition of the first emission. Creation and destruction of income are thus two identical emissions, one positive and the other negative. Consequently, income is issued by its creation (first emission) and its destruction (second emission).

The final expenditure of income is the destruction of the positive quantum deposit and thus defines the macroeconomic 'consumption' of the product. What lives on as wage goods is a purely physical object, a 'value in use', and not a product (a value in exchange). Let us recall that, even though creation and destruction of income define a single operation (in quantum time), these two events are not simultaneous in continuous time, where the existence of income is strictly limited by its final expenditure. A positive interval of continuous time separates the payment of wages from the purchase of the product.

Let us consider these two events, in their chronological succession and in their quantum simultaneity, in relation to the production of a car. At the end of every month a car is completed and emitted as a real product. At the same time a given amount of wages is paid to the workers, and the real emission is transformed into a monetary emission: wages take the place of the car, which is absorbed by the negative quantum deposit at F. The net gain of W is a positive national income defining the product. Now this income, which is fully created in quantum time, is also located in continuous time, where it represents the net credit of *W* to the bank. From this moment to the moment of its final expenditure, *income is the product* and exists as such in continuous time. When *W* spend their wages, the product is destroyed (by the conflation of positive and negative quantum deposits) and the car stays on as 'use-value'. After the second monetary emission (expenditure of wages) all that is left is the car as a commodity in the strict sense, ready to be used by the consumer.

The solution to our previous questions is no longer a mystery. In fact, the simultaneity of the two emissions of wages (positive and negative) allows us to conclude that income is *retroactively* destroyed. When wages are spent on the commodity market, income is destroyed through a monetary emission (negative) which, by retroaction, coincides with the payment of wages (positive emission). Income created by the positive emission is destroyed by the negative emission, and since these two emissions are simultaneous, the quantum destruction of income implies its retroactive destruction in continuous time. 'The positive expenditures locate wages in continuous time and the negative expenditures withdraw them retroactively, the objects maintained in continuous time being physical or merely material, as they result from the real emissions.'[104] Now, it would be wrong to deduce from this retroactive destruction of income that its existence in continuous time is nil. In fact, income is destroyed only after a positive interval of continuous time. Income is retroactively destroyed in continuous time only after the negative emission of wages has taken place. This emission has the same quantum time dimension as the creation of wages, but does not take place at the same moment in continuous time, except retroactively. If, for example, wages are paid at t_1, where $t_0 - t_1$ represents a period of one month, and they are spent at t_2, these two monetary emissions

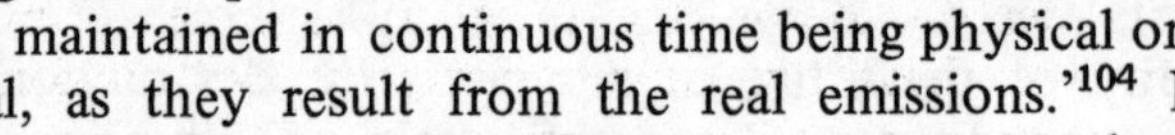

have the same time dimension, equal to $t_0 - t_1$. Thus, the emissions at t_1 and at t_2 coincide in quantum time. However, the interval of continuous time separating t_1 from t_2 is positive. The income created at t_1 by the payment of wages subsists in continuous time until its expenditure at t_2. Yet, this expenditure is a quantum event of the same time dimension as the expenditure taking place at t_1. These two expenditures define the same quantum of time and are simultaneous: the income located at $t_1 - t_2$ is simultaneously withdrawn even if its withdrawal occurs at t_2. Finally:

> Emissions are the very life of economics. They allow the division of labour, the production of homogeneous commodities and the distribution of the product between wages and profits. Having fulfilled their task, incomes are cancelled from their origin in continuous time; real goods remain in the merely physical and essential form which the classics called use-values.[105]

Keynes's definition of national income is fully supported by quantum analysis. Income is determined in quantum time and is identically defined by its creation (supply side) and by its destruction (demand side). The identity between demand and supply is one of the fundamental results of Keynes's analysis, and the clearest statement that creation and destruction are simultaneous events related to the same object. Now, according to quantum analysis, income results from the payment of wages whereas its destruction is due to its final expenditure. The simultaneity of these two quantum events implies, therefore, that the expenditure of wages destroys the totality of the product. But, if wages are the definition of the product and if their expenditure is the destruction of this same product, how can profits be defined?

5. A short note on profits

Let us briefly recall the two monetary emissions defining the creation and the destruction of income. The first emission is the payment of wages and defines a net quantum deposit at *W* (see Figure 3.13). The second emission is the final purchase of the product and defines the destruction of the net

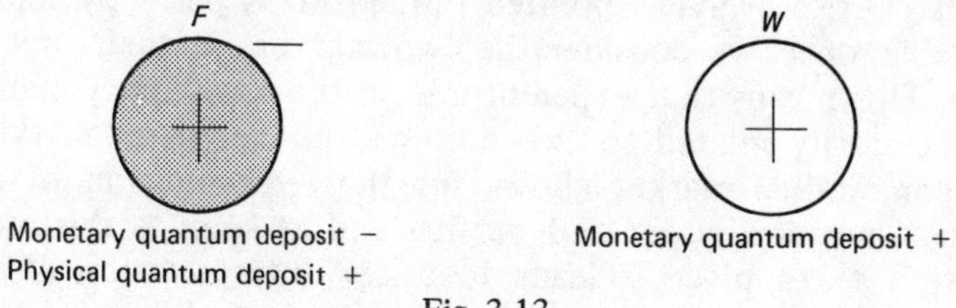

Fig. 3.13

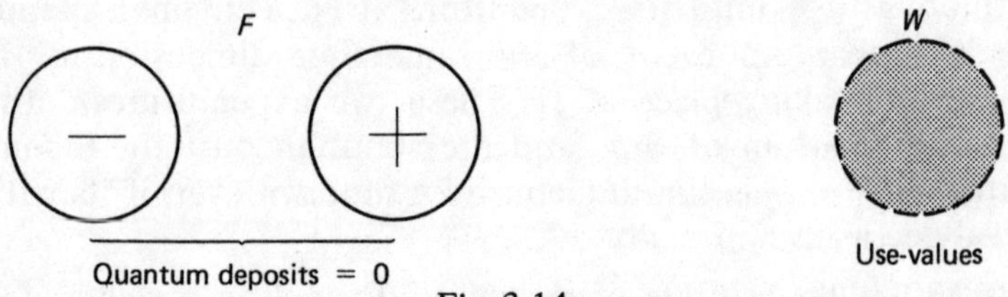

Fig. 3.14

quantum deposit formed at *W* (see Figure 3.14). The final result of these two emissions is therefore the following:

Agents	*F*	*W*
Monetary quantum deposits	$(-x + x)$	$(+x - x)$

where income (the net quantum deposit of *W*) has been totally destroyed and the physical product has been freed from the negative quantum deposit of *F*.

Thus the first emission, which defines the creation of income, has as its exact and necessary counterpart the second emission, its final destruction. The important point here is the exact correspondence between negative and positive quantum deposits. Every expenditure of income, i.e. of a positive quantum deposit, destroys a negative quantum deposit of exactly the same amount and defines the final purchase of an equivalent product. Hence, the final purchase of any product implies an exchange between equal amounts of positive and negative quantum deposits. In other words, income spent is necessarily equivalent to the goods purchased: no distinction can be drawn between price and value. In such a context, profits seem to be necessarily nil. If price equals value and if wages equal product, can distribution still be explained?

If the commodity and factor markets were autonomous, the identity of price and value within a wage units theory of production would be irreconcilable with the existence of positive profits. Yet, as Keynes pointed out, profit is perfectly understandable once we consider the two markets in their organic unity. This means that expenditures on the commodity market are necessarily related to expenditures on the factor markets. The commodity market allows for the redistribution of the product between wages and profits, and as soon as this redistribution takes place it leads to a new interpretation of the transactions concluded on the factor markets. What we have to bear in mind is that the two emissions, income creation and final expenditures, are quantum processes. As such, they coincide, as we already know. Thus, every operation taking place in the commodity market is instantaneously effective on the factor markets. Obviously enough, the final purchase of any given commodity requires the previous creation of a corresponding income. Thus, expenditures on the commodity market are not only based upon, but can also modify, expenditures on the factor markets. This happens when workers receive only part of the physical product in exchange for their wages. Profits, the difference between total wages and workers' purchasable product, transform the initial emission on the factor markets. Payment of wages, in its nominal aspect, is partially and contemporaneously a final purchase. In other words, a positive profit implies an expenditure of income *within* the payment of wages: the payment of wages by *F* is simultaneously a final expenditure of profit. Finally, the realisation of a positive profit on the commodity market must instantaneously be interpreted as an income expenditure on the factor markets. Purchases on the two markets take place in their respect of the identity between price and value, and yet profits are indisputably positive.

A short numerical example may prove useful to illustrate this last point. Suppose that firms, *F*, pay 100 units of wages to workers, *W*, and that the product will finally be shared between wages and profit in a proportion of 4 to 1. Accordingly, workers receive only 80 units of the product from their spending, the remaining 20 units being captured by *F*. Now, these 20 units of profit represent the final expenditure hidden in the payment of wages (see Figure 3.15). The Keynesian identity between expenditures on (I) and (II) is fully respected, as is Marx's identity of price and value: the totality of the product is purchased by the totality of wages independently of its final distribution.

But how can profits be positive since, according to the quantum theory of monetary expenditures, the emission of wages defines the product as a whole? The answer is easy: the distribution of the product between wages and profits is the result of a subsequent operation taking place on the commodity market. In fact, if firms sell the product at a selling price of 125,[106] workers can buy, at most, 80 units of it, which

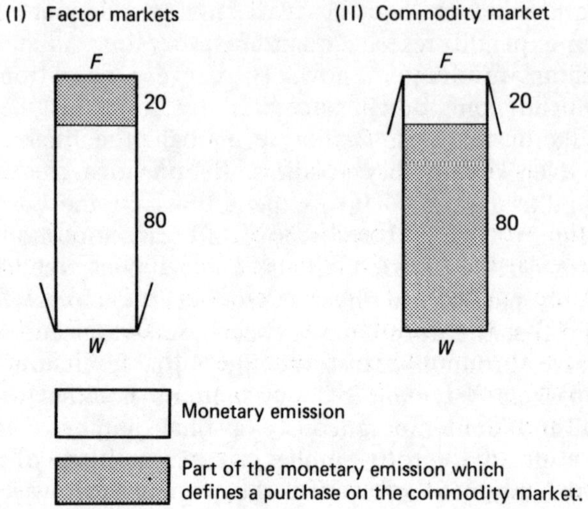

Fig. 3.15

means that only 80 units of income out of the 100 spent by *W* correspond to a final purchase. The remaining 20 units are transferred from *W* to *F*, and define the product still to be sold by *F*. The firms' internal profit is, thus, equal to the 20 units of income they succeed in taking away from *W* on the commodity market.

However, although perfectly correct, this observation is only the first step towards the solution. In fact, it can be proved that the workers' final expenditure on the commodity market retroactively modifies the emission of wages. More precisely, the formation of a positive (internal) profit signifies the inclusion of a positive expenditure on the commodity market *within* the expenditure on the factor markets. Profits are therefore defined as a positive purchase of products which is included in the payment of wages. In other words, the workers' final transfer of income in favour of firms defines a profit which has already been spent in the initial emission of wages. Referring to our previous numerical example, we can see that:

(I) on the commodity market, the workers' expenditure of 100 units of income is in reality a final purchase of 80 since the selling price is equal to 125: firms acquire an income of 20 units corresponding to the value of the remaining product;

(II) the profit of 20 units acquired by firms on the commodity market corresponds to a final purchase of goods which has already taken place on the factor markets.

Finally, the workers' expenditure on the commodity market is the necessary retroactive sanction of a final purchase included in the emission of wages. Hereafter, price and value are identical: value (the amount of wages) is 100 and 100 is also the price, i.e. the amount of income spent for the final purchase of the whole product (80 on the commodity market and 20 on the factor markets).

As a result of this process, the product is shared between wage goods and profit goods. Contrary to any obvious expectation, this result is perfectly consistent with the identity of wages and product. In fact, the complementarity of wages and profits is verified only in real terms, the value of the product being always identical to nominal wages. Thus

$$\text{product} \equiv \text{nominal wages},^{107} \qquad (3.3)$$

and

$$\text{product} \equiv \text{real wages} + \text{real profits}, \qquad (3.4)$$

are simultaneously and consistently verified for any level of production.[108]

6. The factors of production

The classics. Since Adam Smith it has been known that if labour, capital and land are productive in terms of value, then national income is the sum of three different incomes: wages, interest and rent. Now, according to the classics, labour 'is the real measure of the exchangeable value of all commodities'.[109] In Smith's analysis labour 'is alone the ultimate and real standard by which the value of all commodities can at all times and places be estimated and compared'.[110] Value is therefore considered a *substance* whose measure is expressed in terms of labour. As a real standard of value, labour produces the common substance to which physically heterogeneous goods can be reduced in order to be compared. 'Labour, therefore, it appears evidently, is the only universal, as well as the only accurate measure of value, or the only standard by which we can compare the values of different commodities at all times, and at all places.'[111]

It is true that the value thus determined is later shared between the categories of wages, interest and rent. Yet, this operation is logically subsequent to the determination of value: it represents a simple distribution of a value fully determined by labour alone.

As the price or exchangeable value of every particular commodity, taken separately, resolves itself into some one or other or all of those three parts; so that of all the commodities which compose the whole annual produce of the labour of every country, taken complexly, must resolve itself into the same three parts, and be parcelled out among different inhabitants of the country, either as the wages of their labour, the profits of their stock, or the rent of their land. The whole of what is annually either collected or produced by the labour of every society, or what comes to the same thing, the whole price of it, is in this manner originally distributed among some of its different members.[112]

Following Smith, Ricardo elaborates a theory of value in which labour is the sole and objective origin or principle of value. His attempt to determine an invariable measure of value is symptomatic of this conception of value. Labour, being the source of value, must itself be measured by a standard which logically cannot be a pure number. A dimensional unit of measurement is required in order to express a value which is itself dimensional. According to Ricardo, this unit is labour-time. The consequence of this choice of a dimensional unit of measurement is that labour-time can only be defined by money if money is substantially equal to it. Consistently, Ricardo defines money as a commodity. Unfortunately, this analysis leads him to a blind alley: the dimensional definition of money does not adduce an invariable measure of value.

When commodities varied in relative value, it would be desirable to have the means of ascertaining which of them fell and which rose in real value, and this could be effected only by comparing them one after another with some invariable standard measure of value, which should itself be subject to none of the fluctuations to which other commodities are exposed. Of such a measure it is impossible to be possessed, because there is no commodity which is not itself exposed to the same variations as the things, the value of which is to be ascertained; that is, there is none which is not subject to require more or less labour for its production.[113]

With Marx, the distinction between exchange- and use-values becomes very sharp, and labour, though still measured in time units, acquires a very abstract dimension. In much of his work[114] Marx is indeed very near to a non-dimensional definition of value and money. The 'general equivalent' is the best example of his attempt to free the analysis from the concept of a value-substance. Considered as a general equivalent, money is not itself a commodity but the form in which every commodity is expressed. 'But *Ricardo does not examine* the form—the peculiar characteristic of labour that creates exchange values or manifests itself in exchange values—the *nature* of this labour. Hence he does not grasp the connection of *this* labour with *money* or that it must assume the form of *money*.'[115] Money is therefore the form of labour, and since labour is reduced by Marx to the concept of abstract labour, it seems possible to consider money as a non-dimensional definition of value. Yet Marx does not go as far as this, and his abstract labour remains defined as the *substance* of value. 'Exchange value presupposes social labour as the substance of all products, quite apart from their natural make-up.'[116] According to this substantial conception of value, money is not a mere number but a substance which allows the transformation of a particular commodity (like gold) into a general equivalent which remains fundamentally a commodity. 'Money is labour time in the form of a general object, or the objectification of general labour time, labour time as a *general commodity*.'[117] Despite his efforts, Marx does not succeed in building a new theory of value capable of solving Ricardo's problem. As long as value is considered as a substance, no invariable measure can be found, and consequently other problems, such as the heterogeneity of labour[118] and the monetary realisation of surplus value, remain unresolved.

The neoclassics. With the works of Walras, Jevons and Menger, the search for an absolute value is abandoned in favour of the concept of relative value. According to the neoclassical school, the value of goods is determined through their exchange on the commodity market. The central concept of the theory is no longer the commodity as a social 'rod' for measuring production but the physical outputs which are, presumably, exchanged for each other on the outside and internal markets. Within this context, it is obvious that products are considered as originating from more than one category of factor of production. Thus, products are merely physical objects, outputs given by inputs which are also purely physical. Accordingly, the factors of production are evaluated in physical terms.

> We shall suppose the quantities of the services to be measured in the following two types of units: (1) in units of natural or artificial capital, like a hectare of land, an individual person, or a piece of capital proper; and (2) in time units, like a day. Thus we have a certain quantity of land-service per day from a hectare of such and such a piece of land; a certain quantity of labour per day from such and such a person; a certain quantity of capital-service per day from such and such a capital good.[119]

Once production has been defined as a process of physical transformation, the factors of production can be determined almost arbitrarily, according to the function one wants to emphasise. Although other factors have sometimes been introduced, the factors of production have traditionally been identified with labour, land and capital. 'Commodities are products which result from the combination of such factors of production as labour, land and capital goods.'[120]

Most importantly, the physical definition of production calls for a mathematical formulation, the so-called production functions. These functions, which are supposed to represent the production possibilities, are based on the assumption that production is a continuous or discontinuous function of time. A critique of this 'mechanical' analysis of production having already been developed, let us simply note that the production functions are strictly related to the heterogeneity problem. If labour, capital and land are not homogeneous magnitudes, then it is impossible to order them into an equation defining their functional relation. As Bliss also points out, the heterogeneity problem is not confined to capital, but concerns every factor of production as well as the product itself.

> However, before we tackle *K*, what about *Y*? If the production function is to describe the productive activities of the entire economy, and if that economy can, and typically does, produce more than one kind of final output, then is there not a parallel problem of justifying the representation

of Y by a single number? It would be a serious mistake to dismiss this last problem as just 'an index-number problem' (whatever that means) while supposing that the problem of aggregating capital is in some sense more profound and intractable.[121]

The solution to this problem is a necessary condition for the writing of any production function. As has been argued,[122] this solution cannot be found within the neoclassical framework, where products remain necessarily heterogeneous and the factors of production completely undetermined. In fact, indeterminacy is not only limited to the factors of production but concerns the product itself: in neoclassical theory the product is not defined. Consequently, money and product are not mutually integrated and the representation of the economy remains dichotomous. It is not to be doubted that Walras's concept of numéraire is an important step towards a new definition of the product. As the word itself implies, 'numéraire' is really a pure number, that is, a dimensionless unit. When real output is defined in terms of the numéraire it is, therefore, identified with a set of numbers. Unfortunately, here again a commodity is chosen as the numéraire and, even worse, the numéraire is regarded as one of the two terms of a relative exchange: the numéraire is exchanged for the product and not changed into a product. Thus, the numéraire is a substance and the product is its counterpart. Like the classics, the neoclassics consider money as a substance but, in opposition to them, they try to determine only relative values through the exchange of this substance on the commodity market. Analysis shows, however, that this determination cannot be successful since even relative exchange requires the homogeneity of the products exchanged. Ultimately, the neoclassics do not succeed in solving the two problems with which every economic theory is traditionally confronted: heterogeneity and dichotomy are not defeated by relative exchange, and the product as well as the factors of production is left undefined.

The theory of emissions. From both classical and neoclassical theories it is possible to derive useful guidelines for the elaboration of a new analysis of value. From the classics we learn, in fact, that the product must be defined before its exchange on the commodity market, whereas from the neoclassics we learn that its definition must be a numerical one. Absolute values and the numéraire are the fundamentals of the new analysis. Accordingly, production is an emission whose result is not a new substance but a 'bunch of numbers' which literally was not there before. One of the consequences of the theory of emissions is that the factors of production can now be determined. In fact, it can be proved in two different ways that there is only one category of factor of production: labour.

The first proof is related to what Schmitt calls the real emission. As we have already seen, the product is emitted as a whole as soon as it is completed. This real emission is obviously not the creation of a new substance. Even though the product exists as a physical object, its new utility is issued as a quantum. Before acquiring this form, the product does not even exist. What exists is matter and energy, whereas what is created is a product, i.e. new utility. Now, this utility can only be emitted by the industry of mankind: 'The utility form can only be imagined or conceived by people (and for people); it is always the result of a plan.'[123] Given that 'production is the realisation of the project',[124] it follows that labour is the only factor of production. 'People conceive the design and, through their work, force matter and energy to comply with it. Human labour and labour alone can conceive the form of utility, and through its work put the matter into it.'[125]

Capital goods are also the result of a real emission and, as such, are created by work alone. Once they have acquired their utility they can obviously be used in the process of production, but this does not mean that they are an additional factor of production. Capital goods, as well as land or any other natural resource, are not capable of conceiving anything and are therefore not the agents of any real emission. Capital and land can transform matter and energy, but they cannot emit the product which, as we know, is not material even if it exists in physical objects. Ultimately, people and people alone create the product. Matter and energy can be supposed to be continuously transformed in continuous time, but the emission of the product is an instantaneous event defined in quantum time. Taking again the example of the car, we can see that its production takes place instantaneously at the end of the month even if all its physical parts have been continuously transformed during the whole month. The 'labour activity' plans the way these materials have to be put together to form a car. Production is therefore defined as an instantaneous event taking place as soon as this plan is realised, i.e. as soon as the car is finished and matter takes the form of this product. The creation of the real product is thus defined in a quantum of time as the realisation of plans. Now, in a monetary economy this real emission is replaced by a monetary emission and the product is changed into money: *the emission of money identifies itself with the production of real goods*.

The presence of money allows for an alternative proof of the logical existence of only one category of factor of production. Bearing in mind that we are concerned with the factors determining the economic value of the product and not its use-value, let us consider the three traditional factors of land, labour and capital. As we have already shown, production gives rise to three quantum deposits, as depicted in Figure 3.16 where x

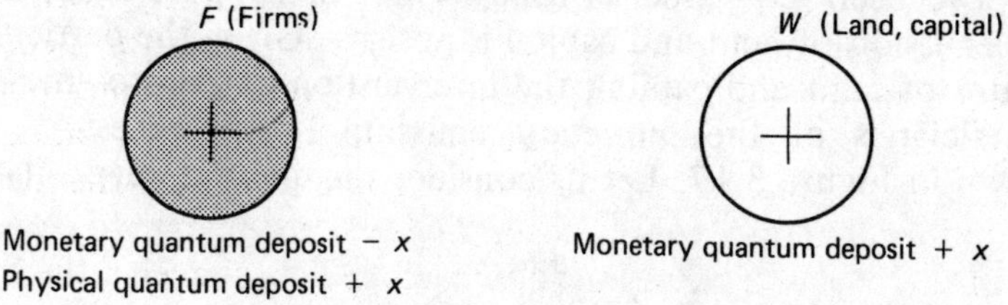

Fig. 3.16

represents the amount of wages paid to the workers. What we now have to prove is that this amount will not be increased by the use of land and capital, so that x is the unique economic definition of the physical product stocked in F.

The amount of wages, x, is a net quantum deposit. It follows that land and capital can increase this deposit only if their activity is an emission. Let us suppose that this is the case. Then, the production of capital and land is represented as in Figure 3.16. Now, the problem is whether or not this exchange of real and monetary emissions can effectively take place given the very nature of money. The answer is obviously in the negative, since the beneficiary of monetary emissions is always a person. Thus, if the real emission of land and capital is positive, the corresponding monetary emission must reach the owners. It follows that land and capital are the agents of the positive real emission but not the beneficiaries of its corresponding monetary emission, while the owners of capital and land are the beneficiaries of the monetary emission but not the agents of its corresponding real emission:

activity of land and capital —— monetary emission = 0 / real emission = 0 —— owners

Monetary and real emissions, however, are two aspects of the same operation. The two emissions, in fact, measure each other. If the real emission of the owners of land and capital is zero, then the corresponding nominal emission is also zero. Similarly, if the monetary emission of land and capital is zero, its corresponding real emission is also zero: land and capital are not the agents of any economic emission.

The preceding proof, first presented by B. Schmitt in 1980,[126] has also been expressed as follows. Let us suppose again that the emission of land and capital is positive. Given the particular nature of land and capital, the intervention of their owners as beneficiaries of the monetary emission is still necessary, as shown in Figure 3.17. Let us consider the quantum deposits of

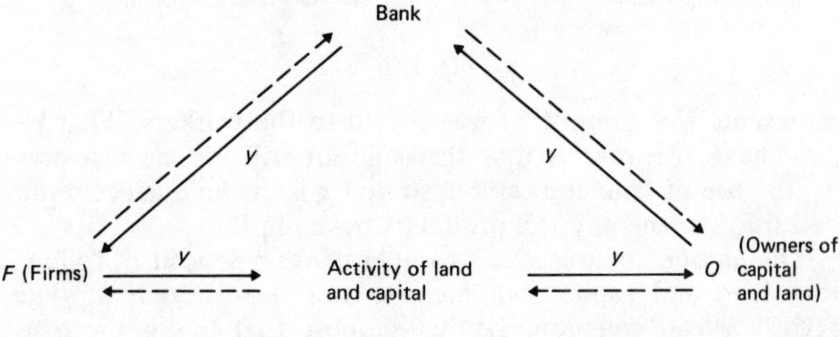

Fig. 3.17.

firms, land and capital, and the owners. As for the emission of wages, the quantum deposits of F, although negative and positive for the same amount, are of a different nature. The positive quantum deposit of F is physical—it represents the physical product stocked while the negative quantum deposit is monetary. At the other vertex of our triangle (see Figure 3.17) the quantum deposit of the owners of capital and land is positive, and represents the monetary form of the product of capital and land. The activity of land and capital functions as a mere intermediary between F and O, and must therefore be characterised by a positive and a negative quantum deposit of the same nature. Finally we have the distribution shown in Table 3.5.

Table 3.5

	Firms	Land and capital	Owners
Monetary quantum deposit	$-y$	$+y$ $-y$	$+y$
Physical quantum deposit	$+y$		

Now it is clear that the existence of the triangle (Figure 3.17) is conditioned by the possibility of capital and land transmitting a positive quantum deposit to the owners. The triangle is, in fact, meaningful only if it results from the union of two distinct operations, as shown in Figure 3.18. Unfortunately operation (I)

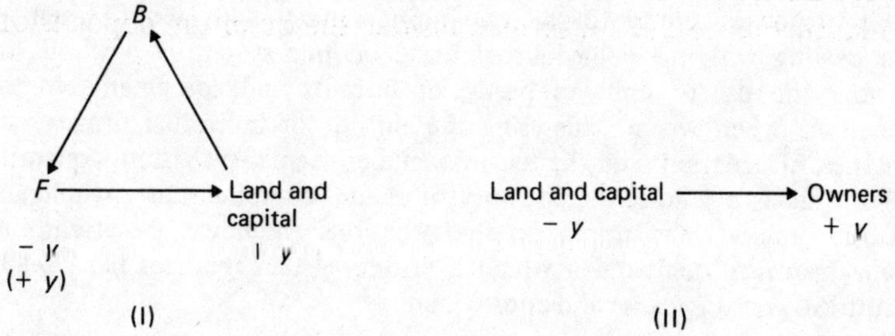

Fig. 3.18

cannot take place, since land and capital are not the beneficiaries of any monetary emission. Because land and capital are not persons, they cannot receive money. Thus, no transmission can take place between them and their owners. The conclusion is straightforward: capital and land cannot transfer to their owners a quantic deposit which they are incapable of receiving.

From the fact that the activity of capital and land does not imply the production of any quantum deposit, it follows that the creation of income due to capital and land is necessarily equal to zero. In other words, wages are the unique definition of income, since labour is the sole factor of production, i.e. the sole factor whose activity creates a net quantum deposit. Obviously, this does not mean that the owners of capital and land do not receive any income. What it does mean is that all the incomes such as rent, profits and dividends are included in the income created by the activity of labour: they are a part, although a non-additive part, of wages.

This conclusion is widely supported by Keynes's analysis. Starting from the *Treatise*, he points out that:

> Human effort and human consumption are the ultimate matters from which alone economic transactions are capable of deriving any significance; and all other forms of expenditure only acquire importance from their having some relationship, sooner or later, to the effort of producers or to the expenditure of consumers.[127]

The central role played by human effort is underlined again in *The General Theory*, where Keynes distinguishes individual from global entities.

> It is my belief that much unnecessary perplexity can be avoided if we limit ourselves strictly to the two units, money and labour, when we are dealing with the behaviour of the economic system as a whole; reserving the use of units of particular outputs and equipments to the occasions when we are analysing the output of individual firms or industries in isolation; and the use of vague concepts, such as the quantity of output as a whole, the quantity of capital equipment as a whole and the general level of prices, to the occasions when we are attempting some historical comparison which is within certain (perhaps fairly wide) limits avowedly uprecise and approximate.[128]

Another step toward the solution is taken when individual magnitudes as well as physical factors of production are confined to a merely physical description of economics, the determination of all significant variables requiring the intervention of money.

> The division of economics between the theory of value and distribution on the one hand and the theory of money on the other hand is, I think, a false division. The right dichotomy is, I suggest, between the theory of the individual industry or firm and of the rewards and the distribution between different uses of a *given* quantity of resources on the one hand, and the theory of output and employment *as a whole* on the other hand. So long as we limit ourselves to the study of the individual industry or firm on the assumption that the aggregate quantity of employed resources is constant,

and, provisionally, that the conditions of other industries or firms are unchanged, it is true that we are not concerned with the significant characteristic of money. But as soon as we pass to the problem of what determines output and employment as a whole, we require the complete theory of a monetary economy.[129]

Finally, money and labour, integrated through the payment of wages, represent the necessary and sufficient condition for the social definition of production.

I sympathise, therefore, with the pre-classical doctrine that everything is *produced* by *labour*, aided by what used to be called art and is now called technique, by natural resources which are free or cost a rent according to their scarcity or abundance, and by the results of past labour, embodied in assets, which also command a price according to their scarcity or abundance. It is preferable to regard labour, including, of course, the personal services of the entrepreneur and his assistants, as the sole factor of production, operating in a given environment of technique, natural resources, capital equipment and effective demand. This partly explains why we have been able to take the unit of labour as the sole physical unit which we require in our economic system, apart from units of money and of time.[130]

Thus, it follows that the purchasing power of money must be derived from the relation between labour and product, such as it results from the process of production. Now, how is this relation determined in terms of money? The answer is familiar to economists: money wages, expressed in wage units, represent the homogeneous measure of labour and product. Stated in this way, this result seems to be too similar to the classical (pre-classical in Keynes's own terms) theory of value. In fact, it differs from it on a small but essential point: the monetary definition of labour. According to the classics, labour is considered as the substance of value and is measured in physical units, whereas Keynes's basic unit is monetary.

Two main difficulties, never overcome by the classics, are here avoided, namely, the physical heterogeneity of labour and the integration of money into the real world. Wages are then the objective link between money and product, a link which is the direct result of the production process.

Unfortunately, Keynes's message has often been misunderstood or treated, like Ricardo's, as a deplorable simplification of reality. This attitude was predicted by Keynes himself and is still very much alive in contemporary economics. The correct understanding of his theory is therefore essential to avoid the fulfilment of the sad prophecy he made in his letter to R. F. Harrod on 27 August 1935.

I am frightfully afraid of the tendency, of which I see some signs in you, to appear to accept my constructive part and to find some accommodation between this and deeply cherished views which would in fact only be possible if my constructive part has been partially misunderstood. That is to say, I expect a great deal of what I write to be water off a duck's back.[131]

Notes

1. R. G. D. Allen, *Macro-Economic Theory*, London, Macmillan, 1968, p. 76.
2. W. C. Hood, 'Some aspects of the treatment of time in economic theory', *Canadian Journal of Economics and Political Science*, Vol. 14, 1948, p. 456.
3. J. Robinson, 'The production function and the theory of capital', *Review of Economic Studies*, 55, 1953–4, p. 85.
4. Allen, op. cit., p. 5.
5. Ibid.
6. Ibid.
7. Ibid., p. 6.
8. R. G. D. Allen, *Mathematical Economics*, London, Macmillan, 1956, p. 179.
9. Ibid.
10. Ibid.
11. Ibid., p. 206.
12. P. A. Samuelson, 'Some notions of causality and teleology in economics', in *The Collected Scientific Papers of Paul A. Samuelson*, ed. Robert C. Merton, Boston, MIT Press, Vol. III, 1972, pp. 439–40.
13. R. Frisch, 'On the notion of equilibrium and disequilibrium', *Review of Economic Studies*, 3, 1935–6, p. 100.
14. Hood, op. cit., p. 455.
15. Ibid., p. 457.
16. R. Courant, *Differential and Integral Calculus*, Vol. I, London and Glasgow, Blackie & Son, 1934, p. 112.
17. Allen, *Macro-Economic Theory*, op. cit., p. 86.
18. The traditional definition of income as a flow is, in fact, now modified by the choice of period analysis. May's assumption that 'in period analysis all quantity variables have the dimension of stocks, whereas in continuous analysis one is forced to distinguish between stocks and flows' (J. May, 'Period analysis and continuous analysis in Patinkin's macroeconomic models', *Journal of Economic Theory*, 2/1–9, 1970, p. 1) is wrong if 'quantity variables' refer to income. As long as we consider chronological time, the fact that income is measured at a point in time does not contradict the assumption that income is determined by the implementation of its instantaneous level over a finite period of time. In other words, even in period analysis income is said to be a flow since its value is given as a function of time and not merely indexed by time. 'So, if Y is the constant rate of income (output) per unit of time,

then the amount of income received or output produced in a period of Δt time-units is simply $Y\Delta t$' (Allen, *Macro-Economic Theory*, op. cit., p. 2). Our analysis is supported by Harrison who, in his article about the stock-flow distinction, claims that May's contribution is one of the reasons for the recent confusion in this theoretical field (see G. W. Harrison, 'The stock–flow distinction: a suggested interpretation', *Journal of Macroeconomics*, Spring 1980, 116–20).

19. M. E. Baron, *The Origins of the Infinitesimal Calculus*, Oxford, Pergamon Press, 1969, p. 7.
20. Ibid., p. 240.
21. Ibid., p. 7.
22. Ibid., p. 240.
23. K. Wicksell, *Lectures on Political Economy*, London, Routledge, 1934, p. 14.
24. B. Russell, *Principles of Philosophy*, quoted by W. Charlton in 'Time', *Philosophy*, April 1981, p. 149.
25. The pre-existence of space is the only logical way out of Zeno's paradoxes of motion.
26. B. Schmitt, 'Time as quantum', in *Advances in Economic Theory*, ed. M. Baranzini, Oxford, Blackwell, 1982, p. 122.
27. B. Schmitt, *Monetary Expenditures and Quantum Time*, Castella/Presses Universitaires de Dijon, forthcoming, p. 28.
28. W. H. Newton-Smith, *The Structure of Time*, London, Routledge & Kegan Paul, 1980, p. 127.
29. Ibid., p. 128.
30. Ibid., p. 127.
31. D. Foley, 'On two specifications of asset equilibrium in macroeconomics', *Journal of Political Economy*, April, 1975, p. 310.
32. B. W. Lindgren, *Statistical Theory*, London, Macmillan, 1968, p. 162.
33. Ibid., p. 161.
34. Ibid., p. 162.
35. F. H. Knight, 'Capitalistic production, time and the rate of return', in *Economic Essays in Honour of Gustav Cassel*, London, Allen & Unwin, 1933, p. 329.
36. May, op. cit., p. 1.
37. Ibid., p. 1.
38. Foley, op. cit., p. 310.
29. Ibid., p. 311.
40. Ibid., p. 310.
41. May, op. cit., p. 3.
42. E. A. Kuska, 'On the fundamental flaw in the portfolio-balance or asset approach to modelling economic systems', *Abstract*, London School of Economics, 1980, pp. 8–9.
43. Ibid., p. 8.
44. Ibid., p. 40.
45. Ibid.
46. Ibid., p. 38.
47. Ibid., p. 40.
48. Foley, op. cit., p. 311.
49. J. Hicks, *Value and Capital*, London, Oxford University Press, 1978, pp. 122–3.
50. Ibid., pp. 131–2.
51. Ibid., p. 184.
52. D. Patinkin, quoted by Harrison, op. cit., p. 115.
53. D. H. Robertson, 'Saving and hoarding', *Economic Journal*, September 1933, p. 399.

54. D. H. Robertson, *The Banking Policy and the Price Level,* London, P. S. King & Son, 1932, p. 59.
55. Robertson, 'Saving and hoarding', op. cit., p. 413.
56. Ibid., p. 411.
57. K. J. Arrow and F. H. Hahn, *General Competitive Analysis*, Amsterdam, North-Holland, 1971, p. 62.
58. Ibid., p. 61.
59. Ibid., p. 62.
60. P. A. Samuelson, 'A quantum theory model of economics: is the co-ordinating entrepreneur just worth his profit?', in Hiroaki Nagatani and Kate Crowley (eds), *The Collected Scientific Papers of Paul A. Samuelson,* Vol. IV, Boston, MIT, 1977, p. 332.
61. Ibid., p. 329.
62. Ibid., p. 330.
63. Ibid., p. 332.
64. Ibid., p. 330.
65. A. Qadir, 'Quantum economics', *Pakistan Economic and Social Review,* **16**/3–4, 1978, p. 117.
66. Schmitt, *Monetary Expenditures,* op. cit., p. 5.
67. P. A. Samuelson, in Stiglitz (ed.) *The Collected Scientific Papers*, op. cit., Vol. II, p. 1155.
68. Schmitt, 'Time as quantum', op. cit., p. 112.
69. See Schmitt, *Monetary expenditures* op. cit., p. 1.
70. The idea of a 'quantum leap' seems to have been present in Bergson's work. Analysing Zeno's paradox of the arrow, Bergson claims that the flight of the arrow is 'a single and unique bound'. Now, Bergson's claim does not really allow for a quantum analysis of Zeno's paradox, since the space covered by the arrow is given before, and independently of, its flight. The trajectory of the flight is not a creation of space, and that is why the displacement of the arrow can be analysed in terms of classical mechanics. A quantum event, on the other hand, does not suppose the pre-existence of its result and therefore cannot be described in terms of continuous analysis.
71. Schmitt, *Monetary Expenditures,* op. cit., p. 4.
72. A. N. Whitehead, *Process and Reality*, London, Macmillan, 1929, p. 53.
73. J. M. Keynes, *The General Theory of Employment, Investment and Money,* London, Macmillan, 1973, p. 39.
74. Ibid., p. 43.
75. Schmitt, *Monetary Expenditures,* op. cit., p. 49.
76. G. L. S. Shackle, *Expectations, Enterprise and Profit*, London, Allen & Unwin, 1970, p. 15.
77. Ibid., p. 15.
78. G. L. S. Shackle, *Epistemics and Economics*, 1972, Cambridge, Cambridge University Press, p. 268.
79. P. A. Samuelson, 'Rejoinder: agreements, disagreements, doubts and the case of induced Harrod-neutral technical change', in Robert C. Merton (ed.), *The Collected Scientific Papers*, Vol. III, Boston, MIT, 1972, p. 174.
80. J. M. Keynes, *A Treatise on Money*, Vol. 1, *The Pure Theory of Money,* London, Macmillan, 1971, p. 111.
81. Ibid., p. 121.
82. Keynes, *The General Theory,* op. cit., p. 38.
83. R. S. Sayers, *Modern Banking,* London, Oxford University Press, 1958, pp. 15–6.
84. Ibid., p. 17.
85. Ibid., p. 12.

86. Ibid.
87. Ibid., p. 15.
88. Ibid., p. 12.
89. Ibid., p. 14.
90. Ibid., p. 12.
91. Ibid., pp. 18–19.
92. A. Smith, *The Wealth of Nations,* Harmondsworth, Pelican Classics, 1978 (first published 1874), p. 388.
93. We call 'relative exchange' any transaction defining the mutual exchange of product and money, and 'absolute exchange' any transaction defining the product as a given sum of money.
94. R. W. Clower, 'The Keynesian counter-revolution: a theoretical appraisal', in *Monetary Theory,* ed. R. W. Clower, Harmondsworth, Penguin Education, 1973, p. 279.
95. P. A. Samuelson, 'Samuelson on the neoclassical dichotomy: a reply', in Hiroaki Nagatani and Kate Crowley (eds), *The Collected Scientific Papers*, Vol. IV, Boston, MIT, 1977, p. 789.
96. Here we are assuming that at the beginning of the process firms do not hold any positive income. In other words, the only money available is the nominal money issued by the bank. However, this assumption does not alter the analysis in any way, and its introduction is purely didactic. In fact, the analysis shows that the theory of emissions applies even when firms own a 'revolving fund'. The payment of wages does not require the expenditure of a positive income, so that if *F* pay their wages out of a 'revolving fund' this does not modify the amount of income finally spent by *F* for the purchase of profit goods. Analytically, the payment of wages is clearly distinguished from the final expenditure of profits, and only the latter can eventually destroy firms' own income.
97. Even if the firms' revolving fund is positive, its expenditure on the factor markets does not modify the analysis.
98. Schmitt, *Monetary Expenditures,* op. cit., p. 46.
99. As we shall see, the real emission is necessarily a twofold operation, so that every monetary emission is in reality only one half of a real emission.
100. Schmitt, *Monetary Expenditures,* op. cit., p. 67.
101. Ibid., p. 48.
102. Ibid.
103. Ibid., p. 43.
104. Ibid., p. 80.
105. Ibid., p. 96.
106. Selling prices should not be confused with macroeconomic prices, which are defined by the amount of income spent for the final purchase of the product.
107. Nominal wages ≡ wages paid to the factors of production.
108. The profit we have briefly analysed here is what Schmitt calls the *internal profit*, i.e. the part of income corresponding to rent, interest and dividends. The analysis also shows the existence of another category of profits called *external profits*, whose origin is to be found in the existence of emissions which allow the creation of false or purely nominal incomes. Symptoms of the pathological condition of our economic system, these external profits are not integrated in the payment of wages. Thus, external profits are clearly defined as the direct appropriation of capital goods resulting from an emission which gives to the workers monetary wages that are 'empty'. For a detailed analysis of external profits see Schmitt, *Monetary Expenditures*, op. cit., pp. 135–9.

109. Smith, op. cit., p. 133.
110. Ibid., p. 136.
111. Ibid., pp. 139–40.
112. Ibid., p. 155.
113. D. Ricardo, *On The Principles of Political Economy and Taxation*, Cambridge, Cambridge University Press, 1975 (first edition J. Murray, 1817), pp. 43–4.
114. See especially K. Marx, *Grundrisse*, Notebook I, Harmondsworth, The Pelican Marx Library, 1973.
115. K. Marx, *Theories of Surplus Value*, Vol. 2, London, Lawrence & Wishart, 1969, p. 164.
116. Marx, *Grundrisse*, op. cit., p. 205.
117. Ibid., p. 168.
118. The attempt to solve this problem through exchange belongs fundamentally to neoclassicism. In fact, even if it is true that Marx himself seems to support this idea sometimes, it is even more true that for him commodity values have to be determined *before exchange*. On the commodity market it is on the basis of these values that commodities are later exchanged. According to Marx and the classics, the common quality which allows the commensurability of physically heterogeneous products is labour, and the relation between labour and products is established within the process of production, and not on the commodity market. In arguing that 'labour becomes social only because it is equalised with some other labour, and this equalisation is carried out by means of exchange' (I. I. Rubin, *Essays on Marx's Theory of Value*, Detroit, Black & Red, 1972, p. 66), Rubin is trying to transform Marx's analysis into a neoclassical model where all the significant variables are determined through exchange.
119. L. Walras, *Elements of Pure Economics*, London, Allen & Unwin, 1965 (first published 1874), p. 237.
120. M. Morishima, *Walras' Economics: A Pure Theory of Capital and Money*, Cambridge, Cambridge University Press, 1977, p. 46.
121. C. J. Bliss, *Capital Theory and the Distribution of Income*, Amsterdam, North-Holland/American Elsevier, 1975, pp. 170–1.
122. See A. Cencini, 'The logical indeterminacy of relative prices', in *Advances in Economic Theory*, ed. M. Baranzini, Oxford, Blackwell, 1982.
123. Schmitt, *Monetary Expenditures*, op. cit., p. 46.
124. Ibid., p. 46.
125. Ibid.
126. Ibid.
127. Keynes, *A Treatise on Money*, Vol. I, op. cit., pp. 120–1.
128. Keynes, *The General Theory*, op. cit., p. 43.
129. Ibid., p. 293.
130. Ibid., pp. 213–4.
131. J. M. Keynes, The Collected Writings of, ed. D. Moggridge, Vol. XIII, *The General Theory and After*, Part I, *Preparation*, London, Macmillan, 1973, p. 548.

4 Ex-Ante and Ex-Post in Chronological and Quantum Time

PART I: THE EX-ANTE DETERMINATION OF INCOME

1. The traditional analysis

The distinction between ex-ante and ex-post variables, first introduced by the Swedish economist G. Myrdal, has traditionally been used to prove the possibility of saving being different from investment. Many economists, feeling uneasy with Keynes's definitions, were looking for a method of reconciling identities and conditions of equilibrium. As a result of this search, the assumption was made that economic entities must be distinguished according to their 'virtual' or 'realised' evaluation. Thus, it was said that ex-ante economic forces like saving and investment are virtual, whereas ex-post these same forces are realised. Accordingly, identities hold good ex-post and conditions of equilibrium ex-ante. Ex-ante, saving and investment can differ; ex-post, they are necessarily equal. This distinction, once it is applied to the theory of income determination, allows for the introduction of a perfect analogy between income and price.

The false analogy between income analysis and price analysis. After the appearance of Keynes's *General Theory* the traditional determination of income seemed seriously challenged. This impression was nevertheless a very fleeting one, since the distinction between ex-ante and ex-post allowed the reintroduction of neoclassical analysis. According to the latter, income is determined by a process exactly similar to that determining prices. As in price analysis, the ex-post income is, therefore, said to result from an adjustment (ex-ante) between two curves: one representing total demand and the other total supply. This is traditionally represented as in Figure 4.1. Every point on the two curves except one (the intersection point) represents either a virtual demand or a virtual supply, and thus corresponds to a virtual level of income. Saving and investment

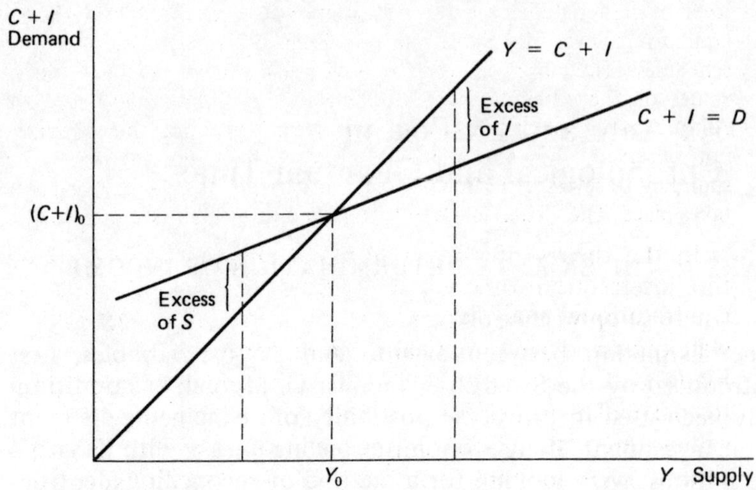

Fig. 4.1

are, therefore, expressed as schedules, i.e. as relations between the values of saving (or investment) and all the possible values of income. The point of intersection of the two curves which represent the saving schedule and the investment schedule determines the realised or 'observable' level of income. At this point saving and investment are also observable and equal, while at all the other points on the curves their values are virtual.

If these two schedules are smooth curves, as we believe them to be, there will exist a unique level of national income such that savings calculated from the savings schedule equal investment calculated from the investment schedule. This is the savings–investment equation in the schedule sense.

The term 'observable savings' refers to that particular level of savings calculated from the savings schedule from a knowledge of the unique equilibrium value of national income which equates savings and investment. Observable investment is calculated from the investment schedule at the same level of national income. The observable values of savings and investment are single points, while the schedules of savings and investment form continuous series of points along curves.[1]

The analogy with the theory of prices is obvious. As for the determination of prices:

The economic process is viewed as made up of a series of intersection or equilibrium points of savings and investment schedules. The observed level of national income for each time point can be considered as the equilibrium level of income corresponding to a set of savings–investment schedules. The observed levels of savings and investment are those two values on the schedules corresponding to the observed level of income. All the other values of savings and investment along the schedules are not observed; they are virtual levels of savings and investment corresponding to levels of national income other than that level which actually takes place. The virtual levels of savings and investment are not equal.[2]

In the theory of price determination price is determined by the intersection of the two curves of demand and supply, where supply and demand are both functions of price. The well-known diagrammatical representation is shown here in Figure 4.2. Each curve represents a set of points corresponding to particular values of demand and supply. Each of these values refers to a virtual price and to a given point on the time axis. Analogously, saving and investment are both functions of income, and their value outside equilibrium is related to a virtual level of income. Moreover, the observable income

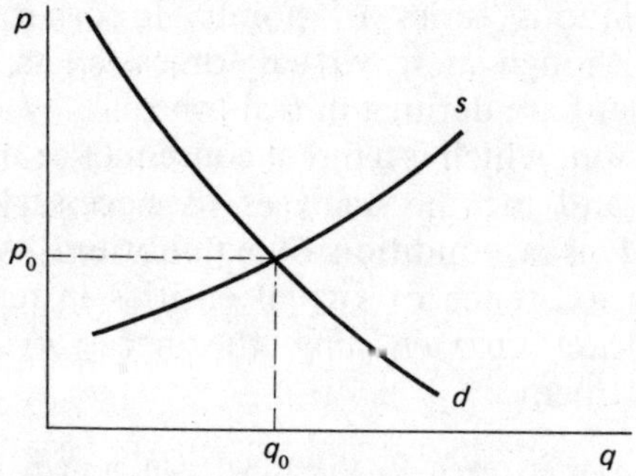

Fig. 4.2

is determined at the intersection of the two curves of saving and investment in the same way that the observable price is determined by the intersection of supply and demand.

The analogy seems, therefore, well founded. In both analyses demand and supply are 'schedules', virtual values of variables whose final determination is a matter of equilibrium and not a definitional identity.

Now it should be clear that the relationship we have here described between amount bought and amount sold is a different one from the definitional identity. Here we have amount sold as a function of price:

$$s = s(p),$$

amount bought as another function of price:

$$d = d(p),$$

and an equilibrium condition

$$s = d$$

which corresponds to the intersection in [Figure 4.2].[3]

This apparently reassuring interpretation of income analysis is nevertheless deeply misleading. The analogy with the theory of price is based on a wrong assumption: unlike supply and demand in price analysis, virtual saving and virtual investment are not real forces whose interaction determines real income.

Virtual saving, virtual investment and time. Klein, as well as Samuelson, Hansen and many others, explicitly assumes that saving and investment are equal at one point in time and different at a continuous series of points. In other words, they assume that, although mere virtual forces, ex-ante saving and ex-ante investment are defined in real time.

This assumption, which is a direct consequence of the analogy between price and income analyses, is necessary in order to consider $S = I$ as a condition of equilibrium. As Samuelson points out, the existence of virtual entities in real time is the essential condition for avoiding the necessary equality of saving and investment.

It is not true, however, even in the Keynesian system that for *virtual* displacements, which by their nature cannot be simultaneously observed, the saving (saving-investment) which households *would* perform out of a given income need equal the investment (saving-investment) which entrepreneurs *would* make at that same income. It is precisely because of their being unequal except at one point that income is uniquely determined. The idea of saving and investment being equilibrated, in the sense of schedule intersections, by income and by the other variables of the system, is implicit in the minds of most Keynesians (e.g., Harrod), but is often badly expressed. The concepts *ex-ante* and *ex-post* attempt to convey the idea, but seem less suitable than the terminology *virtual* and *observable*.[4]

Whatever terms are chosen, it is clearly assumed that saving and investment are equal *only at one point* in time. At all the other points of the time axis, saving and investment are unequal: they are considered as 'virtual' magnitudes located in time.

The utility of such an assumption is obvious. Being located in time, virtual saving and virtual investment can be regarded as real forces capable of making income vary from one level to another. If, on the contrary, virtual saving and virtual investment were not real forces, then income could no longer be determined by their interaction, and its level would remain completely indefinite unless we accepted the reduction of $S = I$ to a pure identity.

The 'equilibrists' are perfectly aware of this problem and do not hesitate to refer to income analysis as 'a process of adjustment which achieves an equilibrium'.

As observables over time, supply and demand are always equal in so far as they just represent opposite sides of the same transaction. But as static schedules, supply and demand are related in a genuine equation and are not identical. In the latter instance one can talk about divergences between supply and demand at *virtual, unobserved* prices. Similarly, one can talk about divergences of savings and investment at *virtual, unobserved* levels of income.[5]

After observing that 'if we construct the theories that supply and demand are equal, at the going market price, and that savings and investment are equal, at the going level of national income, then we have some real analytical tools',[6] Klein claims that national income is the result of a continuous dynamic process.

The idea of regarding any observed value of national income as the equilibrium value corresponding to an equation between savings and investment, in the schedule sense, is somewhat artificial. A more realistic view is that observed levels of national income are observed as the result of a continuous dynamical process.[7]

The traditional analysis could not be expressed more clearly. Let us quote Klein once again.

In this [Keynesian] model, savings depend upon the level of income; investment depends upon the level of income; the rate of change of income depends upon the difference between savings and investment such that income rises when investment exceeds savings, and income falls when savings exceed investment. In equilibrium, income has a zero rate of change; it is neither rising nor falling. The equilibrium, in this sense, implies that there is no difference between savings and investment.

Thus the Keynesian savings-investment equation can be looked upon as the equilibrium solution of a dynamical system. In exactly the same way, the usual supply-demand equation can also be looked upon as the equilibrium solution of a dynamical system.[8]

Because Klein considers the determination of income a dynamic process, he is bound to assume that virtual saving and virtual investment (as well as virtual demand and virtual supply) are real forces positively defined in real time. For an excess of investment over saving to cause a rise in income it is necessary that this difference exerts a real, positive action on income. A mere hypothetical force would not do so. Thus, the traditional analysis can be represented by the following conclusions:

1. virtual saving and virtual investment are real forces in real time; and
2. income is determined by a dynamic process of interaction between these two forces.

This analysis, which was greatly furthered by the debate following the publication of *The General Theory*, is aimed at integrating Keynes's thought into the mainstream of neoclassical theory. Did it succeed? Keynes's analysis would be reduced to a mere alternative approach within the general equilibrium system. Traditionally, the identity of saving and investment is considered a simple, particular case of a process of conditional equalisation. In other words, identity of S and I is supposed only to be valid ex-post, at a particular point in time, while the inequality of S and I occupies all the remaining points. Ex-ante saving and investment are different, and this difference provides the energy necessary to the whole process of income determination. 'Ex-post we have only the point of intersection of the curve, ex-ante we have the whole curves, which determines where the point of intersection will be.'[9]

As we have already pointed out, this attempt to reinterpret Keynes's thought in a more conventional way corresponds to the common belief that income must be determined in very much the same way as are prices in a traditional general equilibrium analysis. Such a reinterpretation required that Keynes's identities be fundamentally transformed in order to allow for an adjustment between total supply and total demand. This was done by differentiating between ex-ante and ex-post magnitudes. The clearest example of the way Keynes's identities were transformed into mere conditions of equilibrium is to be found in Samuelson.

By definition, *national income* (at market prices), Y, can initially be set equal to the sum of consumption expenditure, C, and *net investment*, I:

$$Y = C + I.$$

If Keynes had stopped with this identity, we should be left with an indeterminate system. In his simplest model of income determination, he added the following two hypotheses: (a) consumption is a function of income, and (b) investment may provisionally be taken, at any one time, as a constant. Mathematically, these relations may be written

$$C = C(Y) \text{ and } I = \bar{I}.$$

When we substitute these into our first identity, we come up with the simplest Keynesian income system:

$$Y = C(Y) + \bar{I}. \tag{1}$$

This is a determinate system, being one equation to determine one unknown variable. While much of the anti-Keynesian and Keynesian world was still arguing over the tautological character of the Keynesian concepts, Professor Hansen had quickly cut through the non-essentials to isolate the critically important role of the propensity-to-consume schedule, as embodied in this fundamental equation.

Equation (1) is crucially important for the history of economic thought. It is the nucleus of the Keynesian reasoning. If it *in no way* gives insight into the analysis of employment, then the Keynesian system is sterile and misleading. In its oversimplification, this relationship must be compared with two other seminal single equations which contain by implication much of the remainder of economic theory: namely the equating of supply and demand to determine market price,

$$D(p) - S(p) = 0,$$

and the determination of a firm's best output, q, (or anything else) by the condition that its profits, π, be at a maximum through the balancing of the effect of any decision on *total revenue, R,* and *total cost, C,*

$$\frac{d\pi}{dq} = \frac{dR(q)}{dq} - \frac{dC(q)}{dq} = 0.$$[10]

There is an implicit contradiction in Samuelson's analysis. Having accepted the identity $Y \equiv C + I$, it is logically impossible to assume that Y and $C + I$ are simultaneously the two terms of a condition of equilibrium.[11] It is, therefore, necessary to assume that identity and condition of equilibrium do not refer to the same period of time. This is what the distinction between ex-ante and ex-post should allow. In schedule terms this is expressed by the assertion that, except at the point of intersection of the two curves (or schedules), all the other points represent virtual levels of income where virtual demand can actually differ from virtual supply.

> The observed levels of savings and investment are those two values on the schedules corresponding to the observed level of income. All the other values of savings and investment along the schedules are not observed; they are virtual levels of savings and investment corresponding to levels of national income other than that level which actually takes place. The virtual levels of savings and investment are not equal.[12]

This interpretation of Keynes's work (which is consistent with the traditional analysis of price) has since dominated economic theory. Despite its powerful influence, it is still worth challenging it on a purely logical basis. Before doing so, however, we need to look at Keynes's own appraisal of this attempt at 'dynamising' his analysis.

2. Keynes's analysis

Time and the equality of saving and investment. The inconsistency between the traditional analysis of the multiplier and the necessary equality of saving and investment has already been discussed in Chapter 2. In relation to this we can only once again emphasise that Keynes's theory is logically opposed to the existence of a causal link between successive incomes. This conclusion is largely supported by Keynes himself, namely through his theories of effective demand and the instantaneous multiplier. Another confirmation can be found in the relation he establishes between the equality of S and I and time.

Let us suppose, preposterously, that incomes are functionally related. In this case, what are the forces which make income move from one level to another? A superficial analysis seems to point to the rate of interest. Now, if the rate of interest can explain the new level of income, then it cannot establish a functional relation between this income and the preceding one, except through a variation of S and I. The existence of a causal link can only be based on a temporal difference between saving and investment. In other words, incomes of successive periods only form a concatenation if a non-zero period of time elapses between the variation in investment (saving) and the corresponding variation in saving (investment). In the case, for example, of a rise in the rate of interest, income Y_0 will determine income Y_1 if, and only if, the difference between S and I allowed for by the increase of the rate of interest is not instantaneously cancelled. The passage from Y_0 to Y_1 is, in fact, brought about by the working of real forces deployed in real time. What does Keynes say about this matter? Does he allow for a 'schedule analysis of saving and investment'?

In his letter to G. Hawtrey, dated 24 September 1935, Keynes explicitly admits that according to his theory no adjustment between saving and investment can possibly take place in real time. 'In any passages in which I seem to regard the adjustment of investment and saving as a process occupying time, I agree with you that I am expressing myself incorrectly and am departing from my own ideas.'[13]

Consistent with his definition of national income, Keynes rejects the assumption that the identity of saving and investment can also be considered as a condition of equilibrium. But, if the adjustment of saving and investment is not a process requiring time, it necessarily follows that it is instantaneous. In other words, saving and investment never differ from each other: they are 'the twin result of the system's determinants'.[14] Keynes is obviously not referring here to the possible difference between saving and investment within a given income, i.e. within the identity of suppy and demand, since what has to be established is whether or not successive incomes are functionally linked through the adjustment of Y and D. His conclusion that saving and investment do not adjust in real time has, therefore, to be contrasted with the traditional assumption that income can be determined by the interaction of S and I. In fact, income is still defined by most theorists as a process of adjustments. A short appraisal of the (neo)Walrasian disequilibrium approach will confirm the strength of this assumption.

'A state of equilibrium, by definition, is a state in which something, something relevant, is *not* changing; so the use of an equilibrium concept is a signal that time, in some respect at least, has been put to one side.'[15] Starting from this consideration, several economists have strongly criticised the traditional neoclassical approach of Walras because of its *static* definition of economics. Equilibrium, as shown by the theory of price determination, is a state of affairs which does not describe the workings of the real world. As Hendry and Spanos say: '. . . the demand–supply theory, being proposed as an explanation of the determination and adjustments of the observable prices and quantities, in actual fact has nothing to do with either determination or adjustment'.[16] Following Hahn's sequential analysis, Hendry and Spanos put the emphasis on the adjustment process between plans and expectations. As E. R. Weintraub points out:

> The path through disequilibrium theory requires one to step through analytic time. It seems to require specific partial theories of how time intervals for particular decisions are cut up, then meshed together again. Agents have information from the 'past' and expectations about the future. There are a few future markets which link time periods, or assets which can be carried over period-to-period. Decisions are made, 'mistakes' may be recognized and incompatibilities between plans may or may not show up in the market.[17]

Traditional analysis is, therefore, at least partially rejected by those who believe that equilibrium between two theoretical variables, such as demand and supply, is a '*contextual concept*' and refers to '*a state wherein the forces at work are so adjusted to one another that no inherent tendency to change prevails.* As such, equilibrium is *a characteristic of the model* and not the real world.'[18]

According to this analysis, the general equilibrium approach does not provide a description of reality. Its static definition does not allow any adjustment in real time and wrongly assumes that the observed data are in fact the realised values of the variables. In order to avoid these empirical flaws and to follow the work of Clower, Leijonhufvud and Patinkin, many authors have developed what is known as the Walrasian disequilibrium theory. The detailed analysis of this theory being beyond our present purpose, let us simply note, with Hendry and Spanos, that the disequilibrium approach was introduced as a reaction to 'equilibrium economics' and 'as an alternative method purporting *to provide a better approximation to the real time dimension of the economic processes* by projecting an alternative (to the equilibrium method) image of reality, as concurrent chains of events; *a process not a state*'.[19] From this statement it is clear that the aim of disequilibrium analysis is fundamentally the same as that of traditional neoclassical theory: they both try to establish a functional relation between successive events. Referring again to the paper by Hendry and Spanos, we can see that sequential planning is introduced in order to take 'into consideration the time dimension of the adjustment processes and what that entails—inconsistency of plans and uncertainty about the future'.[20]

Although this is done within the microeconomic framework of price determination, it is possible to claim that income analysis should also be submitted to the disequilibrium approach. For, according to Walrasians and neo-Walrasians alike, macroeconomics is a mere aggregation of microeconomics.

In the change from price to income analysis, supply and demand are simply shifted from the individual to the aggregate level so that, according to these theorists, income can also be analysed as the result of a concurrent chain of events. Now, once the disequilibrium point of view has been introduced, theoretical variables and observed data are clearly distinguished, and the theory must explain how to bridge the gap between plans and realisation. At this stage of their analysis, Hendry and Spanos refer to the distinction between plans and data as the '*temporal facet*'[21] of the more general distinction between theoretical and observed variables. This distinction, which is said to correspond to Myrdal's distinction between ex-ante and ex-post variables, recalls the traditional attempt to explain income determination through the adjustment, ex-ante, of supply and demand. The introduction of the *latent variables framework* does not alter, therefore, the main assumption underlying the neoclassical approach to income determination: income is still considered as the result of a process of adjustment between total demand and total supply.

Now, if we refer to virtual income, the existence of an adjustment between expected demand and virtual supply cannot be denied. It is obvious that plans, expectations and decisions are not totally independent from one another. That past experiences influence expectations and that expectations influence decisions is not to be doubted. The interest of a theory which tries to establish a functional relation between these variables in order to provide a better insight into future economic activities is also not to be disputed.

Yet, this kind of relational analysis does not prove that income can be *logically determined* through the adjustment of supply and demand. The foresight of future income is, in fact, logically distinct from the *determination* or *definition* of such income. Thus, the acceptance of an adjustment between expected demand and virtual supply is compatible with several theories of income determination. According to the theory which underlines the establishment of these behavioural relations, the result is therefore quite different. It is not irrelevant for the forecast of future productions whether income is logically defined as the result of an activity over time (i.e. as a function of continuous or discontinuous time), or as an emission.

Let us say it again. If a functional relation can be established between past experiences, expectations and decisions, this can only represent a relation referring to an hypothetical income whose result can, thus, be either confirmed or disproved once production eventually takes place. It is true that expected demand and virtual supply adjust to each other, but this adjustment can only determine a *virtual* or *hypothetical* income. Moreover, this determination is possible only on the basis of the previous *logical* (as contrasted with terminological)[22] definition or determination of real income. The works of Shackle, Knight and many other economists on this subject still warrant further investigation, provided it is agreed that they must rest on a theory which allows for this logical definition.

Now, in contrast with the theory of prices, the evaluation of future, hypothetical incomes can by no means be identified with a process of adjustment between real supply and real demand, since these two forces can only exist in relation to a realised income. In fact, supply and demand are nothing other than two identical expressions of income in terms of money. Their existence is the existence of two (monetary) expenditures, the payment of wages and the final purchase of the product, which are defined by the actual creation–destruction of income.

What the supporters of neo-Walrasian analysis do not see is that income is the result of an emission. The product is created as a sum of money, and this creation has the instantaneous effect of quantising the whole period of time corresponding to the process of production, i.e. the whole of real time. Thus, income defines the identity of total supply and total demand at every instant of real time. The ex-ante distinction between these two forces if therefore limited to virtual time, which is simply another way of saying that in real time no real forces (such as supply and demand or saving and investment) are available for the functional determination of income.

As far as income analysis is concerned, the neo-Walrasian attempt to avoid static analysis is therefore bound to fail since:

> Science can free itself from the static only if it stops looking for the dynamic. In reality economic magnitudes *are* time. Now, an analysis which allows the definition of these magnitudes not in time but as having temporal nature, is neither static nor dynamic: it is a *quantum analysis*.[23]

Rejection of the functional determination of income (either by static or dynamic analysis) leads us to Keynes's theory of effective demand.

The concept of effective demand and time. In *The General Theory*, Keynes argues that:

> The reader will readily appreciate that the problem here under discussion is a matter of the most fundamental theoretical significance and of overwhelming practical importance. For the economic principle on which the practical advice of economists has been almost invariably based, has assumed, in effect, that, *cet. par.,* a decrease in spending will tend to lower the rate of interest and an increase in investment to raise it. But if what these two quantities determine is, not the rate of interest, but the aggregate volume of employment, then our outlook on the mechanism of the economic system will be profoundly changed. A decreased readiness to spend will be looked on in quite a different light if, instead of being regarded as a factor which will, *cet. par.,* increase investment, it is seen as a factor which will, *cet. par.,* diminish employment.[24]

In accordance with his attempt to challenge classical theory, Keynes reverses the traditional order of causality and considers the level of income, as well as the identity of saving and investment which it defines, as a result and not as a cause. $I = S$ and its corresponding income are thus the dependent variables of the system, while the rate of interest is one of its determinant factors.

> Our independent variables are, in the first instance, the propensity to consume, the schedule of the marginal efficiency of capital and the rate of interest, though, as we have already seen, these are capable of further analysis.

> Our dependent variables are the volume of employment and the national income (or national dividend) measured in wage-units.[25]

Now, these three factors determine the amount of expenditures the community will undergo for the production of consumption and investment goods or, respectively, the amount the community will spend for their final purchase. This amount, which defines virtual demand and can symbolically be represented by $(C + I)$, is what is usually called effective demand. It then follows that virtual income, Y, is finally determined by the level of effective demand.

> The amount of labour (N) which the entrepreneurs decide to employ depends on the sum (D) of *two* quantities, namely D_1, the amount which the community is expected to spend on consumption, and D_2, the amount which it is expected to devote to new investment. D is what we have called above the *effective demand.*[26]

Effective demand determines, therefore, the total amount entrepreneurs decide to spend, and actually spend, for current production. 'The *effective demand* is simply the aggregate income (or proceeds) which the entrepreneurs expect to receive . . . from the amount of current employment which they decide to give.'[27] According to Keynes, this amount depends on three fundamental psychological factors (the psychological propensity to consume, the psychological attitude to liquidity, and the psychological expectation of future yield from capital assets) as well as on the level of wage units and the quantity of money. We shall leave aside any specific analysis of these factors, and retain only their global influence on effective demand.

As Keynes noted:

> Expenditure is determined partly by yesterday's income, partly by today's, partly by expectations of tomorrow's and by many other things too. What primarily matters is the expectation of expenditure formed by the entrepreneur beforehand and secondarily by the gradual revision of this expectation in the light of experience.[28]

Thus, entrepreneurs' decisions are based on their expectations of what will be consumed and what will be invested. According to their expectations, entrepreneurs determine the level of income by the effective production of consumption and investment goods.

According to this first definition of effective demand, income is determined by the adjustment between production and expectations. That this determination concerns *virtual* income is obvious. Before production takes place in real time, entrepreneurs adjust income (Y^*) to an effective demand which is merely virtual, i.e. to a demand which does not exist in real time. The important point here is that income only exists once the decisions are positively realised.

Another definition of the concept of effective demand is, however, possible. According to this definition, which has been proposed by Keynes himself, effective demand corresponds to the final purchase of consumption and investment goods, $C + I$. 'We shall, indeed, designate the two constituents of effective demand as effective investment demand and effective consumption demand.'[29] The definition of income as $C + I$, i.e. as the final sum of investment and consumption expenditures, explains the particular relation which exists between income and effective demand. In fact, once production has taken place, the link between income and effective demand becomes an identity. That is what Keynes's fundamental relations are all about. $Y \equiv C + I$ is the definition of income as the sum of 'effective consumption demand and effective investment demand'. Consequently, income is defined by effective demand, $C + I$, whose amount is correspondingly defined by income. $Y \equiv C + I$ does not mean anything other than Y is $C + I$, and $C + I$ is Y.

This analysis of effective demand is obviously concerned with ex post concepts. C and I are the final demands for consumption and investment goods which do effectively take place, and not their mere expectations. It is true that, before production, decisions are taken on the basis of an effective demand which is only a potential or expected entity. Once production takes place, however, effective demand becomes truly effective, and its value can no longer be distinguished from that of income. That this is what Keynes really meant by effective demand can be definitively established by the following quotation in which he emphasises the originality of his analysis. 'For other economists, I find, lay the whole emphasis, and find the whole explanation in the *differences* between effective demand and income; and they are so convinced that this is the right course that they do not notice that in my treatment this is *not* so.'[30]

Effective demand and the identity of supply and demand. Having defined effective demand as the total demand for consumption and investment goods, we now have to relate it to total supply. As we know, Keynes's definition of income implies the identity of Y and $C' + I'$, where C' and I' represent the total costs of producing consumption and investment goods respectively. $C' + I'$ is therefore the supply side of the relation which Keynes establishes between the production of income and its final expenditure. Now, this relation is an identity: $Y \equiv C' + I'$. It then follows that

$$Y \equiv C' + I' \equiv C + I,$$

since both total supply, $C' + I'$, and total demand, $C + I$, are the definition of income. Thus, being two faces of the same reality, total supply and total demand are necessarily always equal. This also means that effective demand is identically defined either by the total creation of income or by its final expenditure. Moreover, these two concepts apply to the same period of time. Finally, total supply and total demand are ex-post concepts whose necessary equality occupies every instant in real time. It is thus established that, according to Keynes, all the significant concepts (from saving and investment to total supply and total or effective demand) are ex-post. No room is then left for any real difference between S and I or between total supply and total demand, since ex-post it is always true that

$$I \equiv S \quad \text{and} \quad \text{total supply} \equiv \text{total demand}.$$

Finally, there are two main interpretations of the concept of effective demand. According to the first interpretation, effective demand is the firms' expected demand and is, therefore, a virtual magnitude. Ex-ante, this virtual demand $(C + I)^*$ is adjusted to virtual income, Y^*. It is on the basis of this adjustment that decisions are determined. Thus, entrepreneurs' decisions are virtual, or ex-ante, variables. '*Ex-ante* decisions in their influence on effective demand relate solely to entrepreneurs' decisions.'[31] Ex-ante, firms choose to produce the goods and services which are more likely to maximise their profits. Figure 4.3 represents by spheres of different sizes the possibilities open to firms. Each of these spheres represents a possible production. The adjustment which occurs at this

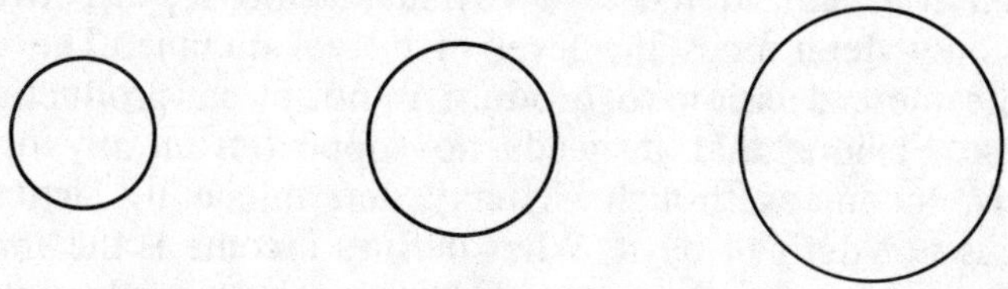

Fig. 4.3

level is not between the spheres but between them and Y^*. Firms aim to produce only goods which will be demanded, and it is on this basis that they choose between the different virtual productions. It is there that virtual demand intervenes. The choice open to firms is determined by the magnitude of virtual demand. The income that will be produced is the one which, given the magnitude of virtual demand, maximises profit. The sphere chosen by firms is therefore the one that corresponds to the greatest production compatible with a given virtual demand and with a desired profit. This adjustment between virtual production and virtual demand is itself virtual since 'in each period income is adjusted to virtual demand, a quantity which, contrary to realized demand, does not exist in real time'.[32]

Now, as soon as firms' decisions are realised, production is defined by the identity of supply (Y) and demand ($C + I$), as shown in Figure 4.4. As realised magnitudes, supply and

Fig. 4.4

demand are necessarily identical since they are the twin aspects of the same emission. Thus, the positive quantum deposit of W is identical to the physical quantum deposit of F, and their unity defines national income. The positive quantum deposit is the realised effective demand. It is this demand that defines income in real time, and that corresponds to the second possible interpretation of the concept of effective demand.

When it is considered as a virtual magnitude, effective demand only determines the level of virtual income. The claim that the mere decision to produce is not a real production at all is so obvious that it needs no support from any further analysis. Income, although virtually determined by virtual demand, is not defined by it. What defines income is the amount of wages firms effectively pay to the workers producing consumption and investment goods: income is an ex-post concept.[33] Thus, income cannot be defined as the result of an ex-ante adjustment between supply and demand since this adjustment is as virtual as the variables adjusted. Once again, the fundamental reason for this logical impossibility is the non-existence of virtual forces in real time. Thus, since no real force is available ex-ante, every income is independently determined from period to period.

Expectations and memory will of course have an influence on decisions and therefore on realised quantities, but this influence can never be confused with a real market force 'for the individual cannot now, at the moment of making his decision, have any contact with its actual and objective consequences, which do not yet exist'.[34] Decisions in themselves, though necessary, are not sufficient for the objective existence of supply and demand. Thus, virtual forces such as expectations can be brought into real time once they have been realised. This evident banality has, however, been too often underestimated or misunderstood in economics. Yet, its validity is certain, as Shackle demonstrates.

> The individual can create situations and events in imagination. If he is content to leave these unrelated to the world of external experience, to the way the world of nature and of human nature works, and to the specific character of the moment-in-being, they are mere fantasies or day-dreams, and no question can legitimately be asked as to the possibility of whatever is thus imagined ever becoming actual. Such a question would be entirely irrelevant to the nature of these mental acts. But he may instead set conscious limits to the scope of these acts of imagination, by constraining them into some supposed congruity or consistency with the permanent and inherent nature of things and with the specific character of the moment-in-being within which his act of imagination takes place. In that case his imaginary situation or chain of situations will seem to him to be possible consequences of acts which are open to him, and these imagined consequences can then be attached to particular calendar debates. They can then be called *expectations*.[35]

These virtual forces become real only when decisions are realised, and once they are realised, that is once a production has taken place, no difference can be found between total supply and total demand. Before production, ex-ante, no real forces exist which could allow a quantitative distinction between demand and supply, and after, ex-post, the necessary equality of supply and demand is logically opposed to their adjustment. As St. Augustine points out:

This indeed I know, that we generally think before on our future actions, and that that forethinking is present, but the action whereof we forethink is not yet, because it is to come. Which, when we have set upon, and have begun to do what we were forethinking, then shall that action be; because then it is no longer future but present.[36]

The determination of the reciprocal importance of ex-ante and ex-post analysis is too complex to be dealt with in a few sentences. For the purposes of our study, however, it is enough to point out the deep divergence existing between the logical theory of income determination and the empirical study of expected behaviour. What we hope to have established here is that Keynes's identities are concerned with the logical definition of income and not with the uncertain pre-vision of the future. Previous to any evaluation about the future, income must be defined, and according to Keynes this determination is carried out in real time by the (ex-post) identity of total supply and total demand (and, correspondingly, by the identity of saving and investment). The logical priority of this determination is indisputable and should be enough to prove the importance of Keynes's ex-post analysis. Hicks, therefore, is missing the point when he writes that:

Ex-post calculations of capital accumulation have their place in economic and statistical *history*; they are a useful measuring-rod for economic progress; but they are of no use to theoretical economists, who are trying to find out how the economic system works, because they have no significance for conduct. The income *ex-post* of any particular week cannot be calculated until the end of the week, and then it involves a comparison between present values and values which belong wholly to the past. On the general principle of 'bygones are bygones', it can have no relevance to present decisions.[37]

In reality, ex-post calculations are of the foremost theoretical importance because they lead to the definition of income. How could it be possible to determine how the economic system works if income could not even be defined? Now, having established his fundamental identities, Keynes introduces the concept of effective demand to explain the level of present income. Here also the analysis is fully ex-post. Effective demand is a demand which effectively takes place, and not a mere hypothetical magnitude. It corresponds to the production effectively undertaken, and not simply to its desired level. In other words, expected demand becomes effective once decisions are transformed into real activity. Before that, production is only hypothetical, as are demand and its corresponding income. Demand, therefore, is the twin definition of income only when it becomes effective, ex-post. Hicks's analysis is mistaken precisely because he does not fully understand the novelty present in the concept of effective demand.

Keynes's alternative way of looking at income is rich in theoretical consequences. One of them refers to the causal relation between the determinates and the determinants, between income, saving and investment on one side, and the rate of interest, the propensity to consume and the schedule of the marginal efficiency of capital on the other. The identity of saving and investment introduces a sharp distinction between the causality implied in the traditional analysis of income and the one implicit in Keynes's theory.

3. One-way causality versus simultaneous causality

Simultaneous causality. Let us start with the general equilibrium analysis. Originating from the works of Walras, the general equilibrium approach is undoubtedly the underlying theoretical framework of most contemporary analysis. Its main idea can be summarised as an attempt to understand economics by reducing it to a system of simultaneous equations. This analysis, which results from a close intimacy with mathematics, is based upon the assumption that, in economics, everything depends upon everything else.

> Another feature which makes analysis difficult is that, typically, everything in the economy depends upon everything else and it is not possible to determine any quantity without doing most of the work needed to determine every quantity. In other words, a model of the economic system does not normally *decompose*. It is not usually allowed to the analyst to divide the primitive postulates into two classes, *A* and *B*; such

that certain variables can be determined from postulates included in class *A* alone without regard to, or without even a knowledge of, the postulates of class *B*.[38]

Thus according to general equilibrium analysis, economic variables are interrelated in such a way that their determination can only be simultaneous.

Within this theory, therefore, it seems possible to conclude that simultaneous or contemporaneous causality is the characteristic form of causal relations in economics. As Hicks points out, a contemporaneous causality is one in which both cause and effect relate to the same time period.[39] In the case of general equilibrium analysis, the causality appears at once as contemporaneous, since the simultaneous equations allow for a simultaneous solution (if any). Finally 'an interdependent market system is a very complicated construction in which all the primitive specifications will normally play a part in influencing any particular magnitude, so that it usually makes no sense to ask for the cause of a particular magnitude while expecting a brief answer'.[40] According to this assumption, the neoclassical attempt to reinterpret Keynes's analysis can also be read as an attempt to express his identities in terms of contemporaneous causality.

At the time of the appearance of *The General Theory*, general equilibrium analysis was still the dominant stream of economics. It is therefore hardly surprising that many leading economists attempted to integrate Keynes's approach into what they considered the more general framework of general equilibrium analysis. Encouraged by what they thought to be Keynes's approval of Hicks's income–expenditure model of *IS* and *LM* schedules, they converted Keynes's theory of income determination into a dynamic process of adjustment between demand and supply. 'Thus the Keynesian saving–investment equation can be looked upon as the equilibrium solution of a dynamical system.'[41] Keynes's analysis, which is said to be the result of the adjustment of a system of simultaneous equations, thus appears to be no exception to contemporaneous causality.

Having proved that virtual forces can only determine virtual income since they do not exist in real time, we must reject as a mere intellectual exercise this attempt, which is sometimes attributed to Keynes himself, to reduce Keynes to Marshall.[42] What can we say, then, about the contemporaneous causality said to be implicit in Keynes's theory? Does the rejection of general equilibrium analysis imply the rejection of simultaneous causality, or does it allow us to retain it as 'the characteristic form of the causal relation in modern economics'?[43]

In fact, as can be seen in Desai's *Applied Econometrics*,[44] there is a large literature in econometrics challenging the notion of simultaneous causality, the ultimate reason being that the system of simultaneous equations is logically opposed to a causal explanation of economics. This can be shown through a rigorous analysis of the concept of contemporaneous causality, which we had provisionally taken for granted. The first thing to notice is that this concept implies the previous definition of simultaneity. However, simultaneity cannot be defined without referring to a co-ordinative system: the conceptual definition of simultaneity can only be relative. As Reichenbach points out:

> To determine the simultaneity of distant events we need to know a velocity, and to measure a velocity we require knowledge of the simultaneity of distant events. The occurrence of this circularity proves that simultaneity is not a matter of knowledge, but of a co-ordinative definition, since the logical circle shows that a knowledge of simultaneity is impossible in principle.[45]

Once the concept of simultaneity has been determined (for example by reference to speed of light) we still have to relate it to causality. Now, causality appears to be the necessary condition of existence of time in physics: '. . . in the absence of the causality assumed in the theory in the form of causal (signal) connectibility, it is altogether unclear how the system of relations between events would possess the kind of *structure* that we call the "time" of physics'.[46] In this context, causality is the most adequate expression of the conceptual definition of simultaneity. In fact, the simultaneity of two events implies the indeterminacy of their time order, so that 'the concept *simultaneous* is to be reduced to the concept *indeterminate as to time order*'.[47] In other words, '. . . two simultaneous events are so situated that a causal chain cannot travel from one to the other in either direction'.[48] Finally simultaneity and causality are reciprocally exclusive since 'the relativity of simultaneity . . . rests solely on the existence of a finite limiting velocity for causal propagation'.[49] The absence of causality being the conceptual definition of simultaneity, it is therefore useless to look for the existence of contemporaneous causality. Thus, the contemporaneous causality attributed to spatially separated events is plainly a contradiction so long as time order is defined in terms of causality (the causal relation is, in fact, the criterion of 'the topological co-ordinative definition of time order').[50]

Applied to economics, this analysis shows that in a general equilibrium system the simultaneous (reciprocal) determination of the variables precludes the existence of any causal relation between them. By assuming a general equilibrium type of analysis we implicitly abandon any causal explanation in economics, whose laws (according to the latter definition) would become totally arbitrary. This conclusion is unavoidable *as long as economic events are identified with physical processes of change*. In physics, the causal relation between spatially distinct events is conceivable only within the limit of the speed of light. There can *therefore be no simultaneous causality* which would imply a velocity of change greater than the speed of light. On this basis, Reichenbach's argument can be applied and the concept of simultaneous causality becomes theoretically inconsistent.

One-way causality. Despite the formal elegance of general equilibrium analysis, it has to be recognised that the simultaneous solutions of the equations do not really allow for an analysis in terms of causality. As Kregel says: '. . . changes in any one variable affect all the others in the system. In such a system it is very difficult to talk about direct causality, for everything determines everything else, determination cannot be discussed outside the scope of the entire system'.[51] This feeling of unease is shared by some outstanding exponents of the general equilibrium system.

> In any event, it should be apparent that an income–expenditure version of Keynes' analysis does not entirely miss the point of *The General Theory*. Further, a neo-Walrasian reconstruction is not a completely inappropriate framework for discussing the systematic interactions in a Keynesian model. What is somewhat unsettling, however, is that the neo-Walrasian bias towards a symmetric treatment of all markets may obscure the economics of their linkages if the symmetry is pursued at the expense of economic analysis.[52]

Confronted with this problem, the post-Keynesians try to

overcome it by introducing one-way causality. Accordingly, they separate their analysis into three distinct stages. In the first, the rate of interest is determined by relating the need for investment funds to the supply of these funds. The second step consists of determining the cost of production of all goods in terms of wage units, given the technique of production. Finally, the rate of output is determined, as well as the capital-output ratio in value terms. The share of profit results from the introduction of demand conditions, taking into account the given technique of production and the given rate of interest. Although totally opposed to the predominance of general equilibrium analysis,[53] post-Keynesians do not completely reject the possibility of simultaneous relations between variables. What they stress is the need to determine some of the variables by means of a one-way causality.

> As against the attitude—so common to marginal economics theorists—that 'everything depends on everything else', Keynes (as Ricardo) takes the opposite attitude that it is one of the tasks of the economic theorist himself also to specify which variables are sufficiently interdependent as to be best represented by simultaneous relations, and which variables exhibit such an overwhelming dependence in one direction (and such a small dependence in the opposite direction) as to be best represented by one-way-direction relations.[54]

An attempt has recently been made by Hicks to widen the concept of contemporaneous causality to include one-way relations. In his latest book on causality in economics, Hicks does in fact claim that

> . . . there are many such relations which are contemporaneous but not reciprocal . . . It is by no means necessary that a theoretical relation, between contemporaneous events (that is to say, between possible contemporaneous events) should be reciprocal; in most of our economic models we have some relations which are reciprocal, but some which are not. We do indeed have a name for elements which can only enter into what, from the point of view of the theory, are non-reciprocal relations; we call them *exogenous*. From the point of view of the theory, an exogenous element (or the taking of some particular value by an exogenous element) cannot be an effect. It can only be a cause.[55]

By reducing Keynes's theory to what he calls the formal theory (i.e. the multiplier and the *IS–LM* model), Hicks maintains the logical priority of contemporaneous causality in modern economics. This, however, does not stop him underlying the importance that sequential causality assumes in economics when we are concerned with decisions.

> But it is not enough, in economic analysis, to refer to the decision; we are also concerned with the reasons for the decision, the causes of the decision. Thus even the simplest case of sequential causation in economics has two steps in it: a prior step, from the objective cause to the decisions that are based on it, or influenced by it, and a posterior step, from the decisions to their (objective) effects.[56]

Hicks's position (which has been interpreted by Davidson as a confirmation of his thesis that 'Sir John is "getting Keynesian" ') is in reality much more traditional than it appears at first sight. Keynes's fundamental theory of income determination is once again reduced to a Marshallian adjustment capable of being expressed by a system of simultaneous equations. The introduction of exogenously determined variables does not imply any fundamental change. The system remains basically a general equilibrium system, even if its heuristic importance is reduced in proportion to the number of exogenous variables.

> It must indeed be conceded that the abundance of exogenous elements in economics is no cause for congratulation; it is an indication of the modesty of the scientific status, which is all that economics can hope to achieve. It is because the range of phenomena with which economics deals is so narrow that economists are so continually butting their heads against its boundaries. If there were such a thing as an inclusive human science—a Sociology in Herbert Spencer's sense—it might not so often be butting against its boundaries; there might be few things which were relevant to it and yet were exogenous to it. But there are so many things which are relevant to economics and which yet are exogenous to it.[57]

Now, Hicks's analysis is not acceptable, since it is based on the false assumption of contemporaneous causality between physical events. On the other hand, Keynes's approach to macroeconomics cannot be reduced to Hicks's formal theory. The contributions of the *Treatise* and *The General Theory* are of a far greater importance than the *IS–LM* schedule suggests, and cannot be understood by reducing economic determination to a set of simultaneous, spatially separated events. It is true that Keynes' definition of income as an identity is, obviously, inconsistent with the assumption of sequential causality, and from a superficial analysis it would seem that Hicks was right in claiming that his concept of contemporaneous causality was supported by Keynes's theory.

Nevertheless, a decisive distinction can easily be found between Keynes's and Hicks's types of simultaneous causality. In Hicks's neoclassical interpretation of Keynes's work, all the variables are determined by the simultaneous solution of a system of equations. In other words, the relation between the variables is such that their determination corresponds to their simultaneous equilibrium. The equations correspond to functional relations and are, therefore, satisfied only by some particular value of the variables. In Keynes's analysis, on the other hand, the determination of income through the payment of wages is represented by a single identity, $Y \equiv C' + I'$, which is valid for every value of C' and I'. Income is not determined through a process involving the simultaneous solution of a system of equations as in Hicks's analysis, but through an instantaneous expenditure of money. The economic example of Hicks's contemporaneous causality is, thus, reduced to a system composed only of an identity.

Our analysis is confirmed here by the logical distinction, so clearly explained by Reichenbach, between the simultaneity of events taking place at the same place and the simultaneity of spatially separated events. In fact, the simultaneity at the same place defines an identity: it 'is strictly speaking not a simultaneity of time points, but an *identity*'.[58] This is obviously the case with production and expenditure. These two events take place simultaneously at the same place, so that space and time are identical for both. The two events can thus no longer be distinguished: production *is* the payment of wages and their identity defines one and the same object: national income.

It is true, as in the case of Hicks's analysis, that there is no causal relation between production and expenditure, but here such a causality is not even postulated. The identity of expenditure and production defines a unique event called an emission, and it would therefore be inconsistent to look for a causal relation between a given event and itself. Now, unlike general equilibrium theory, quantum analysis does not consider production as a physical event. As an instantaneous process, the determination of income cannot logically be distinguished from production. The determination of income is given by the payment of wages, and income is the result of this unique process. Thus, the determination of income is totally explained by the identity of Y and $C' + I'$, and this is because income is the result of an emission and not of a physical transformation.

Our conclusion is therefore completely opposed to the traditional, neoclassical interpretation of Keynes's analysis. We claim that Keynes was perfectly correct in sustaining the identity of total supply and total demand '*ex ante* and *ex post* and *ex* anything else'.[59]

In the first part of this chapter we have been dealing with the concepts of ex-ante and ex-post, emphasising the role they were said to play in the determination of national income. It is within this theoretical framework that we have rejected them as an artificial device used to introduce the general equilibrium system into Keynes's analysis. This rejection is, however, not opposed to a new interpretation of the distinction first proposed by Myrdal. In the second part of this chapter we shall prove that saving and investment can be allowed to vary independently of one another *within a given income*. The adjustment of saving and investment takes place ex-ante as in traditional theory, but, the traditional definition notwithstanding, ex-ante is a category of real time and not a category related to virtual or unobserved magnitudes.

PART II: SAVING AND INVESTMENT IN QUANTUM TIME AND IN CONTINUOUS TIME

1. A reminder on the relations between quantum and chronological time

One of the results of the analysis developed in Chapter 3 is the definition of quantum time. According to this definition, a quantum of time is the slice of real time corresponding to the indivisible and finite period chosen as the period of reference. Quantum time is therefore characterised by its indivisibility. Moreover, the time quantum is given instantaneously. For any given period of reference the quantum corresponding to that finite interval is the instantaneous result of an emission and not the product of a functional relation between continuous time and its related variable. Thus, quantum time is defined by the instantaneous emission of variables related to a quantum of real time. The emission of income is an operation which takes place at a given point in time, and which is nevertheless related to the time covered by the process of production. This time-period is therefore a positive and finite part of real time instantaneously given as a whole.

Let us take quantum time in its relation with chronological (continuous) time. Firstly, it is evident that quantum time is not another or additional category of time. Thus, quantum and chronological time are both made up of real time. Now, whereas chronological time is indefinitely divisible, quantum time is an indivisible and yet finite part of real time. If we take the day as period unit, we can see that, although both quantum and continuous analyses refer to the same real time represented by the day, in chronological terms the day is a continuous succession of hours, minutes, seconds, and so on, while in quantum terms the day is an indivisible and finite part of time. Chronological and quantum time are, therefore, not two different kinds of real time but rather two different states of the same real time.

As we already know, quantum time only becomes a meaningful concept once the existence of emissions has been admitted. Now, in economics, it can be effectively proved that production is an emission. Thus, the economic definition of production (which corresponds to its economic determination and evaluation) is an instantaneous event related to a quantum of time. If the day is represented by a segment of a given length,

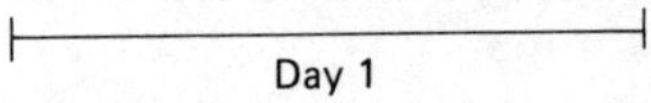

production of day 1 is an instantaneous event, the payment of wages, whose time dimension is represented by this same segment. At the very moment that wages are paid their time dimension is day 1, taken as indivisible. Let us suppose that the payment of wages takes place at the end of the day. We can then represent production as the instantaneous relation between this point in time and the whole of day 1, as in Figure 4.5. It is still true, of course, that day 1 is a period of time equal to a certain amount of hours, minutes, seconds, and so on. Thus, once production has been emitted, it can obviously be divided by 24, 1440, 86400 or any other positive number. The subsequent division of a given production must

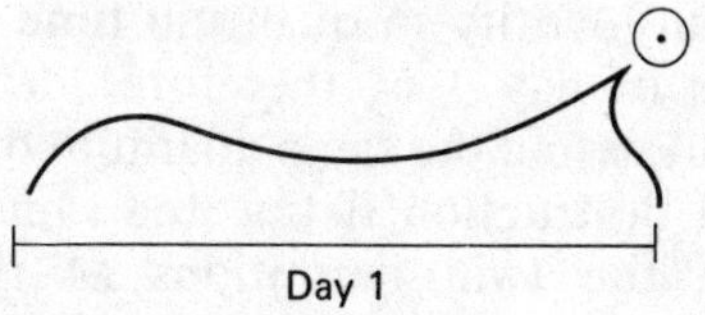

Fig. 4.5

not be mistaken, however, for a process of income determination. If no emission takes place, income, as well as its subdivision, remains undetermined. Correspondingly, once an emission has taken place, income is fully determined and can be divided.

According to the theory, this logical priority of quantum analysis is reaffirmed by the operation of income destruction. The final expenditure of income is, in fact, an emission, and therefore as such it also defines a finite and indivisible period of time. Moreover, creation and destruction being related to the same income, this second emission defines the same quantum of time defined by the first emission. In our example, the final expenditure of income is instantaneously referred to day 1. This relation is verified as soon as the second emission takes place, independently of any chronological subdivision of day 1. In fact, income can be finally spent at any moment in time. The important point is that when it is spent it is retroactively related to day 1 (see Figure 4.6).

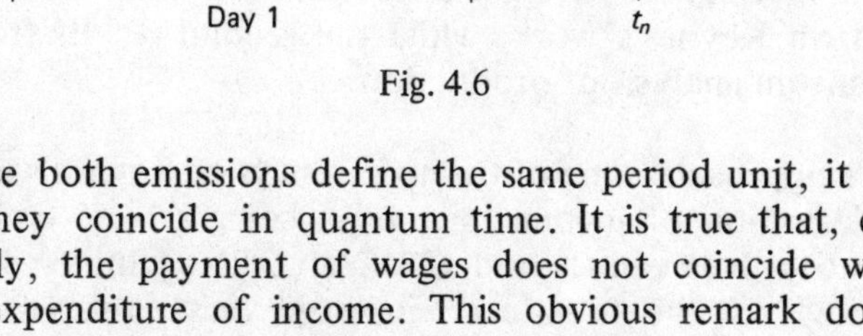

Fig. 4.6

Since both emissions define the same period unit, it follows that they coincide in quantum time. It is true that, chronologically, the payment of wages does not coincide with the final expenditure of income. This obvious remark does not, however, imply their distinction in quantum time, since every emission defines an identity in quantum time. The destruction of the production of day 1 is, therefore, identical to its creation, for they both define the same quantum of time. Reciprocally, creation and destruction define the same 'lump' of time because they are the twin definitions of the same object, income.

This identity in the time dimension of instantaneous events which define the same quantum of time has a striking consequence, namely that the *result of one event can modify the result of the other*. Logically, this modification can only influence the reciprocal importance of the components of each event, and not the magnitude of the event itself. For example, as we already know, the final expenditure of a given income can modify its initial distribution between wages and profits. The total amount of income created and destroyed, however, remains the same; only its subdivision between wage goods and profit goods can vary. Given the time quantum, the variation caused by the second emission has an instantaneous influence on the first emission, each emission thus remaining always identical to the other.

This characteristic of quantum analysis is obviously not verified in continuous time, where what happens at t_n does not modify what happend at t_0. Two successive events never coincide in chronological time. Thus, the instantaneous feedback of one event to another is only possible with respect to those events whose definition is an emission. As we shall see in the following sections of this chapter, the analysis of saving and investment offers another example of instantaneous feedback.

2. Saving and investment: their identity

In this section we shall deal with two ways of defining the quantum identity of saving and investment. The first analysis is based on Keynes's work, while the second results from the new quantum analysis of production.

Keynes's approach. One of the main results of Keynes's analysis is the definition of income. Far from being a mere tautology, the identity between Y and $C' + I'$ tells us that income is determined by the total cost, in wage units, related to the production of consumption and investment goods. $Y \equiv C' + I'$

thus refers to the creation of income, and corresponds to total supply. Now, Keynes also defines income as the sum of the final expenditure on consumption and investment goods: $Y \equiv C + I$. This second definition of income corresponds to its final destruction. This second aspect of national income is therefore called total demand. Because they refer to the same object, Y, these two definitions are necessarily identical. From

$$C' + I' \equiv C + I$$

it then follows that

$$\text{total supply} \equiv \text{total demand.}$$

At this point, it should be remembered that Keynes defines saving as 'that part of the income of the period which has not passed into consumption'.[60] The definition of saving is therefore related to the definition of income as total demand. In other words, in the relation $Y = C + I$ the term investment can always be replaced by the term saving, since they are both defined in the same way: '. . . these two amounts are necessarily equal, since each of them is equal to the excess of income over consumption'.[61] Obviously, this terminological identity between S and I is a mere tautology which does not explain the real significance of the identity so strongly supported by Keynes. In fact, the identity $I \equiv S$ within total demand simply means that the final purchase of investment goods is necessarily equal to the final expenditure on the financial market, since both I and S are the complement of C in the measure of income. Thus, total demand can be expressed either by $C + I$ or by $C + S$. This can be represented diagrammatically, as in Figure 4.7.

The meaning of the identity between saving and investment cannot be understood until total demand is related to total supply. As soon as $C + S$ is related to $C' + I'$ it becomes clear that the non-tautological identity of saving and investment refers to the relation between S and I', where I' represents the cost in wages of producing investment goods. The investment which has to be related to saving is I' and not I. The identity is then established between an element of total supply and an element of total demand. It is only because these two definitions of income are identical that I' and S can be proved to be also necessarily equal.

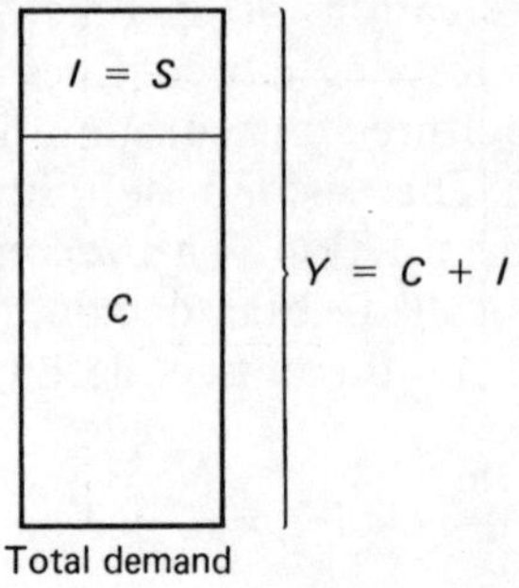

Fig. 4.7

Now, this formal proof requires the intervention of quantum analysis. Not until it has been established that income creation and income destruction are two identical emissions of opposite sign does the identity of I' and S become a logical necessity. For the time being, however, let us accept Keynes's statement that 'in the aggregate the excess of income over consumption, which we call saving, cannot differ from the addition to capital equipment which we call investment'.[62] It then follows that the income created by the production of investment goods, I', is necessarily always equal to the income finally saved. Correspondingly, and given that S is tautologically equal to I, I' is also identical to I: the final expenditure for the purchase of investment goods always corresponds to the production of these same goods. Moreover, given the complementarity of C' and I' in the definition of total supply and that of C and I in the definition of total demand, from $I' \equiv I$ it also follows that $C' \equiv C$. Thus, Keynes's conclusion can only be the following: every production creates the income necessary and sufficient for its final purchase.

This conclusion, which is very similar to Say's law, has not surprisingly been refused by the majority of economists. Before the introduction of quantum analysis it was very difficult to accept the identities $I' \equiv I$ and $C' \equiv C$. Within a continuous perception of time it is impossible to understand the necessary equality of I' and I unless we accept that once I' has been determined I must necessarily adjust to it: that is, unless we accept that the final purchase of investment (consumption) goods is completely predetermined by the production of these

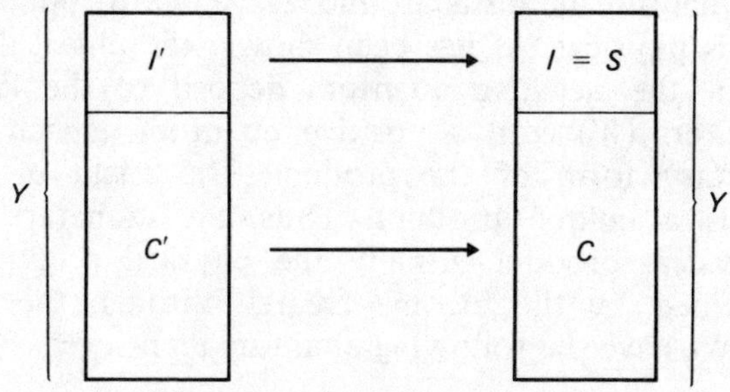

Fig. 4.8

goods. Graphically, this can be represented as in Figure 4.8, where the arrows symbolise a predetermined one-way causality between total supply and total demand. The reluctance to accept such a conclusion is perfectly justified. However, the predetermination becomes a necessary consequence of the analysis if we try to explain Keynes's identities without taking into account the concept of emission and the quantum analysis of time related to it. Before proving this last point let us introduce the new theory of saving and investment.

The new approach. Let us use Schmitt's terminology and call pure physical product (*PPP*) the physical result of production, and monetary physical product (*MPP*) the product in its monetary form. The pure physical product defines the product according to its initial destination in terms of consumption and investment goods. This does not mean that the product is evaluated purely in physical terms. On the contrary, its measure is necessarily monetary. Yet, the monetary expression of *PPP* corresponds to its physical characteristic: the subdivision of the product between consumption and investment goods is expressed monetarily but determined physically. In other words, the production of capital goods is an investment and the intervention of money does not change its nature as far as *PPP* is concerned. Thus, the pure physical product is the product as it is determined by the emission of wages defining the production of consumption and investment goods. According to quantum analysis, the product is the instantaneous result of an event called an emission. This first emission, measured in wage units, defines three quantum deposits. Two of these quantum deposits are monetary and of opposite sign, the third is physical. As has been shown, the physical product vanishes in the negative quantum deposit of the firms (F), while workers (W) earn a positive quantum deposit defining the monetary form of the product. The result of the first emission is a unique product. Thus, the monetary product is the physical product. Finally the physical product is perfectly defined by the income created through the payment of wages. We have the following quantum identities:

$$PPP \equiv Y \equiv C' + I'.$$

The payment of wages which corresponds to the production of consumption and investment goods is, thus, the instantaneous event defining the pure physical product. This first emission, which is analogous to Keynes's income creation, brings about the product in its physical and monetary form, and can also be called total supply. Thus, we have:

$$PPP \equiv Y \equiv C' + I' \equiv \text{total supply}.$$

The decision to call total supply the pure physical product is a matter of terminological convenience. Identity $PPP \equiv$ total supply is therefore purely tautological. Identity between PPP and $C' + I'$, however, is not at all tautological. On the contrary, it is based on the perfect correspondence which the first emission establishes instantaneously between the positive quantum deposit of W and the physical product lodged in the negative quantum deposit of F. Now, given the identity $PPP \equiv C' + I'$, we know that capital goods are defined by the wages paid out for their production: investment is equal to I'.

On the other hand, the *monetary physical product* represents the product in its final form, since it results from the process of its final purchase. The subdivision in consumption and investment goods is no longer physical. The intervention of money transforms PPP into MPP, which can either be consumed or saved. Now, saving and consumption are related to what we have called the second emission. As with any other expenditure, this latter is also an instantaneous event. The two monetary quantum deposits defined by this event are the exact counterpart of the quantum deposits created by the first emission. As a result, the physical product is released from its 'trap' and the monetary quantum deposit destroyed. This second emission is concerned with the final monetary demand of consumption and investment goods, so that, the final purchase being determined by $C + I$, we can write:

$$MPP \equiv C + S \equiv C + I.$$

Having called this second emission total demand,

$$MPP \equiv C + I \equiv \text{total demand},$$

we have now to relate it to total supply. The particular nature of this relation is immediately evident. $C' + I'$ and $C + I$ being definitions of the same income, total supply and total demand are necessarily equal. Moreover, since both the first and the second emissions are emissions which define the same quantum of time, they necessarily coincide in quantum time. *PPP* and *MPP* are therefore two equivalent ways of defining and measuring national income.

The identity between *MPP* and *PPP* is not tautological. It is because of the perfect equivalence between the correspondence of the quantum deposit to the physical product and the correspondence of the quantum deposit to the final expenditure of income that *MPP* and *PPP* are identical, and this equivalence can only be established through quantum analysis. The identity of supply and demand follows from the quantum identity of *PPP* and *MPP*. Bearing in mind that

$$C + I \equiv C + S,$$

it also follows that

$$C + S \equiv C' + I'.$$

Since they are both equivalent to national income, *PPP* and *MPP* are obviously equal. But what about the relation of investment (i.e. the production of capital goods as determined in *PPP*) and saving (the complement of C in *MPP*)? Does the identity of supply and demand imply the necessary equality of saving and investment? Let us note firstly that, unlike Keynes's identities, the necessary equality of *PPP* and *MPP* is established in quantum time. This means that the two emissions defining *PPP* and *MPP* define the same lump of time. Thus, for the whole period of time corresponding to this quantum the initial and final division of the product must necessarily coincide. From

$$PPP \equiv MPP$$

in quantum time, it follows, always in quantum time, that

$$C' \equiv C \text{ and } I' \equiv S \text{ (or } I\text{)}.$$

The answer to our previous question is, thus, positive: saving and investment are necessarily equal in quantum time. The non-tautological character of this identity should be evident by now. Saving and investment are not two different words applied to the same object, but two distinct concepts whose identity has to be logically proved. In fact, being 'that part of income which is not spent for the purchase of consumption goods', saving is a part of demand whereas investment, the production of capital goods, is a part of supply. Thus, saving is related to the monetary physical product (*MPP*) while investment is related to the pure physical product (*PPP*). Ultimately, their identity follows from the identity of *PPP* and *MPP* and not from the erroneous assumption that: 'For the system as a whole, saving and investment, as observable, are defined as the same thing: the difference between income and consumption *when appropriate allowances are made for capital revaluation in the reckoning of income*; or as the value of the increment of capital equipment.'[63]

The identity of *MPP* and *PPP* can be represented as in Figure 4.9, which indicates that, in quantum time, the physical

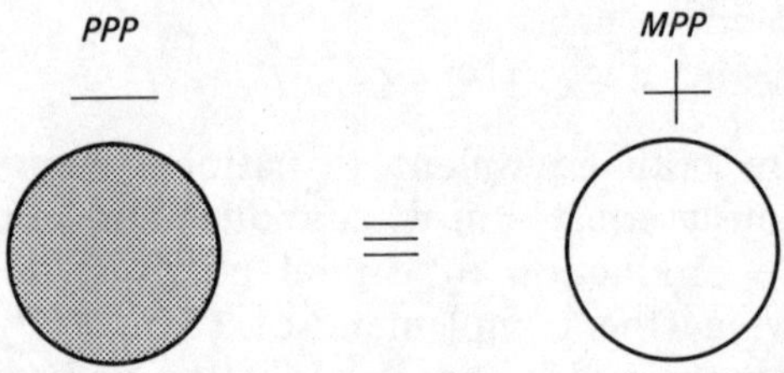

Fig. 4.9

product (as it results from the first emission) is necessarily equal to the final expenditure of its monetary substitute. From this, it is immediately obvious that supply can never be greater or less than its corresponding demand. As a consequence, saving and investment also are always equal. This quantum identity between physical and monetary products allows the final dismissal of the traditional concept of hoarding. Hoarding, conceived as a positive stock of money which is neither invested nor consumed, can only be nil. In fact, if hoarding were positive we would have an excess of demand over supply, which can be represented as in Figure 4.10.

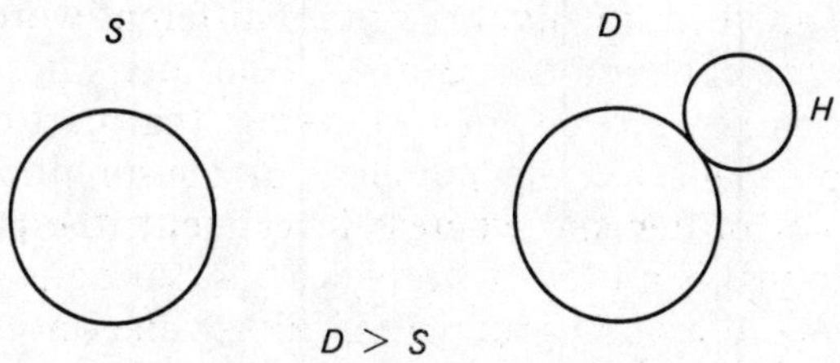

Fig. 4.10

Whether or not we regard hoarding as a part of saving, its existence would still imply a positive difference between *MPP* and *PPP*. Now, such a difference is impossible, since *MPP* and *PPP* are one and the same object. Quantum analysis teaches us that the monetary physical product is the pure physical product. Money defines the product, so that *PPP* is always identical to *MPP* whereas *H* is necessarily always equal to zero.

Hoarding, conceived as a positive difference between Supply and Demand, is the result of a dichotomous appraisal of the economic world, money being somehow, because of individuals' behaviour, different from the product. Once we know that money is defined by the product, we must stop looking for any difference between the product and money.[64]

Let us prove the identity of S and I' once again.

3. Saving and investment in quantum time

What we want to show in this section is how every conceivable difference between the pure physical product and the monetary physical product can be instantaneously cancelled in quantum time. Let us consider the two extreme cases where:

1. a positive saving is compared with a zero investment; and
2. a positive investment is related to a zero saving.

Were we able to establish that, despite any appearance to the contrary, saving and investment are always equal in both cases, then it would be only a matter of arithmetic to show that the same solution applies in every intermediary case.

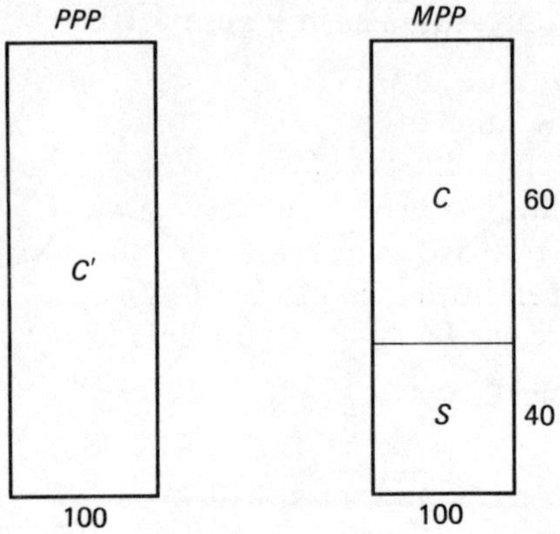

Fig. 4.11

In the first case, which is represented in Figure 4.11, we suppose that production consists of consumption goods only. *PPP* is then measured by *C′*, the amount of wages paid for the production of consumption goods. Let this amount be equal to 100 wage units. On the other hand, we suppose that consumers save part of their income, so that in the monetary physical product saving is equal to 40 wage units. *MPP* is, thus, composed of 60 units of *C* and 40 units of *S*. If we compare *PPP* with *MPP* we find that, far from being equal, saving and investment differ for the total amount of saving. If, nevertheless, saving and investment have to be identical, then a change must take place either in *PPP* or in *MPP*. Leaving aside any change in the consumers' behaviour, the only objective change compatible with the identity of saving and investment must be located on the side of *PPP*. To understand how such a change can intervene, let us start from the concept of saving.

As we know, saving is that part of income which is spent on the financial market. This means that saving is not finally spent by consumers. The final expenditure carried out by consumers is, obviously, the purchase of consumption goods. Now, if saving is not an expenditure which benefits the consumers, it must necessarily be an expenditure in favour of non-consumers, i.e. firms. Such an expenditure, however, does not take place independently of the payment of wages. Every expenditure in favour of *F* is, in fact, an expenditure which takes place on the factor market. That is, the quantum analysis of saving is similar to the quantum analysis of profit.

Both saving and profit represent a transfer of income in favour of firms, and in both cases this transfer represents an income which has already been spent since the emission of wages. Thus, the formation of a positive saving implies the inclusion of a positive expenditure on the commodity market, within the expenditure on the factor market. In the payment of wages is concealed a positive and final expenditure of income defining the final purchase in favour of *F* (see Figure 4.12).

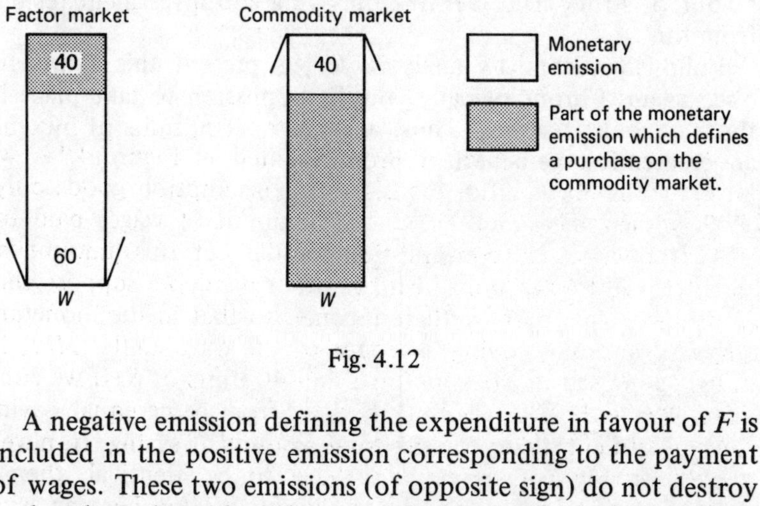

Fig. 4.12

A negative emission defining the expenditure in favour of *F* is included in the positive emission corresponding to the payment of wages. These two emissions (of opposite sign) do not destroy each other, since they do not coincide in chronological time. The payment of wages is prior to the determination of saving, in the same way that the creation of income precedes its destruction. Both emissions, however, define the same quantum of time, which means that in quantum time they necessarily coincide. The chronological distinction and the quantum coincidence of the two emissions defining *PPP* and *MPP* mean, therefore, that:

(a) the emission defining the final expenditure of income

is instantaneously related to the emission of wages; and that

(b) the intervention of the second emission does not modify the first emission but only its *result*.

In our example, the amount saved leaves unaltered the emission of wages (always equal to 100) but modifies its subdivision between consumption and investment goods. Being a positive purchase in favour of F, saving defines a positive investment of the same amount. In fact, the part of wages which is simultaneously a final expenditure on the commodity market defines the goods directly produced for F, i.e. the investment goods. As soon as a part of income is positively saved, it is logically necessary to reinterpret the payment of wages. The income saved is thus, retroactively, a final expenditure in favour of firms. The identity of saving and investment results from this.

Following Schmitt's analysis, let us present this argument once again. Chronologically, the first emission to take place is the payment of wages. Thus, at time t_0, 100 units of income are created for the benefit of producers.

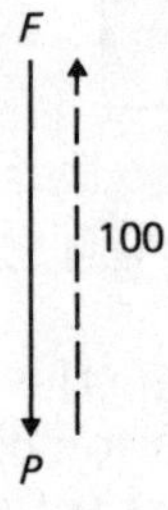

According to our initial assumption, the product consists of consumption goods only, so that 100 wage units are the measure of C. Now, at a subsequent time, t_1, consumers spend a fraction of their income (60) for the purchase of consumption goods and use the rest (40) for the purchase of assets on the financial market. This last purchase defines a saving of 40 units of income by consumers and simultaneously a final expenditure of the same amount in favour of firms. In fact, saving is not an unspent income. It is defined as that part of income which is not spent *by consumers*, and represents the final purchase of firms. Ultimately, the saving taking place at t_1 retroactively modifies the emission of wages taking place at t_0 because:

(a) the emission of saving defines the same quantum of time as the corresponding emission of wages; and because
(b) saving defines an expenditure which can only take place within the payment of wages.

This process can be represented as in Figure 4.13.

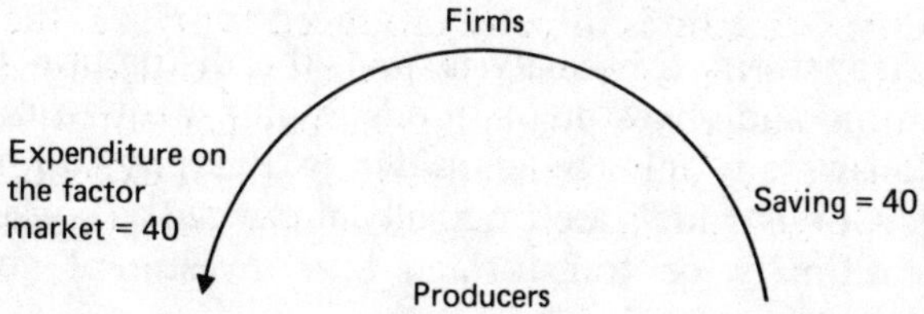

Fig. 4.13

Given the retroactivity of saving, the first emission must be reinterpreted. In the payment of wages for the production of consumption goods there is concealed a final expenditure on the commodity market in favour of firms: the product is partially transformed into investment goods. In other words, the consumption goods purchased by *F*, because of the very nature of this purchase, which takes place within the emission of wages, must be considered as investment goods. Once it has been reinterpreted, the first emission can be represented as in Figure 4.14. The total amount of wages paid to the workers remains unaltered. The real difference between the two representations of the first emission is due to the existence of a positive saving. The creation of income is 100 in both cases, but when savings are positive, 40 units of income are created in favour of firms. Thus, 40 units of the 100 paid as wages represent an income of *F* which is spent as soon as it is created. This expenditure is, by definition, a positive investment, so that finally saving always induces an investment of the same amount. 'Newly created income can be partially saved, in particular by the totality of consumers. Thus, saving defines the purchase of the product in favour of firms: investment.'[65]

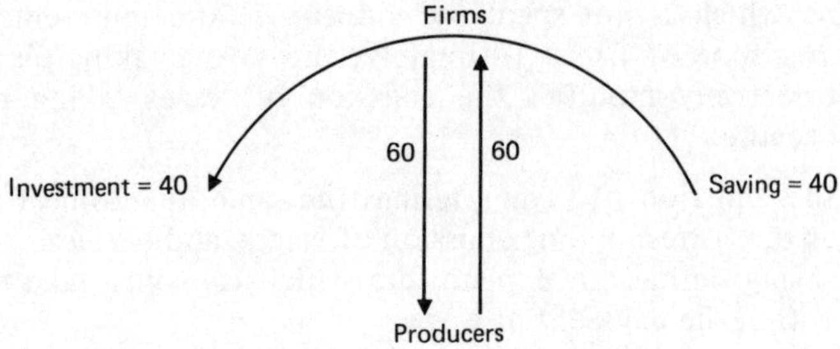

Fig. 4.14

It is clear from this analysis that the distinction between consumption and investment goods is not a question which can be answered only by considering the physical form of products. Goods which are originally produced as consumption goods can finally be transformed into investment goods. As Schmitt points out:

> Investment goods start out as consumption goods. This is perfectly logical; the first form of existence of investment goods is a 'real wage fund', firms acquiring consumption goods which they later transform—in another quantum of time—into all kinds of equipment. For this purpose, it is enough that firms owning the saved consumption goods give them as wages to the workers who produce the equipment. Even in its final form, fixed capital, investment has its source in the saving which creates capital as consumption goods.[66]

The analysis of the second of our extreme cases will confirm this last conclusion.

The assumption on which this second case (represented by Figure 4.15) is based is that consumers spend the totality of their income on the commodity market. Saving is, therefore, supposed to be zero, so that the monetary physical product is totally represented by consumption goods. On the other hand, we are also assuming that the production of capital goods is positive, so that the pure physical product is made up of consumption and investment goods.

Here again, the difference between saving and investment seems inescapable. A closer analysis, however, allows us to overcome this first impression. The emission defining *PPP* must, in fact, be reinterpreted in the light of the second emission. The expenditure, by consumers, of the totality of their

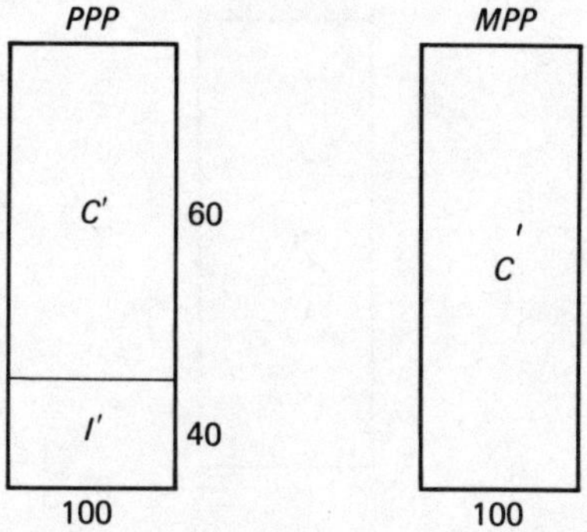

Fig. 4.15

income means in reality that the investment goods produced are consumption goods 'by destination'. This obviously does not mean that a change occurs in the physical form of the produced goods. Capital goods maintain their physical form but, being purchased by consumers and not by firms, they necessarily become the original form of consumption goods. The purchase of investment goods by consumers is then a purchase of consumption goods in the form of capital goods.

Another way to understand this reinterpretation of the first emission is as follows. For the amount corresponding to the production of capital goods, income spent by consumers is a forward purchase of future consumption goods. This forward purchase takes the form of a loan from consumers to firms. The investment goods which consumers purchase today will be substituted by an equivalent amount of consumption goods in a subsequent quantum period. For example, let us suppose that in the following period no investment goods are produced, as shown in Figure. 4.16. Given the previous situation, consumers receive the whole product, but they do not spend the totality of their incomes. A part of the actual production has, in fact, already been purchased in the form of capital goods. Thus, consumers save a part of their income equal to the loan previously granted to firms. The monetary physical product can therefore be represented as in Figure 4.17. As we already know, the positive saving by consumers is an expenditure of income in favour of firms, and takes place on the factor market. Now, given that the debt of F is equal to the amount of saving,

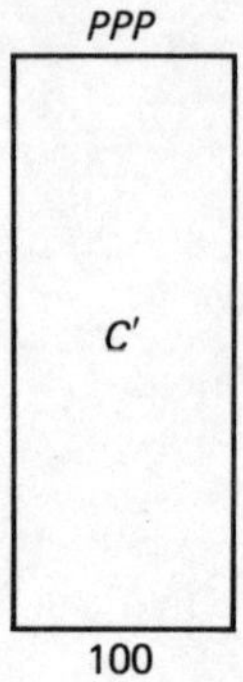

Fig. 4.16

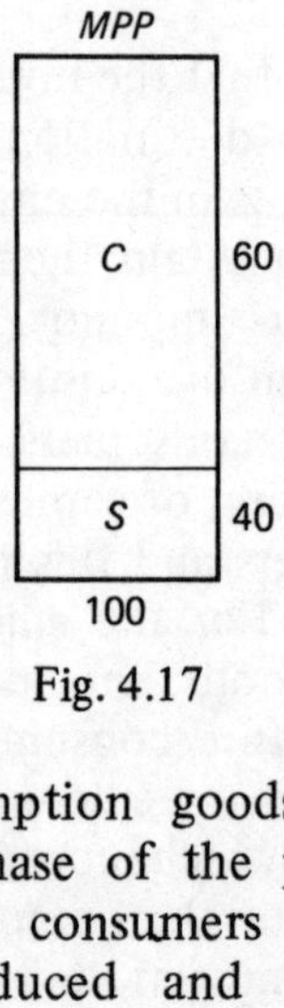

Fig. 4.17

this purchase of consumption goods by F is immediately transformed into a purchase of the previously produced investment goods. Finally, consumers receive the totality of consumption goods produced and firms acquire, through saving, the totality of investment goods. If we consider the two periods together we have the distribution represented in Figure 4.18.

The introduction of a second period is simply a device to allow a better intuitive understanding of the analysis, whose validity is not dependent upon the intervention of such a period. The investment goods actually purchased by consumers are bound to become consumption goods, so that logically they can be considered as consumption goods from their formation: because of the zero saving, the pure physical product is only made up of consumption goods. The quantum

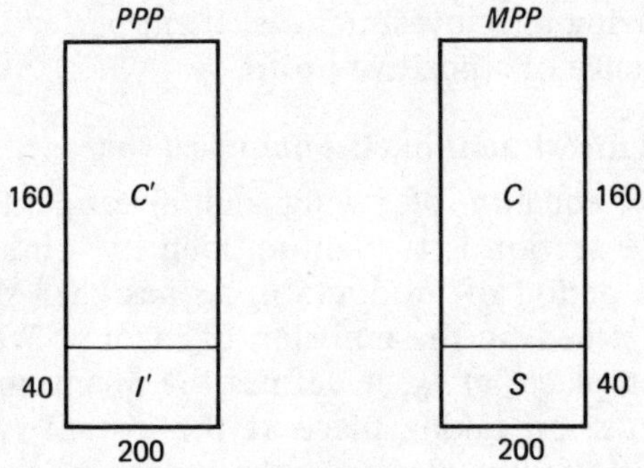

Fig. 4.18

identity between *PPP* and *MPP* is respected once again, as is the quantum identity of saving and investment.

The definition of consumption and investment goods is, therefore, clearly established. The division of the product is not explained by the physical differences in its components. Instead, what determines the distinction between the two categories of goods is the final purchase in favour of firms. If this purchase, i.e. the expenditure of income included in the payment of wages, is positive then investment is positive. We can thus conclude that the amount of investment goods in *PPP* is determined by the amount of income spent in favour of firms.

A short remark on saving, investment and profit. As we have previously noted, the analysis of saving is similar to that of profit. Accordingly, the presence of a positive profit does not modify our result: saving and investment are always equal in quantum time whatever the amount of profit. In fact, a positive profit will only influence the level of the identity but not the identity itself. Profit, being also a part of income spent in favour of firms, increases both investment and saving simultaneously and by the same amount.

Profit, which is defined in exactly the same way as saving (that part of income which is not spent by consumers), differs from the latter only because of its characteristic irreversibility. Saving is a reversible transfer of income whereas profit is not. Ultimately, profit is undoubtedly a category of saving (a forced saving) whose presence as part of national income instantaneously defines a corresponding investment. The quantum identity of saving and investment is, then, perfectly consistent with the existence of a positive profit.

4. Saving and investment in chronological time

The necessary equality of saving and investment established in the previous section is a quantum identity, obtaining during the indivisible period of production. As has been shown, quantum time is defined by the emission of income. When the first emission takes place, at t_0, it defines the quantum p_0, as does the second emission taking place at the instant t_1 (see Figure 4.19). Chronologically distinct, the two emissions coincide in quantum time. As soon as time is quantised, there is no room left for any interaction of saving and investment.

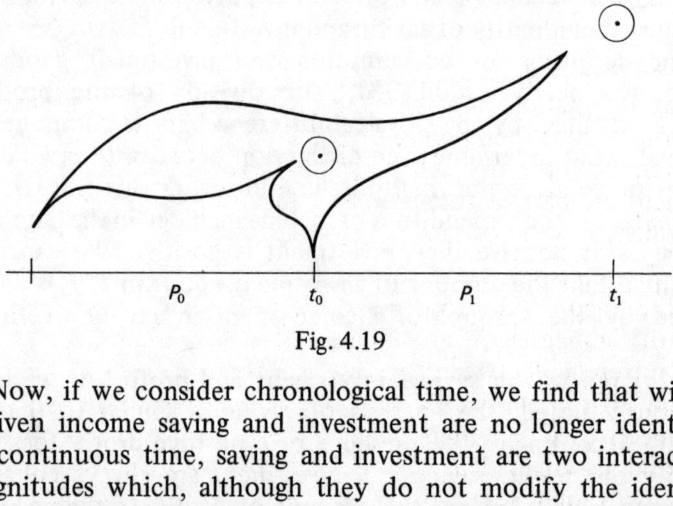

Fig. 4.19

Now, if we consider chronological time, we find that within a given income saving and investment are no longer identical. In continuous time, saving and investment are two interacting magnitudes which, although they do not modify the identity of Y and D, are autonomously determined. The decision to produce a certain amount of capital goods, which leads to the determination of investment, is taken by firms, whereas the decision to save is taken by consumers. As Keynes says in the *Treatise*:

> Saving is the act of the individual consumer and consists in the negative act of refraining from spending the whole of his current income on consumption.
>
> Investment, on the other hand, is the act of the entrepreneur whose function it is to make the decisions which determine the amount of the non-available output, and consists in the positive act of starting or maintaining some processes of production or of witholding liquid goods.

It is measured by the net addition of wealth whether in the form of fixed capital, working capital or liquid capital.[67]

Saving and investment are therefore separately determined, and their eventual equality does not imply their identity. If we refer to Figure 4.19, we can see that in chronological time, between instants t_0 and t_1, saving and investment can differ from one another. Income, as created at t_0 by the first emission (in quantum time), exists in continuous time where it is subject to the separate decisions of firms and consumers.

Saving and investment, whilst autonomously determined in continuous time, are nevertheless subject to the constraint that they are necessarily equal in quantum time. In other words, quantum time is the necessary framework of saving and investment. Their inequality in chronological time can thus only exist within the period elapsing between the two emissions of income. Thus:

1. the interaction of saving and investment in continuous time brings about their equality; and
2. even when the two magnitudes are unequal, saving and investment are part of total demand and total supply respectively, which, as we know, are always identical.

The first emission creates an income which is necessarily equal to the income destroyed by the second emission, and this identity applies to every income. It is thus impossible to find any difference between the two aspects of a given income, the supply (first emission) or demand side (second emission), irrespective of whether analysis is set out in quantum or in continuous time. This can be represented as in Figure 4.20. The two solid rectangles represent the emission of income. They are not only equal, but identical, since they are the two aspects of the same reality. Moreover, final saving, which is instantaneously related to the first emission, necessarily corresponds to investment. On the other hand, between the instants of the two emissions, saving and investment can be fixed at different levels. Yet this variation takes place within an income given once and for all by the first emission.

Products are created and destroyed in quantum time. Between these two events, in continuous time, they can be saved or invested in different proportions. Yet, given the necessary equality of saving and investment in quantum time, we know

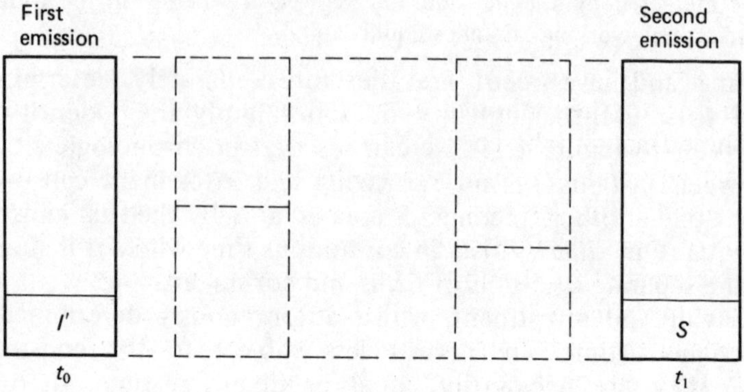

Fig. 4.20

that their difference must finally disappear. It follows that, even in chronological time, saving and investment must finally balance. What has to be proved, then, is that it is always possible to reduce one magnitude to the other.

In the case of an excess of saving over investment, it must be shown that this excess can be reduced either by increasing investment or by decreasing saving. The increase of investment does not present any analytical difficulty. As for a decrease of saving, its logical possibility can be easily established. The excess of saving over investment defines a positive purchase of old bonds and assets which reduces the amount of net saving to the amount of investment. Since it defines a positive saving for the purchaser but a negative saving of the same amount for the seller, the purchase of old bonds and assets is not a net saving. Thus, the total amount of net saving only partially corresponds to the initial amount of saving determined by consumers. Only the purchase of new bonds and assets is a net saving, and this purchase is obviously equal to investment. The remaining saving is counterbalanced by the dis-saving of the sellers of olds bonds and assets.

The other possible instance of a difference between saving and investment is in the case of an excess of investment over saving. What must be shown here is that this difference is cancelled either by increasing saving or by decreasing investment. Since investment is the output of capital goods, it seems impossible to reduce it once production has effectively taken place. Now, as we saw in the previous section, this impossibility is only apparent. As soon as we understand that products are not divided into consumption and investment goods according to their physical form but according to the identity of their final purchasers, it becomes evident that part of the capital equipment really belongs to the category of consumption goods. Just as part of the capital can be created in the form of consumption goods, part of the investment goods can be created in the initial form of consumption goods. Part of the investment goods are effectively purchased on behalf of consumers, and the amount of investment by firms is necessarily reduced for the economy as a whole.

Finally both saving and investment are either increased or decreased in such a way that any difference between them can always be reabsorbed. Now, what is the intermediary through which saving and investment can be equalised in continuous time? In other words, what is the price of the adjustment between saving and investment?

As Schmitt tells us,[68] this adjustment takes place through a variation of the interest rate. On the financial market, consumers supply part of their income and firms demand a certain amount of saving to finance their investment. Because saving is a loan to firms for the production and final purchase of capital goods, investment corresponds to a demand for saving. Thus, on the financial market, supply of and demand for saving determine a rate of interest whose original *raison d'être* has to be found in the process of production. In other words, a financial rate of interest can be determined because that part of income saved by consumers and invested by firms is a loan to producers and not, as Keynes thought, merely a loan to consumers. If the financial rate of interest (Bohm-Bawerk's Leihzins) were not based on the original interest (the Urzins) created by the production of investment goods,[69] Keynes's analysis of the rate of interest would be correct. In that case, saving and investment would always be equal, not because of their quantum identity, but tautologically. Let us briefly return to Keynes's analysis.

According to Keynes, saving and investment are equal, independently of the rate of interest. More precisely, saving and investment do not determine the rate of interest which, in turn, does not determine their equality. The only influence which the rate of interest can exert on saving and investment is not on their equality but on its level.

Given the rate of interest and the marginal efficiency of capital, a change in investment will induce a change of income which brings out, given the propensity to consume, the equality between saving and investment.

The traditional analysis has been aware that saving depends on income but it has overlooked the fact that income depends on investment, in such a fashion that, when investment changes, income must necessarily change in just that degree which is necessary to make the change in saving equal to the change in investment.[70]

As we know, the change in income is related, through the multiplier, to the change in investment. 'The ratio, thus determined, between an increment of investment and the corresponding increment of aggregate income, both measured in wage units, is given by the investment multiplier.'[71]

Calling k the multiplier, we have

$$\Delta Y = k\Delta I,$$

where

$$k = \frac{1}{1-c},$$

c being the propensity to consume. The important point is that, according to Keynes, the increase in income must allow for an increase of saving equivalent to the increase of investment:

$$\Delta S = (1-c)\,\Delta Y = \Delta I,$$

where $(1-c) = s =$ propensity to save.

Now, the supposed relation between income, investment and the marginal propensity to consume is such that the increase of saving is always tautologically equal to the increase of investment. In fact, from

$$\Delta Y = \frac{1}{1-c}\,\Delta I$$

we have

$$\Delta I = (1-c)\,\Delta Y,$$

which is equivalent to

$$\Delta S = (1 - c)\,\Delta Y.$$

It is then obvious that saving and investment are always equal because of their tautological definition. '*Saving* and *investment* have been so defined that they are necessarily equal in amount, being, for the community as a whole, merely different aspects of the same thing.'[72]

This result becomes even more evident once we remember that the multiplier is necessarily always equal to one.[73] In this case, and again according to Keynes, we have

$$\Delta Y = \Delta I = \Delta S.$$

Thus, every increase in income due to an increase of investment must imply a corresponding and equal increase of saving. Obviously, this can only be the case if saving and investment are so defined that they merely represent two different names for the same object. Then the increase in income caused by the increase of investment is equivalent to the increase of saving, since saving is precisely that part of income which is invested.

As we already know from the first part of this chapter, Keynes's rejection of the classical theory of the rate of interest was due to his attempt to allow income to be determined independently of full employment. Unfortunately, this attempt led him to introduce the tautological equivalence of saving and investment.

> Whilst, therefore, the amount of saving is an outcome of the collective behaviour of individual consumers and the amount of investment of the collective behaviour of individual entrepreneurs, these two amounts are necessarily equal, since each of them is equal to the excess of income over consumption.[74]

This analysis, which does not allow for any adjustment between consumers' saving and firms' investment, either in quantum or in continuous time, does not prove the identity of saving and investment. The possibility of determining income without referring to full employment is, therefore, also not established.

We know, however, that the identity of saving and investment and the determination of income irrespective of full employment are both perfectly consistent with the reciprocal adjustment of S and I. Quantum analysis does, in fact, establish the identity of saving and investment (in quantum time) for every income created, and confirms that, being determined by effective demand, income varies independently of the level of employment. Moreover, this new analysis is not opposed to the adjustment of saving and investment in continuous time. This adjustment, which takes place through the variation of the rate of interest, is the logical consequence of the factual distinction between consumers' determination of saving and firms' determination of investment. Thus, the classical theory of the rate of interest does not seem to deserve Keynes's drastic criticism. As we know from quantum analysis, adjustment of saving and investment through the variation of the rate of interest is not inconsistent with Keynes's main results (the identity of total supply and total demand and the determination of income by effective demand). This also means that the variation of the rate of interest does not necessarily bring income to its full-employment level. Let us explain this last point in some detail.

Keynes, arguing against the classical theory, claims that if saving and investment are made equal through the variation of the rate of interest, income will increase until it reaches the full-employment level. What he is saying is that if saving and investment can be made equal whatever the level of income, there is no reason for this level not to be that of full employment. On the contrary, in stating that saving and investment are equal whatever the rate of interest, Keynes is stressing the possibility of determining income independently of its full-employment level. In other words, according to Keynes, if the equivalence of saving and investment is assured through the variation of r (the rate of interest) then income will increase until it reaches the level of full employment, while, if this equivalence is assured through the variation of income, the level of income will usually not correspond to the level of full employment, since income will be determined by the given magnitudes of the rate of interest and the marginal efficiency of capital.

Keynes's main criticism of the classical theory of interest is, thus, addressed to the mechanism assuring equality of saving and investment.

> It is fairly clear, however, that this tradition has regarded the rate of interest as the factor which brings the demand for investment and the willingness to save into equilibrium with one another. Investment represents

the demand for investible resources and saving represents the supply, whilst the rate of interest is the 'price' of investible resources at which the two are equated. Just as the price of a commodity is necessarily fixed at that point where the demand for it is equal to the supply, so the rate of interest necessarily comes to rest under the play of market forces at the point where the amount of investment at that rate of interest is equal to the amount of saving at that rate.[75]

Now, Keynes's argument against this process of equalisation of saving and investment obviously does not take into account quantum analysis. Only once it has been proved that saving and investment are identical in quantum time is it possible to let them adjust to each other in continuous time. If quantum analysis did not provide the fundamental reason for the identity between saving and investment, it would be impossible to explain their adjustment. Consequently, it is because they are identical in quantum time that saving and investment can adjust in continuous time. Keynes could not see that it is not because of the variation of the rate of interest that this adjustment ends up with the necessary equivalence of saving and investment. Even if the rate of interest fails to bring them into equality in chronological time, the second emission will unfailingly fulfil this task.

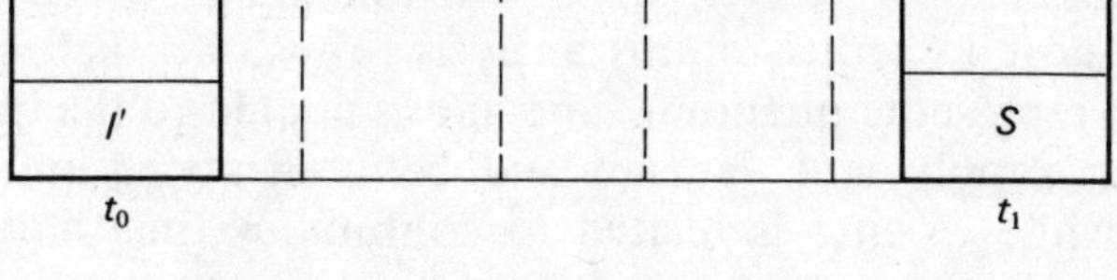

Fig. 4.21

Within the interval $t_0 - t_1$ (see Figure 4.21) the difference between saving and investment can be reduced through a variation of the rate of interest. However, whether successful or not this adjustment is instantaneously taken over and, if necessary, finally accomplished as soon as the second emission takes place in t_1. A difference between saving and investment is always possible in continuous time (in the interval $t_0 - t_1$), despite the variation of the rate of interest, but not in quantum time. Thus, the variation of the rate of interest is neither a necessary nor sufficient condition for the equivalence between saving and investment. Once the logical priority of quantum analysis has been established, however, it becomes clear that the rate of interest is the price of the adjustment, in chronological time, of saving and investment. Within this limit, the classical theory of interest supported by Robertson and Ohlin against Keynes finds new life. As Ohlin said, 'The rate of interest is the price of credit'[76] as determined on the financial market. Now, Ohlin's theory of interest was deeply rooted in the Swedish distinction between ex-ante and ex-post. It is, therefore, worth showing how quantum analysis modifies the traditional interpretation of this distinction.

5. Quantum analysis and the distinction between ex-ante and ex-post variables

The traditional distinction between ex-ante and ex-post variables was concerned only with continuous time. This is the main reason why it was logically impossible for the theory to explain the necessary equality of saving and investment. The eventual adjustment, in continuous time, between these two forces was not sufficient to establish their identity ex-post. Something more rigorous is required. As we know, quantum analysis establishes the identity of saving and investment without being opposed to their adjustment in continuous time. It is then possible to reinterpret the distinction between ex-ante and ex-post in terms of this analysis. Thus, we shall say that ex-post represents quantum time and is related to the identities between supply and demand and between saving and investment, while ex-ante is related to continuous time and to the adjustment of saving and investment.

This new definition of the distinction between ex-ante and ex-post allows for a final comment on the traditional analysis of income determination. According to this dynamic analysis, the determination of income is based on the ex-ante adjustment of supply and demand. This adjustment, it is said, takes place either between virtual forces if it is concerned with the determination of a first income, or between real forces if it is situated between two successive incomes. In both cases, total supply and total demand are supposed to vary ex-ante, while they are necessarily equal ex-post. Now, it has been proved formally by quantum analysis that:

1. the adjustment between saving and investment in continuous time can only be explained by their necessary equality in quantum time; and that
2. the quantum identity of saving and investment results from the quantum identity of total demand and total supply.

This last identity, i.e. the necessary equivalence between the pure physical product (*PPP*) and the monetary physical product (*MPP*), is, however, always verified in both quantum and continuous time. Total supply and total demand are not submitted to any process of adjustment, so that between the two instants corresponding to the emission of *PPP* (t_0) and the emission of *MPP* (t_1), income does not undergo any change. In fact, income can only be affected by its creation or its expenditure. Both these operations take place in quantum time, and in quantum time income is defined identically by its total supply or its total demand. In continuous time, where income is neither created nor spent, it necessarily remains unchanged.

Every expenditure defining either a creation or a destruction of income is an emission and, as such, is inscribed in quantum time. It is, therefore, impossible to introduce any difference between total supply and total demand by the manipulation of these two processes. Thus, it is no longer possible to sustain that, for example, an excess of saving over investment defines a positive difference between supply and demand. The adjustment between saving and investment does not imply any adjustment between total demand and total supply. In continuous time, ex-ante, the adjustment of saving and investment takes place within a given income and therefore does not involve its variation. In other words, income is not determined by the adjustment, ex-ante, of total supply and total demand, since these two forces are always equal. Let us prove this once again in a different way.

Traditional theory claims that total demand and total supply can differ ex-ante. Two inequalities are conceivable according to whether supply is greater than demand or demand is greater than supply. Logically, they must both be rejected.

$$D > S \tag{4.1}$$

This first inequality can obviously not be accepted since total demand can never be greater than the available income from which it comes. Total supply represents the amount of income available for the purchase of a given production and sets the upper limit to total demand.

$$D < S \tag{4.2}$$

This second inequality seems to be more acceptable than the first. In fact, if it were possible to keep a positive part of income away from expenditure, then total demand would necessarily shrink by this amount. This possibility, which is based on an insufficient analysis of money, can, however, never be verified. Two arguments can be presented here. The first refers to Keynes's definition of saving as the part of income which is spent on the financial market. According to this analysis, saving cannot be mixed up with hoarding since it represents a positive expenditure of income (on behalf of firms). Moreover, and again according to Keynes, available income is totally shared between consumption and saving so that hoarding can only be equal to zero. The necessary equality of total demand and total supply then follows immediately.

The second argument is even more straightforward. The theory of emissions establishes the perfect identity of money and output so that it will never be possible to find any difference whatsoever between total demand and total supply. It will be remembered that in quantum analysis the determination of income corresponds to the emission of wages. As soon as wages are paid out, a perfect correspondence is created between the positive quantum deposit of workers, W, and the negative quantum deposit of firms, F, as is shown in Figure 4.22. The physical product is located in F and fills the negative quantum deposit. In other words, national product is thus totally defined by the monetary income earned by W. The positive quantum deposit of W is the product, and not its monetary counterpart, since income and product are not two different objects confronting each other, but one and the same object. The traditional dichotomy which has for

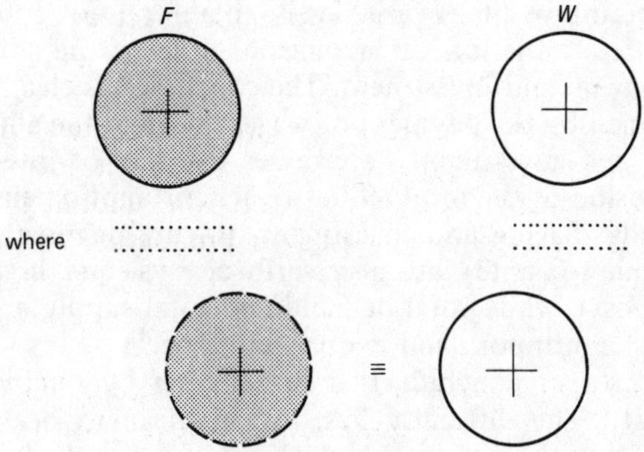

Fig. 4.22

such a long time tormented the nights of many economists is thus definitively overthrown: through the payment of wages, money and product are so closely integrated that one becomes the definition of the other. In these circumstances the search for a difference between product and money is in vain.

The same result is reached when we refer to the second emission. The final expenditure of income relates the positive quantum deposit of W to the negative quantum deposit of F. This operation does not in any way alter the perfect correspondence of income and product. On the contrary, every time an income is finally spent an equivalent part of the physical product is freed from the negative quantum deposit of F, which means that the definition of income is the economic[77] destruction of the product. This is perfectly consistent with the analytical fact that money and product are so strictly related that they cannot exist without one another. This relation of identity between product and money, which is established by production, is therefore the main theoretical reason for the identity between total demand and total supply. Money can never differ from the product which it defines, so that total demand can also never differ from total supply.

Having proved that total demand can neither be greater nor smaller than total supply, we can now conclude that the adjustment of saving and investment in continuous time in no way contributes to the determination of income. The newly discovered distinction between ex-ante (continuous time) and ex-post (quantum time) variables is, therefore, not comparable with the determination of income in terms of the adjustment between saving and investment. The conclusion is clear. Income is determined by the payment of wages, whereas the adjustment of saving and investment determines the rate of interest and the subdivision of the product between consumption and investment goods. Saving and investment, usually different in continuous time (ex-ante), are necessarily always equal in quantum time (ex-post), while total demand and total supply are always identical in continuous and in quantum time.

Finally, let us conclude this last chapter by reminding the reader that: 'The difficulty lies, not in the new ideas, but in escaping from the old ones, which ramify, for those brought up as most of us have been, into every corner of our minds'.[78]

NOTES

1. L. R. Klein, *The Keynesian Revolution*, London, Macmillan, 1968, pp. 110–11.
2. Ibid., p. 111.
3. G. Ackley, *Macroeconomic Theory*, New York, Macmillan, 1961, p. 106.
4. P. A. Samuelson, 'Professor Pigou's employment and equilibrium', in *The Collected Scientific Papers of Paul A. Samuelson*, ed. J. E. Stiglitz, Vol. I, Boston, MIT Press, 1966, p. 546.
5. Klein, op. cit., pp. 111–12.
6. Ibid., p. 112.
7. Ibid.
8. Ibid., pp. 112–13.
9. B. Ohlin, 'Alternative theories of the rate of interest', *Economic Journal*, September 1937, p. 424, Note 1.
10. P. A. Samuelson, in Stiglitz (ed.), *The Collected Scientific Papers*, Vol. II, op. cit., pp. 1198–9.
11. For a detailed critique of Samuelson see B. Schmitt, *Macroeconomic Theory: A Fundamental Revision*, Albeuve (Switzerland), Castella, 1972, pp. 32–8.
12. Klein, op. cit., p. 111.
13. K. M. Keynes, *The Collected Writings of*, ed. D. Moggridge, Vol. XII, London, Macmillan, 1973, p. 581.
14. J. M. Keynes, *The General Theory of Employment, Interest and Money*, London, Macmillan, 1973, p. 183.
15. J. Hicks, 'Some questions of time in economics', in A. M. Tang, *Evolution, Welfare and Time in Economics*, Lexington Mass., Lexington Books, 1976, p. 140.
16. D. F. Hendry and A. Spanos, 'Disequilibrium and latent variables', unpublished paper, London School of Economics, May 1980, p. 7.
17. E. R. Weintraub, *Microfoundations*, Cambridge, Cambridge University Press, 1979, p. 125.
18. Hendry and Spanos, op. cit., p. 8.
19. Ibid., p. 12.
20. Ibid., p. 8.

21. Ibid., p. 12.
22. See Chapter 1, Part II, Section 5.
23. B. Schmitt, *Monetary Expenditures and Quantum Time,* Albeuve, Switzerland, Castella/Presses Universitaires de Dijon, forthcoming, p. 3.
24. Keynes, *The General Theory*, op. cit., pp. 184–5.
25. Ibid., p. 245.
26. Ibid., p. 29.
27. Ibid., p. 55.
28. Keynes, *The Collected Writings of*, op. cit., Vol. XIV, pp. 181–2.
29. Ibid., Vols XIII, p. 433.
30. Ibid., Vol. XIV, p. 181.
31. Ibid., pp. 182–3.
32. Schmitt, *Macroeconomic Theory*, op. cit., p. 70.
33. Keynes, *The Collected Writings of,* op. cit., Vol. XIV, p. 183.
34. G. L. S. Shackle, *Time and Economics*, Amsterdam, North-Holland, p. 21.
35. Ibid., p. 15.
36. St. Augustine, 'Some questions about time', in *The Philosophy of Time,* ed. E. M. Gale, Brighton, Harvester Press, 1968, p. 43.
37. J. Hicks, *Value and Capital*, London, Oxford University Press, 1978, p. 197.
38. C. J. Bliss, *Capital Theory and the Distribution of Income,* Amsterdam, North-Holland/American Elsevier, 1975, p. 119.
39. J. Hicks, *Causality in Economics,* Oxford, Blackwell, 1979, p. 26.
40. Bliss, op. cit., p. 37.
41. Klein, op. cit., p. 113.
42. See Weintraub, op. cit., p. 39.
43. Hicks, *Causality in Economics,* op. cit., p. 62.
44. M. Desai, *Applied Econometrics,* New York, McGraw-Hill, 1976.
45. H. Reichenbach, *The Philosophy of Space and Time,* New York, Dover Publications, 1957, pp. 126–7.
46. A. Grünbaum, 'The status of temporal becoming', in Gale (ed.), *The Philosophy of Time,* op. cit., p. 354.
47. Reichenbach, op. cit., p. 145.
48. Ibid.
49. Ibid., p. 146.
50. Reichenbach's causal theory of temporal order has been criticised by W. H. Newton-Smith in his book *The Structure of Time* (London, Routledge & Kegan Paul, 1980) as well as by A. Grünbaum in *Philosophical Problems of Space and Time* (Dordrecht, Reidel, 1973). Despite the epistemological importance of these criticisms, it remains true that causality can be considered as the conceptual definition of time order as long as we do not employ some notion of temporal order to establish causal connections between separate events. Now, even if causality were defined in terms of temporal order, it would nevertheless be impossible to explain a relation of simultaneous causality. Thus, within this theoretical framework (causality between physical events) it is always true that contemporaneous causality is a logical impossibility.
51. J. A. Kregel, *The Reconstruction of Political Economy: An Introduction to Post-Keynesian Economics,* London, Macmillan, 1973, p. 45.
52. Weintraub, op. cit., p. 47.
53. 'The Hicks' reinterpretation also helps to illustrate how the replacement of causally ordered relations with a system of simultaneous equations is not used only as a purely formal device but as a medium to introduce a basically different interpretative model of economic reality.' (L. Pasinetti, *Growth and Income Distribution*, Cambridge, Cambridge University Press, 1974, p. 47.)

54. Ibid., p. 44.
55. Hicks, *Causality in Economics*, op. cit., p. 21–2.
56. Ibid., p. 88.
57. Ibid., p. 22.
58. Reichenbach, op. cit., p. 124.
59. Keynes, *The Collected Writings of*, op. cit., Vol. XIV, p. 222.
60. Keynes, *The General Theory*, op. cit., p. 62.
61. Ibid., p. 63.
62. Ibid., p. 64.
63. Samuelson, 'Professor Pigou's employment and equilibrium', op. cit., p. 1184.
64. Schmitt, *Monetary Expenditures*, op. cit., p. 117, Note 1.
65. Ibid., p. 108.
66. Ibid.
67. J. M. Keynes, *A Treatise on Money*, Vol. I, *The Pure Theory of Money*, London, Macmillan, 1971, p. 155.
68. See Schmitt, *Monetary Expenditures*, op. cit., p. 114.
69. Ibid., p. 114.
70. Keynes, *The General Theory*, op. cit., p. 184.
71. Ibid., p. 248.
72. Ibid., p. 74.
73. See Chapter 2.
74. Keynes, *The General Theory*, op. cit., p. 63.
75. Ibid., p. 175.
76. Ohlin, op. cit., p. 427.
77. Obviously, the economic destruction of a product does not imply its physical destruction, which depends purely on physical factors.
78. Keynes, *The General Theory*, op. cit., p. xxiii.

Bibliography

Ackley, G., *Macroeconomic Theory*, New York, Macmillan, 1961.

Allen, R. G. D., *Mathematical Economics,* London, Macmillan, 1956.

—*Macro-Economic Theory*, London, Macmillan, 1968.

Arrow, K. J. and Hahn, F. H., *General Competitive Analysis,* Amsterdam, North-Holland, 1971.

St. Augustine, 'Some questions about time', in *The Philosophy of Time,* ed. R. M. Gale, Brighton, Harvester Press, 1968.

Baron, M. E., *The Origins of the Infinitesimal Calculus,* Oxford, Pergamon Press, 1969.

Barrow, Sir Isaac, *Lectiones Geometricae*, London, 1670.

Bergson, H., 'Form and becoming', in *The Philosophy of Time,* ed. R. M. Gale, Brighton, Harvester Press, 1968.

Bliss, C. J., *Capital Theory and the Distribution of Income*, Amsterdam, North-Holland/American Elsevier, 1975.

Cencini, A., 'The Logical indeterminacy of relative prices', in *Advances in Economic Theory,* ed. M. Baranzini, Oxford, Blackwell, 1982.

— and Schmitt, B., 'Wages and profits in a theory of emissions', in *Advances in Economic Theory,* ed. M. Baranzini, Oxford, Blackwell, 1982.

Charlton, W., 'Time', *Philosophy* (Journal of the Royal Institute of Philosophy), April 1981.

Clower, R. W., 'The Keynesian counter-revolution: a theoretical appraisal', in *Monetary Theory,* ed. R. W. Clower, Harmondsworth, Penguin Education, 1973.

Courant, R., *Differential and Integral Calculus,* London and Glasgow, Blackie & Son, 1934.

Curtis, M., 'Is money saving equal to investment?', *Quarterly Journal of Economics,* 1937.

Davidson, P., 'Why money matters: lessons from a half-century of monetary theory', *Journal of Post Keynesian Economics,* Autumn 1978.

Desai, M., *Applied Econometrics,* New York, McGraw-Hill, 1976.

— *Testing Monetarism,* London, Frances Pinter, 1982.

— 'The task of monetary theory: the Hayek–Sraffa debate in a modern perspective', in *Advances in Economic Theory,* ed. M. Baranzini, Oxford, Blackwell, 1982.

Einstein, A., 'Paper on quantum theory', in *The World of the Atom,* eds H. A. Boorse and L. Motz, New York, Basic Books, 1966.

Fisher, I., *Nature of Capital and Income,* London, Macmillan, 1912.

Foley, D., 'On two specifications of asset equilibrium in macroeconomic models', *Journal of Political Economy,* April 1975.

Frankel, S. H., ' "Psychic" and "accounting" concepts of income and welfare', in *Readings in the Concept and Measurement of Income,* eds R. H. Parker and G. C. Harcourt, Cambridge, Cambridge University Press, 1969.

Frisch, R., 'On the notion of equilibrium and disequilibrium', *Review of Economic Studies,* **3**, 1935-6.

Gale, R. M., *The Philosophy of Time,* Brighton, Harvester Press, 1968.

Goodwin, R., 'The multiplier', in *The New Economics,* ed. S. E. Harris, London, Dennis Dobson & Co., 1947.

Grünbaum, A., 'The status of temporal becoming', in *The Philosophy of Time,* ed. R. M. Gale, Brighton, Harvester Press, 1968.

— *Philosophical Problems of Space and Time,* Dordrecht, Reidel, 1973.

Haberler, G., 'Mr. Keynes' theory of the "multiplier": a methodological criticism', in *Readings in Business Cycle Theory*, London, Allen & Unwin, 1950.

Hansen, A. H., 'A note on savings and investment', *Review of Economics and Statistics,* Vol. 30, 1948.

— *A Guide to Keynes,* New York, McGraw-Hill, 1953.

— *Business Cycles and National Income,* London, Allen & Unwin, 1964.

Harrison, G. W., 'The stock-flow distinction: a suggested interpretation', *Journal of Macroeconomics,* Spring 1980, 116-20.

Hendry, D. F. and Spanos, A., 'Disequilibrium and latent variables', unpublished paper, London School of Economics, May 1980.

Hicks, J. R., *Value and Capital,* London, Oxford University Press, 1939.

— *Capital and Growth,* London, Oxford University Press, 1965.

— 'Maintaining capital intact: a further suggestion', in *Readings in the Concept and Measurement of Income,* eds R. H. Parker and G. Harcourt, Cambridge, Cambridge University Press, 1969.

— *Capital and Time,* London, Oxford University Press, 1973.

— *The Crisis in Keynesian Economics,* Oxford, Blackwell, 1974.

— 'Some questions of time in economics', in *Evolution, Welfare and Time in Economics,* ed. A. M. Tang, Lexington Mass., Lexington Books, 1976.

— *Causality in Economics,* Oxford, Blackwell, 1979.

Hood, W. C., 'Some aspects of the treatment of time in economic theory', *Canadian Journal of Economics and Political Science*, Vol. 14, 1948.

Kaldor, N., 'The concepts of income in economic theory', in *Readings in the Concept and Measurement of Income*, eds R. H. Parker and G. Harcourt, Cambridge, Cambridge University Press, 1969.

Kalecki, M., *Essays on the Theory of Economic Fluctuations,* London, Allen & Unwin, 1939.

Keynes, J. M., *A Treatise on Money*, London, Macmillan, 1930.

— *The General Theory of Employment, Interest and Money,* London, Macmillan, 1936.

Keynes, J. M., *The Collected Writings of,* ed. D. Moggridge, London, Macmillan, 1973.

Klappholz, K. and Mishan, E. J. 'Identities in economic models', *Economica,* May 1962.

Klein, L. R., *The Keynesian Revolution,* London, Macmillan, 1968.

Knight, F. H., 'Capitalistic production, time and the rate of return', in *Economic Essays in Honour of Gustav Cassel,* London, Allen & Unwin, 1933 (new impression: Frank Cass & Co., London, 1967).

Kregel, J. A., *The Reconstruction of Political Economy: An Introduction to Post-Keynesian Economics,* London, Macmillan, 1973.

Kuska, E. A., 'On the fundamental flaw in the portfolio balance or asset approach to modelling economic systems', Abstract, London School of Economics, 1980.

Lerner, A. P., 'Mr. Keynes' *General Theory of Employment, Interest and Money*', *International Labour Review,* 1936.

— 'Saving equals investment', *Quarterly Journal of Economics,* 1938.

— '*The General Theory*', in *The New Economics,* ed. S. E. Harris, London, Dennis Dobson & Co., 1948.

— *Economics of Employment,* New York, McGraw-Hill, 1951.

— 'From the *Treatise on Money* to *The General Theory*', *Journal of Economic Literature,* Vol. 12, 1974.

Lindgren, B. W., *Statistical Theory,* London, Macmillan, 1968.

Lipsey, R. G., 'The foundations of the theory of national income: an analysis of some fundamental errors', in *Essays in Honour of Lord Robbins,* eds M. Peston and B. Corry, London, Weidenfeld and Nicolson, 1972.

— *An Introduction to Positive Economics,* Weidenfeld and Nicolson, London, 1979.

Lutz, F. A., 'The outcome of the saving investment discussion', *Quarterly Journal of Economics,* August 1938.

Marshall, A., *Principles of Economics,* Macmillan, 1950.

Marx, K., *Theories of Surplus Value,* 3 vols., London, Lawrence & Wishart, 1969.

— *Grundrisse*, Harmondsworth, The Pelican Marx Library, 1973.

— *Capital,* 3 vols., Harmondsworth, Penguin, 1976.

May, J., 'Period analysis and continuous analysis in Patinkin's macroeconomic model', *Journal of Economic Theory*, Vol. 2, 1-9, 1970.

Morishima, M., *Walras' Economics: A Pure Theory of Capital and Money,* Cambridge, Cambridge University Press, 1977.

Myrdal, G., *Monetary Equilibrium,* London, William Hodge & Co., 1939.

Newton, I., 'Absolute and relative space, time, and motion', in *Philosophy of Science*, eds A. Danto and S. Morgenbesser, New York, New Amsterdam Library, 1974.

Newton-Smith, W. H. *The Structure of Time,* London, Routledge & Kegan Paul, 1980.

Ohlin, B., 'Some notes on the Stockholm theory', *Economic Journal,* 1937.

— 'Alternative theories of the rate of interest', *Economic Journal,* September 1937.

Pasinetti, L. L., *Growth and Income Distribution,* Cambridge, Cambridge University Press, 1974.

Pasinetti, L. L., *Structural Change and Economic Growth: A Theoretical Essay on the Dynamics of the Wealth of Nations,* Cambridge, Cambridge University Press, 1981.

Patinkin, D., 'The process of writing *The General Theory*: a critical survey', in *Keynes, Cambridge and 'The General Theory',* eds D. Patinkin and J. C. Leith, London, Macmillan, 1977.

Qadir, A., 'Quantum economics', *Pakistan Economic and Social Review,* **16**/3-4, 1978.

Reichenbach, H., *The Philosophical Foundations of Quantum Mechanics,* Berkeley, University of California Press, 1944.

— *The Philosophy of Space and Time,* New York, Dover Publications, 1957.

Ricardo, D., *On the Principles of Political Economy and Taxation,* Cambridge, Cambridge University Press, 1975 (first edition J. Murray, 1817).

— *The Works and Correspondence of David Ricardo,* ed. P. Sraffa, Cambridge, Cambridge University Press, 1951-5.

Robertson, D. H., *Money,* Cambridge, Cambridge Economic Handbooks, 1970 (first edition 1922).

— *The Banking Policy and the Price Level,* London, P. S. King & Son, 1932.

— 'Saving and hoarding', *Economic Journal,* September 1933.

— 'Some notes on Mr. Keynes' *General Theory of Employment*', *Quarterly Journal of Economics*, November 1936.

— 'Alternative theories of the rate of interest', *Economic Journal,* September, 1937.

Robinson, J., 'The production function and the theory of capital', *Review of Economics Studies,* **55**, 1953-4.

— *Collected Economic Papers,* 5 vols., Oxford, Blackwell, 1951-79.

Russell, B., *The Principles of Mathematics,* Cambridge, Cambridge University Press, 1903.

Samuelson, P. A., *The Collected Scientific Writings of Paul A. Samuelson,* 4 vols., ed. J. E. Stiglitz, Robert C. Merton, Hiroaki Nagatani and Kate Crowley, MIT Press, Boston, 1966-77.

Sayers, R. S., *Modern Banking,* London, Oxford University Press, 1958.

Schmitt, B., *La Formation du pouvoir d'achat*, Paris, Sirey, 1960.

— *Monnaie, salaires et profits,* Paris, Presses Universitaires de France, 1966.

— L'Analyse macroéconomique des revenus, Paris, Dalloz, 1971.

— *Macroeconomic Theory: A Fundamental Revision,* Albeuve (Switzerland), Castella, 1972.

— *Theorie unitaire de la monnaie, nationale et internationale,* Albeuve (Switzerland), Castella, 1975.

Schmitt, B., *La Monnaie européenne*, Paris, Presses Universitaires de France, 1977.

— 'Time as quantum', in *Advances in Economic Theory*, ed. M. Baranzini, Oxford, Blackwell, 1982.

— *Monetary Expenditures and Quantum Time,* Castella/Presses Universitaires de Dijon, forthcoming.

Shackle, G. L. S., *Time and Economics,* Amsterdam, North-Holland, 1958.

— *Expectations, Investment and Income,* London, Oxford University Press, 1968.

— *Expectations, Enterprise and Profit,* London, Allen & Unwin, 1970.

Smith, A., *The Wealth of Nations,* Harmondsworth, Pelican Classics, 1978 (first published 1776).

Walras, L., *Elements of Pure Economics,* London, Allen & Unwin, 1965 (first published 1874).

Weintraub, E. R., *Microfoundations,* Cambridge, Cambridge University Press, 1979.

Whitehead, A. N., *Process and Reality,* London, Macmillan, 1929.

Wicksell, K., *Lectures on Political Economy,* London, Routledge, 1934.

Index of Names

Analytical Index